DEVICE DRIVER REFERENCE

UNIX SVR4.2

Edited by Robert M. Hines and Spence Wilcox

UNIX
Press

Published by Prentice-Hall, Inc.
A Simon & Schuster Company
Englewood Cliffs, New Jersey 07632

IMPORTANT NOTE TO USERS

While every effort has been made to ensure the accuracy and completeness of all information in this document, USL assumes no liability to any party for any loss or damage caused by errors or omissions or by statements of any kind in this document, its updates, supplements, or special editions, whether such errors, omissions, or statements result from negligence, accident, or any other cause. USL further assumes no liability arising out of the application or use of any product or system described herein; nor any liability for incidental or consequential damages arising from the use of this document. **USL disclaims all warranties regarding the information contained herein, whether expressed, implied or statutory, including implied warranties of merchantability or fitness for a particular purpose.** USL makes no representation that the interconnection of products in the manner described herein will not infringe on existing or future patent rights, nor do the descriptions contained herein imply the granting of any license to make, use or sell equipment constructed in accordance with this description.

USL reserves the right to make changes to any products herein without further notice.

TRADEMARKS

UNIX is a registered trademark of UNIX System Laboratories, Inc. in the USA and other countries. Intel386, Intel486 and Intel860 are trademarks of Intel Corp.

Cover photo: Doug Wilson/Westlight

10 9 8 7 6 5 4 3 2 1

ISBN 0-13-042631-8

UNIX PRESS
A Prentice Hall Title

P R E N T I C E   H A L L

ORDERING INFORMATION

UNIX® SYSTEM V RELEASE 4.2 DOCUMENTATION

To order single copies of UNIX® SYSTEM V Release 4.2 documentation, please call (515) 284-6761.

ATTENTION DOCUMENTATION MANAGERS AND TRAINING DIRECTORS:
For bulk purchases in excess of 30 copies, please write to:

Corporate Sales Department
PTR Prentice Hall
113 Sylvan Avenue
Englewood Cliffs, N.J. 07632

or

Phone: (201) 592-2863
FAX: (201) 592-2249

ATTENTION GOVERNMENT CUSTOMERS:

For GSA and other pricing information, please call (201) 461-7107.

Prentice-Hall International (UK) Limited, *London*
Prentice-Hall of Australia Pty. Limited, *Sydney*
Prentice-Hall Canada Inc., *Toronto*
Prentice-Hall Hispanoamericana, S.A., *Mexico*
Prentice-Hall of India Private Limited, *New Delhi*
Prentice-Hall of Japan, Inc., *Tokyo*
Simon & Schuster Asia Pte. Ltd., *Singapore*
Editora Prentice-Hall do Brasil, Ltda., *Rio de Janeiro*

Preface

This *Device Driver Reference* consists of two primary parts:

- The first part describes the Device Driver Interface/Driver–Kernel Interface (DDI/DKI). The DDI/DKI is a mature interface between drivers and the devices they control, and between drivers and the rest of the kernel. For software conforming to the DDI/DKI, we make certain guarantees about portability of that software to future releases of UNIX System V Release 4. See the introduction in the DDI/DKI section.
- The second part describes routines of the Portable Device Interface (PDI). The PDI is an architecture for block-oriented devices. The PDI presents a framework for driver development that emphasizes the separation of hardware-dependent and hardware-independent pieces of drivers. The routines described in this section are less mature than those of the DDI/DKI. Though future versions of PDI routines are likely to be highly compatible with the versions described in this manual, we do not yet guarantee this compatibility.

NOTE Drivers may have to change as the PDI evolves.

For more information on the DDI/DKI and the PDI, see the device driver programming guides.

Table of Contents

Introduction to the Device Driver Interface/Driver-Kernel Interface

D1. Driver Data

D2. Driver Entry Point Routines

D3. Kernel Utility Routines

D4. Kernel Data Structures

D5. Kernel Defines

Introduction to the Portable Device Interface

D2H. PDI Host Bus Adaptor Driver Entry Point Routines

D3I. PDI SCSI Device Interface (SDI) Utility Routines

D4I. PDI SCSI Device Interface (SDI) Data Structures

Appendix A. Migration from Release 3.2 to Release 4.0

Appendix B. Migration from Release 4.0 to Release 4 Multi-Processor

Appendix C. Additions to the DDI/DKI in Release 4.2

Introduction to the Permuted Index

Permuted Index

Introduction

The Device Driver Interface/Driver–Kernel Interface (DDI/DKI) manual pages provide reference information needed to write device drivers for the UNIX System V Release 4 environment.

This DDI/DKI specification supports driver development on UNIX System V Release 4.0 (SVR4.0), Release 4.1 Enhanced Security (SVR4.1 ES), Release 4 Multi-Processor (SVR4 MP), and Release 4.2 (SVR4.2) for the Intel386, Intel486 and Intel860 family of processors.

The intent of the DDI/DKI is to:

- promote source portability across successive releases of UNIX System V on different machines
- promote source portability and binary compatibility across successive releases of UNIX System V on a particular machine

As its name implies, the DDI/DKI is a set of defined service interfaces for:

- the calling and return syntax of the kernel utility functions used for communication between drivers and the devices they control
- the calling and return syntax of the entry point routines and kernel utility functions used for communication between drivers and the kernel
- the contents of the data structures used to exchange information between drivers and the kernel

Most DDI/DKI manual pages are processor–independent. Drivers written to conform to these generic DDI/DKI interfaces are more likely to be portable to future releases of the UNIX System V operating system on all machines.

Some DDI/DKI manual pages are processor–specific. Drivers written to conform to these non-generic DDI/DKI interfaces are more likely to be portable to future releases of the UNIX System V operating system on a particular machine.

As interfaces are removed from the DDI/DKI specification, they will be retained in the operating system for at least three years to provide compatibility with drivers written to use them. Any driver interfaces not documented in this manual are specifically not part of the DDI/DKI.

Scope of Interfaces

Developers attempting to port device drivers have special challenges. Device drivers are kernel modules that control data transferred to and received from peripheral devices. Although drivers are configured into the UNIX system as part of the kernel, they can be developed independently from the rest of the kernel. If the goal of achieving complete freedom in modifying the kernel is to be reconciled with the goal of compatibility with existing drivers, the interaction between drivers and the kernel must be rigorously regulated. This driver/kernel service interface is one of the three distinguishable interfaces for a driver, summarized as follows:

- Driver–Kernel. I/O System calls result in calls to driver entry point routines. These make up the kernel-to-driver part of the service interface, described in Section 2 of this manual. Drivers may call any of the functions described in Section 3. These are the driver-to-kernel part of the interface.
- Driver–Hardware. Most hardware drivers include an interrupt handling entry point, and may also perform direct memory access (DMA). These and other hardware-specific interactions make up the driver/hardware interface, and are described in Sections 1, 2, 3 and 4 of this manual.
- Driver–Boot/Configuration Software. At boot time, the existence of a driver is made known to the system through information in system files, enabling the system to include the driver. Administrators may also load and unload drivers while the system is running. The interaction between the driver and the boot and configuration software is the third interface affecting drivers. Refer to the device driver programming guides for more information.

To achieve the goal of source and binary compatibility, the functions, routines, and structures specified in the DDI/DKI must be used according to these rules:

- Drivers cannot access system state structures (for example, `u` and `sysinfo`) directly.
- For structures external to the driver that may be accessed directly, only the functions provided in Section 3 of this manual should be used. More generally, these functions should be used wherever possible.
- The header file `ddi.h` must be included at the end of the list of system header files. This header file "undefines" several macros that are reimplemented as functions. Device driver-specific include files should be listed after `ddi.h` to insure only the DDI/DKI interface is used by the driver.

General-Purpose Utilities

The DDI/DKI provides several general-purpose utility functions that are useful for performing certain tasks within drivers, such as character and string manipulation. Although these functions are included in the DDI/DKI, they are not considered part of the driver/kernel or driver/hardware service interfaces.

Uniprocessor vs. Multiprocessor Considerations

This manual applies to both uniprocessor and multiprocessor hardware environments. Drivers that are written in such a way that their code may be safely executed on multiple processors concurrently are said to be multithreaded (or multiprocessor-safe). Drivers which are not written in this way are said to be singlethreaded. Although the DDI/DKI includes interfaces that permit the development of multithreaded drivers, drivers are not required to be multithreaded in order to benefit from conformance to the DDI/DKI. The source portability of DDI/DKI conforming drivers across both uniprocessor and multiprocessor hardware platforms can be summarized as follows:

- Multithreaded drivers which conform to the DDI/DKI will be portable across both uniprocessor and multiprocessor implementations which support the DDI/DKI.
- Singlethreaded drivers which conform to the DDI/DKI will be portable across uniprocessor implementations which support the DDI/DKI.
- Multiprocessor implementations which support the DDI/DKI are not required to support singlethreaded drivers that conform to the DDI/DKI, although some multiprocessor implementations may choose to support such drivers by preventing concurrent execution of code within a given singlethreaded driver.

Driver writers are encouraged to write multithreaded rather than singlethreaded drivers, as these will be more widely portable and can benefit from the parallelism inherent on a multiprocessor. Writing a multithreaded driver requires that shared data within the driver be protected against certain forms of concurrent access. This is done by using appropriate locking primitives to prevent concurrent execution of code which accesses a given piece of shared data. This manual defines interfaces to several types of locking and synchronization primitives, namely basic locks, read/write locks, sleep locks and synchronization variables. Basic locks and read/write locks are intended for use within multithreaded drivers, while sleep locks and synchronization variables are useful in both singlethreaded and multithreaded drivers. The characteristics of the various locking and synchronization primitives are described on the relevant manual pages in Section 3.

Audience

This manual is for experienced C programmers responsible for creating, modifying, or maintaining drivers that run on UNIX System V Release 4 for the Intel386, Intel486 and Intel860 architectures and beyond. It assumes that the reader is familiar with UNIX system internals and the advanced capabilities of the C Programming Language.

How to Use This Manual

This manual is organized into an introduction, five reference sections, and three appendices:

- "Introduction" introduces the DDI, DKI, and other driver interfaces, and explains the notational conventions used in this manual.
- "Section 1: Driver Data" contains reference pages for all driver-defined data needed by the system.
- "Section 2: Driver Entry Point Routines" contains reference pages for all driver entry point routines.
- "Section 3: Kernel Utility Routines" contains reference pages for all kernel functions used in DDI/DKI drivers.
- "Section 4: Kernel Data Structures" contains reference pages for structures used in DDI/DKI drivers.
- "Section 5: Kernel Defines" contains reference pages for kernel **#define**'s used in DDI/DKI drivers.
- Appendices A through C describe migration from one System V Release 4 release to another. These appendices list all existing routines that have been modified or removed for a particular release, and all new routines added.
    - Appendix A describes the changes between Release 3.2 and Release 4.0.
    - Appendix B describes the changes between Release 4.0 and Release 4 Multi-Processor.
    - Appendix C describes the changes between Release 4 Multi-Processor and Release 4.2.

Organization of the DDI/DKI Manual Pages

Driver reference manual pages are similar to those in other reference manuals, with the page name followed by a section number in parentheses. All driver reference manual entries begin with a "D" to distinguish them as driver reference pages. For example, **open**(D2) refers to the **open** entry point routine for a driver, not to the **open**(2) system call documented in the *Operating System API Reference*.

Table 1 describes the headings used in the driver reference manual pages.

Table 1: Section Headings Used in This Manual

Heading	Contents
NAME	Gives the routine's name and a short summary of its purpose.
SYNOPSIS	Summarizes the routine's calling and return syntax.
Arguments	Summarizes each of the routine's arguments.
DESCRIPTION	Describes what the routine does, from the perspective of the software.
Return Values	Summarizes the return values from the routine.
USAGE	Describes how to use the routine, from the perspective of the programmer.
Structure Members	Describes all accessible data structure members.
Level	Gives an indication of when the routine can be used.
Synchronization Constraints	Describes the routine's ability to sleep and hold locking primitives.
Warnings	Provides restrictions on use and cautionary information.
Examples	Provides an example of common usage.
REFERENCES	Lists related manual pages.
NOTICES	Provides supplementary contextual information.
Availability	Identifies the UNIX System V Release 4 releases in which the routine is supported.
Portability	Identifies the processor (and, where appropriate, the hardware platform) on which the routine—as described on the manual page—is supported.

Table 1: Section Headings Used in This Manual (continued)

Heading	Contents
Interface	Identifies the type of interface. "Driver–Hardware" indicates the routine is primarily used to interact with hardware. "Driver–Kernel" indicates the routine is primarily used for kernel-to-driver and driver-to-kernel interactions. "General-purpose utility" indicates the routine is useful in device drivers, but is not part of the driver/hardware or the driver/kernel service interfaces.
Commitment	Gives the support level guaranteed for the routine. Level 1 routines will remain in the DDI/DKI and can be modified only in upward compatible ways. Any change in the definition of the routine will preserve the previous source-code interface and run-time behavior to ensure that the routine remains upwardly compatible. A Level 1 routine may however contain some features that are defined as Level 2. This occurs in cases in which a portion of a routine is evolving in a non_upwardly compatible way, but the basic functionality of the routine remains unchanged. Level 1 routines may be moved to Level 2. The date of their entry into Level 2 will be the date of the reissue of the DDI/DKI in which the change is made. Level 2 routines will remain unchanged for at least three years following entry into Level 2, after which time the routine may be modified in a non-upwardly compatible way or may be dropped from the DDI/DKI. This mechanism also applies to Level 2 portions of a Level 1 routine. Level 2 routines are labeled with the starting date of this three-year period.
Future Directions	Describes how the routine will change in the future, or warns about plans to discontinue support for the routine.

Conventions Used in This Manual

Table 2 lists the textual conventions used in this manual.

Table 2: Textual Conventions Used in This Manual

Item	Style	Example
C Reserved Words	`Constant Width`	`typedef`
C `typedef` Declarations	`Constant Width`	`caddr_t`
Driver Routines	`Constant Width`	`open` routine
Error Values	`Constant Width`	`EINTR`
File Names	`Constant Width`	`sys/conf.h`
Flag Names	`Constant Width`	`B_WRITE`
Kernel Macros	`Constant Width`	`minor`
Kernel Functions	`Constant Width`	`kmem_alloc`
Kernel Function Arguments	*Italics*	*bp*
Structure Members	`Constant Width`	`b_addr`
Structure Names	`Constant Width`	`buf` structure
Symbolic Constants	`Constant Width`	`NULL`
System Calls	`Constant Width`	`ioctl`(2)
C Library Calls	`Constant Width`	`printf`(3S)
Shell Commands	`Constant Width`	`layers`(1)
User-Defined Variable	*Italics*	*prefix*`close`

Related Documentation

Driver Development

Device Driver Programming contains information on writing, installing and testing UNIX System V device drivers. This guide includes instructions for making drivers dynamically loadable. Loadable drivers can be added to a running system without rebuilding the kernel and without having to bring the system down and reboot it. The guide also explains how to install and configure drivers using Installable Driver Tools (idtools) and Driver Software Packages (DSPs).

Portable Device Interface (PDI) explains the PDI, a UNIX System V programmatic interface for creating easily portable, DDI/DKI-compliant device drivers for block-oriented devices. This guide shows how to use the PDI to organize, simplify, and standardize drivers in ways that make them easier to create and maintain.

STREAMS

STREAMS Modules and Drivers describes programming using the UNIX System V STREAMS mechanism at the kernel level. STREAMS is a general, flexible facility for development of UNIX system communication services. Topics addressed in this guide include an overview to the STREAMS module paradigm, details of STREAMS message types and their management, and techniques of multiplexing and clone drivers. Descriptions of the STREAMS-based Transport Provider Interface (TPI) and Data Link Provider Interface (DPLI)— both part of the Open System Interconnection (OSI) Reference Model—are also provided.

Operating System

The UNIX System V reference manuals are the standard reference material for the UNIX operating system. This information is organized into five manuals, including:

- The two-volume *Command Reference* describes all user and administrative commands in the UNIX system, including file handling, basic networking, shell programming, and system management commands.
- *Operating System API Reference* describes UNIX system calls and library functions, including C language, math, networking, and specialized libraries.
- *Windowing System API Reference* describes graphical and character-based UNIX libraries, critical elements for building powerful user-interfaces on workstations, X, and character terminals.
- *System Files and Devices Reference* describes the file formats for important UNIX system files, such as password, hosts, system initialization, and special (device) files.
- *Device Driver Reference* is the manual you are currently reading.

Software Development and Packaging

UNIX Software Development Tools describes tools for developing and packaging application software that can also be used in device driver development and packaging. This guide contains instructions for a variety of UNIX system utilities such as **make**, **SCCS** and **pkgadd**.

Programming in Standard C discusses the UNIX system programming environment and utilities, and provides details of the C language, file formats, link editor, libraries, and tools.

NAME

`intro` – introduction to driver data

SYNOPSIS

```
#include <sys/types.h>
#include <sys/ddi.h>
```

DESCRIPTION

This section describes the data definitions a developer needs to include in a device driver. The system finds this information in an implementation-specific manner, usually tied to the way system configuration is handled.

USAGE

Each driver is uniquely identified by a prefix string specified in its configuration file. The name of all the driver-supplied routines and global variables should begin with this prefix. This will reduce the chance of a symbol collision with another driver. Any private routines defined by a driver that are not entry point routines should be declared as `static`. Also, any global variables that are private to the driver should be declared as `static`.

devflag (D1)

NAME

`devflag` – driver flags

SYNOPSIS

```
#include <sys/conf.h>
#include <sys/ddi.h>

int prefixdevflag = 0;
```

DESCRIPTION

Every driver must define a global integer variable called *prefix*`devflag`. This variable contains a bitmask of flags used to specify the driver's characteristics to the system.

USAGE

The valid flags that may be set in *prefix*`devflag` are:

`D_DMA`	The driver uses DMA (Direct Memory Access).
`D_TAPE`	The driver controls a tape device (mount read-only).
`D_NOBRKUP`	The driver understands page lists (the I/O job is not broken up along page boundaries into multiple jobs by the kernel.)

The following flag is valid for multiprocessor systems only:

`D_MP`	The driver is multithreaded (it handles its own locking and serialization).

The following flags are valid only for systems on which the Enhanced Security Utilities are installed:

`D_NOSPECMACDATA`	MAC (Mandatory Access Control) checking is not performed during data transfers to and from the device controlled by the driver, and the access time field in the inode is not updated.
`D_INITPUB`	The device controlled by the driver is, by default, accessible by non-privileged processes. This setting can be changed using a security system call.
`D_RDWEQ`	All accesses of the device controlled by the driver (both read and write) require strict equality under the MAC policy.

If the driver sets the `D_DMA` flag, it does not have to worry about making kernel buffers addressable to its DMA controller. The kernel will make sure that any kernel buffer addresses passed to the driver's entry points will be addressable by the driver's hardware.

If the driver uses `rdma_filter`(D3) for DMA transfer, the `D_DMA` flag should not be set.

If no flags are set for the driver, then *prefix*`devflag` should be set to 0.

REFERENCES

`rdma_filter`(D3)

NOTICES

Availability

SVR4.0, SVR4.1ES, SVR4MP, SVR4.2

Portability

Intel386, Intel486, Intel860

Interface

Driver-Kernel

Commitment

Level 1

info(D1)

NAME

`info` – STREAMS driver and module information

SYNOPSIS

```
#include <sys/stream.h>
#include <sys/ddi.h>

struct streamtab prefixinfo = { . . . };
```

DESCRIPTION

Every STREAMS driver and module must define a global **streamtab**(D4) structure so that the system can identify the entry points and interface parameters.

REFERENCES

streamtab(D4)

NOTICES

Availability

SVR4.0, SVR4.1ES, SVR4MP, SVR4.2

Portability

All processors

Interface

Driver-Kernel (STREAMS)

Commitment

Level 1

NAME

prefix – driver prefix

SYNOPSIS

```
int prefixclose();
int prefixopen();
. . .
```

DESCRIPTION

Every driver must define a unique prefix. This enables driver entry points to be identified by configuration software and decreases the possibility of global symbol collisions in the kernel.

USAGE

The prefix is usually specified in a configuration file. The maximum length of the prefix is implementation-defined. Driver entry points names are created by concatenating the driver prefix with the name for the entry point.

Examples

An ETHERNET driver might use a driver prefix of "**en**." It would define the following entry points: **enclose**, **eninit**, **enintr**, **enopen**, **enwput**, **enrsrv**, and **enwsrv**. It would also define the data symbols **endevflag** and **eninfo**.

REFERENCES

devflag(D1), **info**(D1), **chpoll**(D2), **close**(D2), **halt**(D2), **init**(D2), **intr**(D2), **ioctl**(D2), **_load**(D2), **mmap**(D2), **open**(D2), **print**(D2), **put**(D2), **read**(D2), **size**(D2), **srv**(D2), **start**(D2), **strategy**(D2), **_unload**(D2), **write**(D2)

NOTICES

Availability

SVR4.0, SVR4.1ES, SVR4MP, SVR4.2

Portability

All processors

Interface

Driver-Kernel

Commitment

Level 1

NAME

`intro` – introduction to driver entry point routines

SYNOPSIS

```
#include <sys/types.h>
#include <sys/ddi.h>
```

DESCRIPTION

This section describes the routines a developer needs to include in a device driver or STREAMS module.

USAGE

The routines described in this section are called "entry point routines" because they provide the interfaces that the kernel needs from drivers and STREAMS modules. The kernel calls these routines when needed. Some are called at well-defined times, such as system start up and system shut down. Others are called as a result of I/O-related system calls or external events, such as interrupts from peripheral devices.

Each driver or module is organized into two logical parts: the base level and the interrupt level. The base level interacts with the kernel and the device on behalf of processes performing I/O operations. The interrupt level interacts with the device and the kernel as a result of an event such as data arrival, and usually cannot be associated with any particular process.

Each driver or module is uniquely identified by a prefix string specified in its configuration file. The name of all the driver-supplied routines and global variables should begin with this prefix. This will reduce the chance of a symbol collision with another driver or module. Any private routines defined by a driver or module that are not entry point routines should be declared as `static`. Also, any global variables that are private to the driver or module should be declared as `static`.

In general, any number of instances of the same driver (or module) entry point routine can be running concurrently. It is the responsibility of the driver or module to synchronize access to its private data structures.

chpoll (D2)

NAME

chpoll – poll entry point for a non-STREAMS character driver

SYNOPSIS

```
#include <sys/poll.h>
#include <sys/ddi.h>

int prefixchpoll(dev_t dev, short events, int anyyet, short *reventsp,
     struct pollhead **phpp);
```

Arguments

dev	The device number for the device to be polled.
events	Mask (bit-wise **OR**) indicating the events being polled.
anyyet	A flag that indicates whether the driver should return a pointer to its **pollhead** structure to the caller.
reventsp	A pointer to a bitmask of the returned events satisfied.
phpp	A pointer to a pointer to a **pollhead** structure (defined in **sys/poll.h**).

DESCRIPTION

The **chpoll** entry point indicates whether certain I/O events have occurred on a given device. It must be provided by any non-STREAMS character device driver that wishes to support polling [see **poll**(2)].

Return Values

The **chpoll** routine should return 0 for success, or the appropriate error number.

USAGE

This entry point is optional, and is valid for character device drivers only.

Valid values for *events* are:

POLLIN	Data is available to be read (either normal or out-of-band).
POLLOUT	Data may be written without blocking.
POLLPRI	High priority data are available to be read.
POLLHUP	A device hangup.
POLLERR	A device error.
POLLRDNORM	Normal data is available to be read.
POLLWRNORM	Normal data may be written without blocking (same as **POLLOUT**).
POLLRDBAND	Out-of-band data is available to be read.
POLLWRBAND	Out-of-band data may be written without blocking.

A driver that supports polling must provide a **pollhead** structure for each minor device supported by the driver. On systems where they are available, the driver should use the **phalloc**(D3) function to allocate the **pollhead** structure, and use the **phfree**(D3) function to free the **pollhead** structure, if necessary.

The **pollhead** structure must be initialized to zeros prior to its first use (when **phalloc** is used to allocate the structure, this is done automatically).

The definition of the **pollhead** structure is not included in the DDI/DKI, and can change across releases. It should be treated as a "black box" by the driver; none of its fields may be referenced. Although the size of the **pollhead** structure is guaranteed to remain the same across releases, it is good practice for drivers not to depend on the size of the structure.

The driver must implement the polling discipline itself. Each time the driver detects a pollable event, it should call **pollwakeup**(D3), passing to it the event that occurred and the address of the **pollhead** structure associated with the device. Note that **pollwakeup** should be called with only one event at a time.

When the driver's **chpoll** entry point is called, the driver should check if any of the events requested in *events* have occurred. The driver should store the mask, consisting of the subset of **events** that are pending, in the **short** pointed to by *reventsp*. Note that this mask may be 0 if none of the events are pending. In this case, the driver should check the *anyyet* flag and, if it is zero, store the address of the device's **pollhead** structure in the pointer pointed at by *phpp*. The canonical **chpoll** algorithm is:

```
if (events_are_satisfied_now) {
        *reventsp = events & mask_of_satisfied_events;
} else {
        *reventsp = 0;
        if (!anyyet)
                *phpp = my_local_pollhead_pointer;
}
return (0);
```

Synchronization Constraints

On uniprocessor systems, user context is available in the **chpoll** routine, but if the driver sleeps, it must do so such that signals do not cause the sleep to longjump [see **sleep**(D3)].

On multiprocessor systems, the **chpoll** routine may not call any function that sleeps.

REFERENCES

bzero(D3), **phalloc**(D3), **phfree**(D3), **poll**(2), **pollwakeup**(D3)

NOTICES

Availability

SVR4.0, SVR4.1ES, SVR4MP, SVR4.2

Portability

All processors

Interface

Driver-Kernel

Commitment

Level 1

NAME

`close` – relinquish access to a device

SYNOPSIS

Block and Character Synopsis

```
#include <sys/types.h>
#include <sys/file.h>
#include <sys/errno.h>
#include <sys/open.h>
#include <sys/cred.h>
#include <sys/ddi.h>

int prefixclose(dev_t dev, int flag, int otyp, cred_t *crp);
```

Block and Character Arguments

dev Device number.

flag File status flags.

otyp Parameter supplied so that the driver can determine how many times a device was opened and for what reasons.

crp Pointer to the user credential structure.

STREAMS Synopsis

```
#include <sys/types.h>
#include <sys/stream.h>
#include <sys/file.h>
#include <sys/errno.h>
#include <sys/cred.h>
#include <sys/ddi.h>

int prefixclose(queue_t *q, int flag, cred_t *crp);
```

STREAMS Arguments

q Pointer to queue used to reference the read side of the driver.

flag File status flag.

crp Pointer to the user credential structure.

DESCRIPTION

Block and Character Description

The `close` routine ends the connection between the user process and the device, and prepares the device (hardware and software) so that it is ready to be opened again.

Valid values for *flag* and their definitions can be found in **open**(D2).

The values for *otyp* are mutually exclusive:

`OTYP_BLK` Close was through the block interface for the device.

`OTYP_CHR` Close was through the raw/character interface for the device.

`OTYP_LYR` Close a layered device. This flag is used when one driver calls another driver's `close` routine.

For **OTYP_BLK** and **OTYP_CHR**, a device may be opened simultaneously by multiple processes and the driver **open** routine is called for each open, but the kernel will only call the **close** routine when the last process using the device issues a **close**(2) system call or exits.

There is one exception to this rule. If a device is opened through both its character and its block interfaces, then there will be one close per interface. For example, if the same device is opened twice through its block interface and three times through its character interface, then there will be two calls to the driver's close routine; one when the block interface is finished being used, and one when the character interface is finished being used.

For **OTYP_LYR**, there will be one such close for every corresponding open. Here, the driver should count each open and close based on the *otyp* parameter to determine when the device should really be closed.

STREAMS Description

The **close** routines of STREAMS drivers and modules are called when a stream is dismantled or a module popped. The steps for dismantling a stream are performed in the following order. First, any non-persistent multiplexor links present are unlinked and the lower streams are closed. Next, the following steps are performed for each module or driver on the stream, starting at the head and working toward the tail:

1. The write queue is given a chance to drain.
2. Interrupts from STREAMS devices are blocked.
3. The **close** routine is called.
4. The module or driver is removed from the stream.
5. Any remaining messages on the queues are freed.

Return Values

The **close** routine should return 0 for success, or the appropriate error number. Refer to **errnos**(D5) for a list of DDI/DKI error numbers. Return errors rarely occur, but if a failure is detected, the driver should still close the device and then decide whether the severity of the problem warrants displaying a message on the console.

USAGE

This entry point is required in all drivers and STREAMS modules.

A **close** routine could perform any of the following general functions, depending on the type of device and the service provided:

disable device interrupts

hang up phone lines

rewind a tape

deallocate buffers from a private buffering scheme

unlock an unsharable device (that was locked in the **open** routine) flush buffers

notify a device of the close

cancel any pending timeout or bufcall routines that access data that are deinitialized or deallocated during close

deallocate any resources allocated on open

Multithreaded STREAMS drivers and modules must call **qprocsoff**(D3) to disable their **put**(D2) and service [**srv**(D2)] routines before returning from the **close** routine.

Synchronization Constraints

The **close** routine has user context and can sleep. However, STREAMS drivers and modules must sleep such that signals do not cause the sleep to longjump [see **sleep**(D3)]. Also, if a **close** routine does sleep, it is important that the driver writer synchronize the driver's **open** and **close** routines, since a driver can be reopened while being closed.

If the **FNDELAY** or **FNONBLOCK** flags are specified in the *flag* argument, the driver should try to avoid sleeping, if possible, during close processing.

REFERENCES

drv_priv(D3), **errnos**(D5), **qprocsoff**(D3), **open**(D2), **queue**(D4), **unbufcall**(D3), **untimeout**(D3), **sleep**(D3)

NOTICES

Availability

SVR4.0, SVR4.1ES, SVR4MP, SVR4.2

Portability

All processors

Interface

Driver-Kernel

Commitment

Level 1

halt (D2)

NAME

`halt` – shut down the driver when the system shuts down

SYNOPSIS

`void` *prefix*`halt(void);`

DESCRIPTION

The **`halt`** routine if present, is called to shut down the driver when the system is shut down. After the **`halt`** routine is called, no more calls will be made to the driver entry points.

Return Values

None

USAGE

This entry point is optional.

The device driver shouldn't assume that the interrupts are enabled. The driver should make sure that no interrupts are pending from its device, and inform the device that no more interrupts should be generated.

Synchronization Constraints

User context is not available, so the driver's **`halt`** routine should not sleep.

NOTICES

Availability

SVR4.0, SVR4.1ES, SVR4MP, SVR4.2

Portability

All processors

Interface

Driver-Kernel

Commitment

Level 1

NAME

`init` – initialize a device

SYNOPSIS

`void` *prefix*`init(void);`

DESCRIPTION

The `init` routine executes during system initialization to initialize drivers and the devices they control.

Return Values

None

USAGE

This entry point is optional.

Although `init` and `start` routines both perform initialization tasks, they execute at different times during system start-up. For this reason, they should be used to handle different types of initialization tasks.

`init` routines:

> execute during system initialization
>
> handle any driver and device setup and initialization that must take place before system services are initialized (for example, perform any setup and initialization that must be done before device interrupts are enabled)
>
> may only call the kernel functions listed below

`start` routines:

> execute after system services are initialized
>
> handle all driver and device setup and initialization that can take place after system services are initialized (most driver setup and initialization tasks can be performed at this time, using a `start` routine)
>
> handle any driver and device setup and initialization that can only take place after system services are initialized (for example, perform any setup and initialization that must be done after device interrupts are enabled)

Types of activities performed by the `init` routine include initializing data structures, allocating memory for private data, mapping the device into virtual address space, and initializing hardware

The following kernel functions can be called from the driver's `init` routine:

ASSERT	dma_swstart	makedevice
bcmp	drv_gethardware	max
bcopy	drv_getparm	min
bioreset	drv_hztousec	outb
btop	drv_usectohz	outl
btopr	drv_usecwait	outw
bzero	etoimajor	physmap
cmn_err	getemajor	physmap_free
dma_disable	geteminor	repinsb

dma_enable	getmajor	repinsl
dma_free_buf	getminor	repinsw
dma_free_cb	inb	repoutsb
dma_get_best_mode	inl	repoutsl
dma_get_buf	inw	repoutsw
dma_get_cb	itoemajor	rmalloc
dma_prog	kmem_alloc	rminit
dma_stop	kmem_free	rmfree
dma_swsetup	kmem_zalloc	vtop

On multiprocessor systems, the folllowing additional kernel functions can be called from the driver's `init` routine:

LOCK_ALLOC	rmallocmap	SLEEP_ALLOC
phalloc	rmfreemap	SV_ALLOC
phfree	RW_ALLOC	

`init` routines for dynamically loadable modules are not called during system start-up as they are for statically linked modules. A loadable module's initialization is performed by its `_load`(D2) routine, which is called each time the module is loaded into a running system. However, if the processing done by a module's `init` routine when the module is configured as a statically linked module can also be used when the module is configured as a loadable module, the module can call its `init` routine from its `_load` routine.

Synchronization Constraints

Functions that can result in the caller sleeping, or that require user context, such as `sleep`(D3), may not be called from `init`. Any function that provides a flag to prevent it from sleeping must be called such that the function does not sleep.

REFERENCES

`_load`(D2), `start`(D2)

NOTICES

Availability

SVR4.0, SVR4.1ES, SVR4MP, SVR4.2

Portability

Intel386, Intel486, Intel860

Interface

Driver-Kernel

Commitment

Level 1

NAME

`intr` – process a device interrupt

SYNOPSIS

`void` *prefix*`intr(int` *ivec*`);`

Arguments

ivec Number used by the operating system to associate a driver's interrupt handler with an interrupting device. The makeup and interpretation of *ivec* is specific to each system implementation. On some systems, this number may be the logical device number, or a combination of logical device and logical controller numbers, used to map the correct interrupt routine with a subdevice. On others, this number could be the interrupt vector number.

DESCRIPTION

The **intr** routine is the interrupt handler for both block and character hardware drivers, as well as for non-driver hardware modules.

Return Values

None

USAGE

This entry point is only required for those modules that interface to hardware that interrupts the host computer. It is not used with software drivers.

The interrupt handler is responsible for determining the reason for an interrupt, servicing the interrupt, and waking up any base-level driver processes sleeping on any events associated with the interrupt.

For example, when a disk drive has transferred information to the host to satisfy a read request, the disk drive's controller generates an interrupt. The CPU acknowledges the interrupt and calls the interrupt handler associated with that controller and disk drive. The interrupt routine services the interrupt and then wakes up the driver base-level process waiting for data. The base-level portion of the driver then conveys the data to the user.

In general, most interrupt routines do the following tasks:

keep a record of interrupt occurrences

return immediately if no devices controlled by a driver caused the interrupt (only for systems supporting shared interrupts)

interpret the interrupt routine argument *ivec*

reject requests for devices that are not served by the device's controller

process interrupts that happen without cause (called spurious interrupts)

handle all possible device errors

wake processes that are sleeping on any events associated with the interrupt

There are also many tasks the **intr** routine must perform that are driver-type and device specific. For example, the following types of drivers require different functions from their **intr** routines:

A block driver dequeues requests and wakes up processes sleeping on an I/O request.

A terminal driver receives and sends characters.

A printer driver ensures that characters are sent.

In addition, the functions of an **intr** routine are device dependent. You should know the exact chip set that produces the interrupt for your device. You need to know the exact bit patterns of the device's control and status register and how data is transmitted into and out of your computer. These specifics differ for every device you access.

The **intr** routine for an intelligent controller that does not use individual interrupt vectors for each subdevice must access the completion queue to determine which subdevice generated the interrupt. It must also update the status information, set/clear flags, set/clear error indicators, and so forth to complete the handling of a job. The code should also be able to handle a spurious completion interrupt identified by an empty completion queue. When the routine finishes, it should advance the unload pointer to the next entry in the completion queue.

If the driver called **biowait**(D3) or **sleep**(D3) [or, for multithreaded drivers, called **SV_WAIT**(D3) or **SV_WAIT_SIG**(D3)] to await the completion of an operation, the **intr** routine must call **biodone**(D3) or **wakeup**(D3) [or, for multithreaded drivers, call **SV_SIGNAL**(D3) or **SV_BROADCAST**(D3)] to signal the process to resume.

The interrupt routine runs at the processor level associated with the interrupt level for the given device. Lower priority interrupts are deferred while the interrupt routine is active. Certain processor levels can block different interrupts. See **spl**(D3) for more information.

uiomove(D3), **ureadc**(D3), and **uwritec**(D3) cannot be used in an interrupt routine when the **uio_segflg** member of the **uio**(D4) structure is set to **UIO_USERSPACE** (indicating a transfer between user and kernel space).

Synchronization Constraints

The **intr** routine must never:

use functions that sleep

drop the interrupt priority level below the level at which the interrupt routine was entered

call any function or routine that requires user context (that is, if it accesses or alters information associated with the running process)

REFERENCES

biodone(D3), **biowait**(D3), **spl**(D3), **SV_BROADCAST**(D3), **SV_SIGNAL**(D3), **SV_WAIT**(D3), **SV_WAIT_SIG**(D3), **wakeup**(D3)

NOTICES

Availability

SVR4.0, SVR4.1ES, SVR4MP, SVR4.2

Portability

Intel386, Intel486, Intel860

Interface
Driver-Kernel

Commitment
Level 1

ioctl (D2)

NAME

`ioctl` – control a character device

SYNOPSIS

```
#include <sys/types.h>
#include <sys/cred.h>
#include <sys/file.h>
#include <sys/errno.h>
#include <sys/ddi.h>
```

`int` *prefix*`ioctl(dev_t` *dev*`, int` *cmd*`, void *`*arg*`, int` *mode*`, cred_t *`*crp*`,`
`int *`*rvalp*`);`

Arguments

dev Device number.

cmd Command argument the driver **`ioctl`** routine interprets as the operation to be performed.

arg Passes parameters between the user and the driver. The interpretation of the argument is dependent on the command and the driver. For example, the argument can be an integer, or it can be the address of a user structure containing driver or hardware settings.

mode Contains the file modes set when the device was opened. The driver can use this to determine if the device was opened for reading (**`FREAD`**), writing (**`FWRITE`**), and so on. See **open**(D2) for a description of the values.

crp Pointer to the user credential structure.

rvalp Pointer to the return value for the calling process. The driver may elect to set the value if the `ioctl`(D2) succeeds.

DESCRIPTION

The `ioctl`(D2) routine provides non-STREAMS character drivers with an alternate entry point that can be used for almost any operation other than a simple transfer of data.

The `ioctl` routine is basically a **`switch`** statement, with each **`case`** definition corresponding to a different `ioctl` command identifying the action to be taken.

Return Values

The `ioctl` routine should return 0 on success, or the appropriate error number on failure. The system call will usually return 0 on success or –1 on failure. However, the driver can choose to have the system call return a different value on success by passing the value through the *rvalp* pointer.

USAGE

This entry point is optional, and is valid for character device drivers only.

Most often, `ioctl` is used to control device hardware parameters and establish the protocol used by the driver in processing data. I/O control commands are used to implement terminal settings, to format disk devices, to implement a trace driver for debugging, and to flush queues.

If the third argument, *arg*, is a pointer to user space, the driver can use **copyin**(D3) and **copyout**(D3) to transfer data between kernel and user space.

STREAMS drivers do not have **ioctl** routines. The stream head converts I/O control commands to **M_IOCTL** messages, which are handled by the driver's **put**(D2) or **srv**(D2) routine.

Synchronization Constraints

The **ioctl** routine has user context and can sleep.

Warnings

An attempt should be made to keep the values for driver-specific I/O control commands distinct from others in the system. Each driver's I/O control commands are unique, but it is possible for user-level code to access a driver with an I/O control command that is intended for another driver, which can have serious results.

A common method to assign I/O control command values that are less apt to be duplicated is to compose the commands from some component unique to the driver (such as a module name or ID), and a counter, as in:

```
#define PREFIX          ('h'<<16|'d'<<8)
#define COMMAND1        (PREFIX|1)
#define COMMAND2        (PREFIX|2)
#define COMMAND3        (PREFIX|3)
```

REFERENCES

copyin(D3), **copyout**(D3), **drv_priv**(D3), **errnos**(D5), **open**(D2)

NOTICES

Availability

SVR4.0, SVR4.1ES, SVR4MP, SVR4.2

Portability

All processors

Interface

Driver-Kernel

Commitment

Level 1

_load (D2)

NAME

`_load` – initialize a loadable kernel module

SYNOPSIS

```
#include <sys/moddefs.h>
#include <sys/ddi.h>

int prefix_load(void);
```

DESCRIPTION

The module **`_load`** routine routine performs any module-specific setup and initialization needed to dynamically load a kernel module into a running system.

Return Values

The **`_load`** routine should return 0 for success, or the appropriate error number.

USAGE

This entry point is optional.

Types of modules that can be dynamically loaded include:

- device drivers (block, character, STREAMS and pseudo)
- Host Bus Adapter drivers
- Direct Coupled Device controller drivers
- STREAMS modules
- file systems
- miscellaneous modules, such as modules containing code for support routines shared among multiple loadable modules which are not needed in the statically configured kernel

A loadable module's **`_load`** routine is defined in module-specific initialization code called wrapper code. The **`_load`** routine can perform activities such as:

- allocate memory for private data
- initialize driver data structures
- install and enable device interrupts by calling the **`mod_drvattach`**(D3) routine
- initialize devices

`sys/moddefs.h` provides a set a macros that can be used to generate wrappers for loadable modules. The macros are of the form:

type`(`*prefix*`,` *load*`,` *unload*`,` *halt*`,` *desc*`);`

where

type is the type of wrapper macro. Valid types are:

`MOD_DRV_WRAPPER`	Generates wrappers for device drivers.
`MOD_HDRV_WRAPPER`	Generates wrappers for Host Bus Adapter drivers.

`MOD_STR_WRAPPER`	Generates wrappers for STREAMS modules.
`MOD_FS_WRAPPER`	Generates wrappers for file systems.
`MOD_MISC_WRAPPER`	Generates wrappers for miscellaneous modules.

prefix Specifies the module's prefix [see **prefix**(D1)].

load Specifies the name of the module's **_load** routine.

unload Specifies the name of the module's **_unload** routine [see **_unload**(D2)].

halt This optional keyword specifies the name of the module's **halt** routine, if any [see **halt**(D2)].

desc Supplies a character string that identifies the module.

Synchronization Constraints

The **_load** routine can sleep.

Warnings

Loadable file system modules should not attempt to manipulate entries in the **vfssw[]** table with their **_load** routines. The **vfssw[]** table is updated automatically at the time the file system is loaded into the system.

Examples

The example shows sample wrapper code for the m320 mouse driver.

```
#include    <sys/moddefs.h>
#include    <sys/ddi.h>

static      int   mse3_load(), mse3_unload();
void mse3start();

MOD_DRV_WRAPPER(mse3, mse3_load, mse3_unload, "320 Mouse Driver");

static      int mse3_load(void)
{
      mod_drvattach(&mse3_attach_info);
      mse3start();
      return(0);
}

static      int mse3_unload(void)
{
      mod_drvdetach(&mse3_attach_info);
      return(0);
}
```

REFERENCES

halt(D2), **init**(D2), **mod_drvattach**(D3), **start**(D2), **_unload**(D2)

NOTICES

Availability

SVR4.2

Portability

All processors

_load (D2)

Interface

Driver-Kernel

Commitment

Level 1

NAME

mmap – support virtual mapping for memory-mapped device

SYNOPSIS

```
#include <sys/types.h>
#include <sys/mman.h>
#include <sys/vm.h>
#include <sys/ddi.h>

int prefixmmap(dev_t dev, off_t off, int prot);
```

Arguments

dev Device whose memory is to be mapped.

off Offset within device memory at which mapping begins.

prot Protection flags from **mman.h**.

DESCRIPTION

The **mmap** entry point provides a way to support character drivers for memory-mapped devices. A memory-mapped device has memory that can be mapped into a process's address space. The **mmap**(2) system call, when applied to a character special file, allows this device memory to be mapped into user space for direct access by the user application (this way no kernel buffering or system call overhead is incurred).

The **mmap** routine checks if the offset is within the range of pages supported by the device. For example, a device that has 32K bytes of memory that can be mapped into user space should not support offsets greater than, or equal to, 32K. If the offset does not exist, then **NOPAGE** is returned. If the offset does exist, the **mmap** routine returns the physical page ID for the page at offset *off* in the device's memory.

Return Values

If the protection and offset are valid for the device, the driver should return the physical page ID. Otherwise, **NOPAGE** should be returned.

USAGE

This entry point is optional, and valid for memory-mapped character device or character pseudo-device drivers only.

Valid values for *prot* are:

PROT_READ	Page can be read.
PROT_WRITE	Page can be written.
PROT_EXEC	Page can be executed.
PROT_USER	Page is accessible from user-level.
PROT_ALL	All of the above.

A physical page ID is a machine-specific token that uniquely identifies a page of physical memory in the system (either kernel memory or device memory). To get the physical page ID for a given virtual address, drivers should use the **hat_getkpfnum**(D3) function (on SVR4.0, SVR4.1ES and SVR4.2 systems) or the **kvtoppid**(D3) function (on SVR4MP systems). To get the physical page ID for a given physical address, drivers should use the **hat_getppfnum**(D3) function (on SVR4.0, SVR4.1ES and SVR4.2 systems) or the **phystoppid**(D3) function (on

SVR4MP systems).

No assumptions should be made about the format of a physical page ID.

Synchronization Constraints

The **mmap** routine has user context and can sleep.

REFERENCES

hat_getkpfnum(D3), **hat_getppfnum**(D3), **kvtoppid**(D3), **mmap**(2), **phystoppid**(D3)

NOTICES

Availability

SVR4.0, SVR4.1ES, SVR4MP, SVR4.2

Portability

All processors

Interface

Driver-Kernel

Commitment

Level 1

NAME

open – gain access to a device

SYNOPSIS

Block and Character Synopsis

```
#include <sys/types.h>
#include <sys/file.h>
#include <sys/errno.h>
#include <sys/open.h>
#include <sys/cred.h>
#include <sys/ddi.h>
```

`int` *prefix*`open(dev_t *`*devp*`, int` *oflag*`, int` *otyp*`, cred_t *`*crp*`);`

Block and Character Arguments

devp Pointer to a device number.

oflag Information passed from the user that instructs the driver on how to open the file.

otyp Parameter supplied so that the driver can determine how many times a device was opened and for what reasons.

crp Pointer to the user credential structure.

STREAMS Synopsis

```
#include <sys/types.h>
#include <sys/file.h>
#include <sys/stream.h>
#include <sys/errno.h>
#include <sys/cred.h>
#include <sys/ddi.h>
```

`int` *prefix*`open(queue_t *`*q*`, dev_t *`*devp*`, int` *oflag*`, int` *sflag*`, cred_t *`*crp*`);`

STREAMS Arguments

q Pointer to the queue used to reference the read side of the driver.

devp Pointer to a device number. For modules, *devp* always points to the device number associated with the driver at the end (tail) of the stream.

oflag Open flags.

sflag STREAMS flag.

crp Pointer to the user credential structure.

Return Values

The **open** routine should return 0 for success, or the appropriate error number.

DESCRIPTION

Block and Character Description

The driver's **open** routine is called to prepare a device for further access. It is called by the kernel during an **open**(2) or a **mount**(2) of the device special file. For non-STREAMS drivers, it can also be called from another (layered) driver.

The bit settings for **oflag** are found in **file.h**. Valid settings are:

- **FEXCL** Interpreted in a driver-dependent manner. Some drivers interpret this flag to mean open the device with exclusive access (fail all other attempts to open the device.)
- **FNDELAY** Open the device and return immediately without sleeping (do not block the open even if there is a problem.)
- **FNONBLOCK** Open the device and return immediately without sleeping (do not block the open even if there is a problem.)
- **FREAD** Open the device with read access permission.
- **FWRITE** Open the device with write access permission.

Valid values for *otyp* are defined in **open.h**. The values are mutually exclusive:

- **OTYP_BLK** Open occurred through block interface for the device.
- **OTYP_CHR** Open occurred through the raw/character interface for the device.
- **OTYP_LYR** Open a layered device. This flag is used when one driver calls another driver's **open** routine.

STREAMS Description

The STREAMS module **open** routine is called by the kernel during an **I_PUSH** **ioctl**(2) or an autopush-style open [see **autopush**(1M)].

Values for *oflag* are the same as those described for the block and character open flags above.

The values for *sflag* are mutually exclusive:

- **CLONEOPEN** Indicates a clone open (see below.) If the driver supports cloning, it must assign and return a device number of an unused device by changing the value of the device number to which *devp* points.
- **MODOPEN** Indicates that an **open** routine is being called for a module, not a driver. This is useful in detecting configuration errors and in determining how the driver is being used, since STREAMS drivers can also be configured as STREAMS modules.
- 0 Indicates a driver is being opened directly, without cloning.

USAGE

This entry point is required in all drivers and STREAMS modules.

The **open** routine could perform any of the following general functions, depending on the type of device and the service provided:

enable device interrupts

allocate buffers or other resources needed to use the device

lock an unsharable device

notify the device of the open

change the device number if this is a clone open

enable put and service procedures for multithreaded drivers

The **open** routine should verify that the minor number component of *devp* is valid, that the type of access requested by *otyp* and *oflag* is appropriate for the device, and, if required, check permissions using the user credentials pointed to by *crp* [see **drv_priv**(D3)].

For STREAMS drivers and modules, the **open** routine is called with interrupts blocked from all STREAMS devices. If the driver sets stream head options by sending an **M_SETOPTS** message upstream from the **open** routine, then the changes are guaranteed to take effect when the system call completes.

Support of cloning is optional. Cloning is the process of the driver selecting an unused device for the user. It eliminates the need to poll many devices when looking for an unused one. Both STREAMS and Non-STREAMS drivers may implement cloning behavior by changing the device number pointed to by *devp*. A driver may designate certain minor devices as special clone entry points into the driver. When these are opened, the driver searches for an unused device and returns the new device number by changing the value of the device number to which *devp* points. Both the major device number and the minor device number can be changed, although usually just the minor number is changed. The major number is only changed when the clone controls more than one device.

Using this method of cloning, a STREAMS driver will never see *sflag* set to **CLONEOPEN**. A different method makes use of this flag. STREAMS drivers can take advantage of a special driver, known as the *clone driver*, to perform clone opens. This frees the driver from having to reserve special minors for the clone entry points. Here, the device node is actually that of the clone driver (the major number is the major number from the clone driver and the minor number is the major number from the real driver.) When the clone driver is opened, it will call the real driver open routine with *sflag* set to **CLONEOPEN**.

For STREAMS drivers and modules, for a given device number (queue), only one instance of the **open** routine can be running at any given time. However, multiple opens on any two different device numbers (queues) can be running concurrently. It is the responsibility of the driver or module to synchronize access to its private data structures in this case. For clone opens, multiple clone opens can run concurrently, and it is the driver's responsibility to synchronize access to its private data structures, as well as allocation and deallocation of device numbers.

Synchronization Constraints

The **open** routine has user context and can sleep. However, STREAMS drivers and modules must sleep such that signals do not cause the sleep to longjump [see **sleep**(D3)].

REFERENCES

close(D2), **drv_priv**(D3), **errnos**(D5), **qprocson**(D3), **queue**(D4)

NOTICES

Availability

SVR4.0, SVR4.1ES, SVR4MP, SVR4.2

Portability

All processors

Interface

Driver-Kernel

Commitment

Level 1

NAME

`print` – display a driver message on the system console

SYNOPSIS

```
#include <sys/types.h>
#include <sys/errno.h>
#include <sys/ddi.h>

int prefixprint(dev_t dev, char *str);
```

Arguments

dev Device number.

str Pointer to a NULL-terminated character string describing the problem.

DESCRIPTION

The `print` routine is called indirectly by the kernel for the block device when the kernel has detected an exceptional condition (such as out of space) in the device. The driver should print the message on the console along with any driver-specific information.

Return Values

Ignored

USAGE

This entry point is optional, and is valid for block device drivers only.

To display the message on the console, the driver should use the `cmn_err`(D3) function.

The driver should not try to interpret the text string passed to it.

Synchronization Constraints

The `print` routine should not call any functions that sleep.

REFERENCES

`cmn_err`(D3)

NOTICES

Availability

SVR4.0, SVR4.1ES, SVR4MP, SVR4.2

Portability

All processors

Interface

Driver-Kernel

Commitment

Level 1

put(D2)

NAME

put – receive messages from the preceding queue

SYNOPSIS

```
#include <sys/types.h>
#include <sys/stream.h>
#include <sys/stropts.h>
#include <sys/ddi.h>

int prefixrput(queue_t *q, mblk_t *mp);   /* read side */

int prefixwput(queue_t *q, mblk_t *mp);   /* write side */
```

Arguments

q Pointer to the queue.

mp Pointer to the message block.

DESCRIPTION

The primary task of the **put** routine is to coordinate the passing of messages from one queue to the next in a stream. The **put** routine is called by the preceding component (module, driver, or stream head) in the stream. **put** routines are designated "write" or "read" depending on the direction of message flow.

Return Values

Ignored

USAGE

This entry point is required in all STREAMS drivers and modules.

Both modules and drivers must have write **put** routines. Modules must have read **put** routines, but drivers don't really need them because their interrupt handler can do the work intended for the read **put** routine. A message is passed to the **put** routine. If immediate processing is desired, the **put** routine can process the message, or it can enqueue it so that the service routine [see **srv**(D2)] can process it later.

The **put** routine must do at least one of the following when it receives a message:

- pass the message to the next component in the stream by calling the **putnext**(D3) function
- process the message, if immediate processing is required (for example, high priority messages)
- enqueue the message with the **putq**(D3) function for deferred processing by the service routine

Typically, the **put** routine will switch on the message type, which is contained in **mp->b_datap->db_type**, taking different actions depending on the message type. For example, a **put** routine might process high priority messages and enqueue normal messages.

The **putq** function can be used as a module's **put** routine when no special processing is required and all messages are to be enqueued for the service routine.

Although it can be done in the service routine, drivers and modules usually handle queue flushing in their **put** routines.

The canonical flushing algorithm for driver write put routines is as follows:

```
queue_t *q;      /* the write queue */
if (*mp->b_rptr & FLUSHBAND) { /* if driver recognizes bands */
      if (*mp->b_rptr & FLUSHW) {
            flushband(q, FLUSHDATA, *(mp->b_rptr + 1));
            *mp->b_rptr &= ~FLUSHW;
      }
      if (*mp->b_rptr & FLUSHR) {
            flushband(RD(q), FLUSHDATA, *(mp->b_rptr + 1));
            qreply(q, mp);
      } else {
            freemsg(mp);
      }
} else {
      if (*mp->b_rptr & FLUSHW) {
            flushq(q, FLUSHDATA);
            *mp->b_rptr &= ~FLUSHW;
      }
      if (*mp->b_rptr & FLUSHR) {
            flushq(RD(q), FLUSHDATA);
            qreply(q, mp);
      } else {
            freemsg(mp);
      }
}
```

The canonical flushing algorithm for module write put routines is as follows:

```
queue_t *q;      /* the write queue */
if (*mp->b_rptr & FLUSHBAND) { /* if module recognizes bands */
      if (*mp->b_rptr & FLUSHW)
            flushband(q, FLUSHDATA, *(mp->b_rptr + 1));
      if (*mp->b_rptr & FLUSHR)
            flushband(RD(q), FLUSHDATA, *(mp->b_rptr + 1));
} else {
      if (*mp->b_rptr & FLUSHW)
            flushq(q, FLUSHDATA);
      if (*mp->b_rptr & FLUSHR)
            flushq(RD(q), FLUSHDATA);
}
if (!SAMESTR(q)) {
      switch (*mp->b_rptr & FLUSHRW) {
      case FLUSHR:
            *mp->b_rptr = (*mp->b_rptr & ~FLUSHR) | FLUSHW;
            break;
      case FLUSHW:
            *mp->b_rptr = (*mp->b_rptr & ~FLUSHW) | FLUSHR;
            break;
      }
}
putnext(q, mp);
```

The algorithms for the read side are similar. In both examples, the **FLUSHBAND** flag need only be checked if the driver or module cares about priority bands.

Drivers and modules should not call **put** routines directly.

Drivers should free any messages they do not recognize.

Modules should pass on any messages they do not recognize.

Drivers should fail any unrecognized **M_IOCTL** messages by converting them into **M_IOCNAK** messages and sending them upstream.

Modules should pass on any unrecognized **M_IOCTL** messages.

Synchronization Constraints

put routines do not have user context and so may not call any function that sleeps.

Multithreaded drivers must not hold locks when passing messages to other queues in the stream.

With multithreaded drivers, multiple copies of the same **put** routine for a given queue, as well as the service routine for the queue, can be running concurrently. Drivers and modules are responsible for synchronizing access to their own private data structures accordingly.

REFERENCES

datab(D4), **flushband**(D3), **flushq**(D3), **msgb**(D4), **putctl**(D3), **putctl1**(D3), **putnext**(D3), **putq**(D3), **qreply**(D3), **queue**(D4), **srv**(D2)

NOTICES

Availability

SVR4.0, SVR4.1ES, SVR4MP, SVR4.2

Portability

All processors

Interface

Driver-Kernel (STREAMS)

Commitment

Level 1

NAME

read – read data from a device

SYNOPSIS

```
#include <sys/types.h>
#include <sys/errno.h>
#include <sys/uio.h>
#include <sys/cred.h>
#include <sys/ddi.h>

int prefixread(dev_t dev, uio_t *uiop, cred_t *crp);
```

Arguments

dev Device number.

uiop Pointer to the **uio**(D4) structure that describes where the data is to be stored in user space.

crp Pointer to the user credential structure for the I/O transaction.

DESCRIPTION

The driver **read** routine is called during the **read**(2) system call. The **read** routine is responsible for transferring data from the device to the user data area.

Return Values

The **read** routine should return 0 for success, or the appropriate error number.

USAGE

This entry point is optional, and is valid for character device drivers only.

The pointer to the user credentials, *crp*, is available so the driver can check to see if the user can read privileged information, if the driver provides access to any. The **uio** structure provides the information necessary to determine how much data should be transferred. The **uiomove**(D3) function provides a convenient way to copy data using the **uio** structure.

Block drivers that provide a character interface can use **physiock**(D3) to perform the data transfer with the driver's **strategy**(D2) routine.

Synchronization Constraints

The **read** routine has user context and can sleep.

REFERENCES

drv_priv(D3), **errnos**(D5), **physiock**(D3), **strategy**(D2), **uio**(D4), **uiomove**(D3), **ureadc**(D3), **write**(D2)

NOTICES

Availability

SVR4.0, SVR4.1ES, SVR4MP, SVR4.2

Portability

All processors

Interface

Driver-Kernel

read (D2)

Commitment

Level 1

NAME

`size` – return size of logical block device

SYNOPSIS

```
#include <sys/types.h>
#include <sys/param.h>
#include <sys/ddi.h>

int prefixsize(dev_t dev);
```

Arguments

dev The logical device number.

DESCRIPTION

The `size` entry point returns the number of `NBPSCTR`-byte units on a logical block device (partition). `NBPSCTR`, defined in `param.h`, is the number of bytes per logical disk sector.

Return Values

On success, the `size` routine should return the number of `NBPSCTR`-byte units on the logical block device specified by *dev*; on failure, `size` should return –1.

USAGE

This entry point is required in all block device drivers.

Synchronization Constraints

The `size` routine has user context and can sleep. However, it should be careful not to spend much time sleeping, especially if the routine is called when the logical device is not open.

NOTICES

Availability

SVR4.0, SVR4.1ES, SVR4MP, SVR4.2

Portability

All processors

Interface

Driver-Kernel

Commitment

Level 1

srv (D2)

NAME

srv – service queued messages

SYNOPSIS

```
#include <sys/types.h>
#include <sys/stream.h>
#include <sys/stropts.h>
#include <sys/ddi.h>
```

```
int prefixrsrv(queue_t *q);     /* read side */
int prefixwsrv(queue_t *q);     /* write side */
```

Arguments

q Pointer to the queue.

DESCRIPTION

The **srv** (service) routine may be included in a STREAMS module or driver for a number of reasons. It provides greater control over the flow of messages in a stream by allowing the module or driver to reorder messages, defer the processing of some messages, or fragment and reassemble messages. The service routine also provides a way to recover from resource allocation failures.

Return Values

Ignored

USAGE

This entry point is optional, and is valid for STREAMS drivers and modules only.

A message is first passed to a module's or driver's **put**(D2) routine, which may or may not process it. The **put** routine can place the message on the queue for processing by the service routine.

Once a message has been enqueued, the STREAMS scheduler calls the service routine at some later time. Drivers and modules should not depend on the order in which service procedures are run. This is an implementation-dependent characteristic. In particular, applications should not rely on service procedures running before returning to user-level processing.

Every STREAMS queue [see **queue**(D4)] has limit values it uses to implement flow control. High and low water marks are checked to stop and restart the flow of message processing. Flow control limits apply only between two adjacent queues with service routines. Flow control occurs by service routines following certain rules before passing messages along. By convention, high priority messages are not affected by flow control.

STREAMS messages can be defined to have up to 256 different priorities to support some networking protocol requirements for multiple bands of data flow. At a minimum, a stream must distinguish between normal (priority band zero) messages and high priority messages (such as **M_IOCACK**). High priority messages are always placed at the head of the queue, after any other high priority messages already enqueued. Next are messages from all included priority bands, which are enqueued in decreasing order of priority. Each priority band has its own flow control limits. By convention, if a band is flow-controlled, all lower priority bands are also stopped.

Once a service routine is called by the STREAMS scheduler it must provide for processing all messages on its queue, restarting itself if necessary. Message processing must continue until either the queue is empty, the stream is flow-controlled, or an allocation error occurs. Typically, the service routine will switch on the message type, which is contained in **mp->b_datap->db_type**, taking different actions depending on the message type.

For singlethreaded modules and drivers, the framework for the canonical service procedure algorithm is as follows:

```
queue_t *q;
mblk_t *mp;
while ((mp = getq(q)) != NULL) {
      if (mp->b_datap->db_type > QPCTL ||
         canput(q->q_next)) {
           /* process the message */
           putnext(q, mp);
      } else {
           putbq(q, mp);
           return;
      }
}
```

If the singlethreaded module or driver cares about priority bands, the algorithm becomes:

```
queue_t *q;
mblk_t *mp;
while ((mp = getq(q)) != NULL) {
      if (mp->b_datap->db_type > QPCTL ||
         bcanput(q->q_next, mp->b_band)) {
           /* process the message */
           putnext(q, mp);
      } else {
           putbq(q, mp);
           return;
      }
}
```

For multithreaded modules and drivers, the framework for the canonical service procedure algorithm is as follows:

```
queue_t *q;
mblk_t *mp;
   while ((mp = getq(q)) != NULL) {
      if (pcmsg(mp->b_datap->db_type) ||
              canputnext(q) {
                   /* process the message */
                   putnext(q, mp);
      } else {
                   putbq(q, mp);
                   return;
      }
}
```

If the multithreaded module or driver cares about priority bands, the algorithm becomes:

```
queue_t *q;
mblk_t *mp;
   while ((mp = getq(q)) != NULL) {
      if (pcmsg(mp->b_datap->db_type) ||
               bcanputnext(q, mp->b_band)) {
                     /* process the message */
                     putnext(q, mp);
      } else {
                     putbq(q, mp);
                     return;
      }
}
```

Each STREAMS module and driver can have a read and write service routine. If a service routine is not needed (because the **put** routine processes all messages), a **NULL** pointer should be placed in the module's **qinit**(D4) structure.

If the service routine finishes running because of any reason other than flow control or an empty queue, then it must explicitly arrange for its rescheduling. For example, if an allocation error occurs during the processing of a message, the service routine can put the message back on the queue with **putbq**, and, before returning, arrange to have itself rescheduled [see **qenable**(D3)] at some later time [see **bufcall**(D3) and **timeout**(D3)].

Service routines can be interrupted by **put** routines, unless the processor interrupt level is raised.

put routines can interrupt and run concurrently with service routines.

Only one copy of a queue's service routine will run at a time.

Drivers and modules should not call service routines directly. **qenable**(D3) should be used to schedule service routines to run.

Drivers (excepting multiplexors) should free any messages they do not recognize.

Modules should pass on any messages they do not recognize.

Drivers should fail any unrecognized **M_IOCTL** messages by converting them into **M_IOCNAK** messages and sending them upstream.

Modules should pass on any unrecognized **M_IOCTL** messages.

Service routines should never put high priority messages back on their queues.

Synchronization Constraints

Service routines do not have user context and so may not call any function that sleeps.

REFERENCES

bcanput(D3), **bcanputnext**(D3), **bufcall**(D3), **canput**(D3), **canputnext**(D3), **datab**(D4), **getq**(D3), **msgb**(D4), **pcmsg**(D3), **put**(D2), **putbq**(D3), **putnext**(D3), **putq**(D3), **qenable**(D3), **qinit**(D4), **queue**(D4), **timeout**(D3)

NOTICES

Availability

SVR4.0, SVR4.1ES, SVR4MP, SVR4.2

Portability

All processors

Interface

Driver-Kernel (STREAMS)

Commitment

Level 1

start (D2)

NAME

`start` – initialize a device at system start-up

SYNOPSIS

`void` *prefix*`start(void);`

DESCRIPTION

The **start** routine is called at system boot time (after system services are available and interrupts have been enabled) to initialize drivers and the devices they control.

Return Values

None

USAGE

This entry point is optional.

The **start** routine can perform the following types of activities:

initialize data structures

allocate buffers for private buffering schemes

map the device into virtual address space

initialize hardware

initialize timeouts

A driver that needs to perform setup and initialization tasks that must take place before system services are available and interrupts are enabled should use the **init**(D2) routine to perform such tasks. The **start** routine should be used for all other initialization tasks.

start routines for dynamically loadable modules are not called during system start-up as they are for statically linked modules. A loadable module's initialization is performed by its **_load**(D2) routine, which is called each time the module is loaded into a running system. However, if the processing done by a module's **start** routine when the module is configured as a statically linked module can also be used when the module is configured as a loadable module, the module can call its **start** routine from its **_load** routine.

Synchronization Constraints

Functions that can result in the caller sleeping, or that require user context, such as **sleep**(D3), may not be called from the **start** routine.

REFERENCES

init(D2), **_load**(D2)

NOTICES

Availability

SVR4.0, SVR4.1ES, SVR4MP, SVR4.2

Portability

All processors

Interface

Driver-Kernel

Commitment
Level 1

strategy (D2)

NAME

strategy – perform block I/O

SYNOPSIS

```
#include <sys/types.h>
#include <sys/buf.h>
#include <sys/errno.h>
#include <sys/ddi.h>

int prefixstrategy(struct buf *bp);
```

Arguments

bp Pointer to the buffer header structure.

DESCRIPTION

The **strategy** routine is called by the kernel to read and write blocks of data on the block device. **strategy** may also be called directly or indirectly (via a call to the **physiock**(D3) function) to support the raw character interface of a block device from **read**(D2), **write**(D2) or **ioctl**(D2). The **strategy** routine's responsibility is to set up and initiate the data transfer.

Return Values

Ignored. Errors are returned by using the **bioerror**(D3) function to mark the buffer as being in error. On systems where the **bioerror** function is not available, errors can be returned by setting the **B_ERROR** flag in the **b_flags** field of the **buf** structure, and setting the error number in the **b_error** field of the **buf** structure.

USAGE

This entry point is required in all block device drivers.

Generally, the first validation test performed by the **strategy** routine is to see if the I/O is within the bounds of the device. If the starting block number, given by **bp->b_blkno**, is less than 0 or greater than the number of blocks on the device, the error number in the buffer header should be set to **ENXIO**, and the **B_ERROR** flag should be set in **bp->b_flags**. If the **bioerror** routine is available, **bioerror** should be used to set the buffer error number to **ENXIO**. Then, the buffer should be marked done by calling **biodone**(D3), and the driver should return. If **bp->b_blkno** is equal to the number of blocks on the device and the operation is a write, indicated by the absence of the **B_READ** flag in **bp->b_flags** (**!(bp->b_flags & B_READ)**), then the same action should be taken. However, if the operation is a read and **bp->b_blkno** is equal to the number of blocks on the device, then the driver should set **bp->b_resid** equal to **bp->b_bcount**, mark the buffer done by calling **biodone**, and return. This will cause the read to return 0.

Once the I/O request has been validated, the **strategy** routine should queue the request. If there is not already a transfer under way, the I/O is started. Then the **strategy** routine returns. When the I/O is complete, the driver will call **biodone** to free the buffer and notify anyone who has called **biowait**(D3) to wait for the I/O to finish.

There are two kinds of I/O requests passed to **strategy** routines by the kernel: normal block I/O requests and paged-I/O requests. Normal block I/O requests are identified by the absence of the **B_PAGEIO** flag in **bp->b_flags**. Here, the starting kernel virtual address of the data transfer will be found in **bp->b_un.b_addr**. Paged-I/O requests are identified by the presence of the **B_PAGEIO** flag in **bp-**

>b_flags. These will not occur unless the driver has set the **D_NOBRKUP** flag [see **devflag**(D1)]. The driver has several ways to perform a paged-I/O request.

If the driver wants to use virtual addresses, it can call **bp_mapin**(D3) to get a virtually contiguous mapping for the pages. If the driver wants to use physical addresses, it can also use **bp_mapin**, but only transfer one page at a time. The physical address can be obtained by calling **vtop**(D3) for each page in the virtual range. The size of a page can be determined by calling **ptob**(D3). However, a more efficient way to use physical addresses is to use **getnextpg**(D3) and **pptophys**(D3) (if these routines are available) for each page in the page list.

If the amount of data to be transferred is more than can be transferred, the driver can transfer as much as possible (if it supports partial reads and writes), and then use the **bioerror** function to set the buffer error number to EIO. If the **bioerror** function is not available, the driver should then set the **B_ERROR** flag, and set **bp->b_resid** equal to the number of bytes not transferred (if all of the data were transferred, **bp->b_resid** should be set to 0).

Synchronization Constraints

The **strategy** entry point has the necessary context to sleep, but it cannot assume it is called from the same context of the process that initiated the I/O request. Furthermore, the process that initiated the I/O might not even be in existence when the **strategy** routine is called.

REFERENCES

biodone(D3), **bioerror**(D3), **biowait**(D3), **bp_mapin**(D3), **buf**(D4), **devflag**(D1), **errnos**(D5), **getnextpg**(D3), **physiock**(D3), **pptophys**(D3), **read**(D2), **write**(D2)

NOTICES

Availability

SVR4.0, SVR4.1ES, SVR4MP, SVR4.2

Portability

All processors

Interface

Driver-Kernel

Commitment

Level 1

_unload (D2)

NAME

`_unload` – clean up a loadable kernel module

SYNOPSIS

```
#include <sys/moddefs.h>
#include <sys/ddi.h>

int prefix_unload(void);
```

DESCRIPTION

The module **_unload** routine handles any cleanup a loadable kernel module must perform before it can be dynamically unloaded from a running system. Typically, a module's **_unload** routine undoes whatever was done in the module's **_load**(D2) routine.

Return Values

The **_unload** routine should return 0 for success, or the appropriate error number.

USAGE

This entry point is optional.

A loadable module's **_unload** routine is defined in module-specific initialization code called wrapper code. The **_unload** routine can perform activities such as:

- disable and remove device interrupts by calling the **mod_drvdetach**(D3) routine
- deallocate memory acquired for private data
- cancel any outstanding **timeout**(D3) or **bufcall**(D3) requests made by the module

Synchronization Constraints

The **_unload** routine should not sleep, and should not call any functions that sleep.

Examples

See **_load**(D2) for an example of **_unload**.

REFERENCES

_load(D2), **mod_drvdetach**(D3)

NOTICES

Availability

SVR4.2

Portability

All processors

Interface

Driver-Kernel

Commitment

Level 1

NAME

`write` – write data to a device

SYNOPSIS

```
#include <sys/types.h>
#include <sys/errno.h>
#include <sys/uio.h>
#include <sys/cred.h>
#include <sys/ddi.h>

int prefixwrite(dev_t dev, uio_t *uiop, cred_t *crp);
```

Arguments

dev Device number.

uiop Pointer to the **uio**(D4) structure that describes where the data is to be fetched from user space.

crp Pointer to the user credential structure for the I/O transaction.

DESCRIPTION

The driver **write** routine is called during the **write**(2) system call. The **write** routine is responsible for transferring data from the user data area to the device.

Return Values

The **write** routine should return 0 for success, or the appropriate error number.

USAGE

This entry point is optional, and is valid for character device drivers only.

The pointer to the user credentials, *crp*, is available so the driver can check to see if the user can write privileged information, if the driver provides access to any. The **uio** structure provides the information necessary to determine how much data should be transferred. The **uiomove**(D3) function provides a convenient way to copy data using the **uio** structure.

Block drivers that provide a character interface can use **physiock**(D3) to perform the data transfer with the driver's **strategy**(D2) routine.

Synchronization Constraints

The **write** routine has user context and can sleep.

The write operation is intended to be synchronous from the caller's perspective. Minimally, the driver **write** routine should not return until the caller's buffer is no longer needed. For drivers that care about returning errors, the data should be committed to the device. For others, the data might only be copied to local staging buffers. Then the data will be committed to the device asynchronously to the user's request, losing the ability to return an error with the associated request.

REFERENCES

drv_priv(D3), **errnos**(D5), **physiock**(D3), **read**(D2), **strategy**(D2), **uio**(D4), **uiomove**(D3), **uwritec**(D3)

NOTICES

Availability

SVR4.0, SVR4.1ES, SVR4MP, SVR4.2

write (D2)

Portability
All processors

Interface
Driver-Kernel

Commitment
Level 1

NAME

`intro` – introduction to kernel utility routines

SYNOPSIS

```
#include <sys/types.h>
#include <sys/ddi.h>
```

DESCRIPTION

This section describes the kernel utility functions available for use by device drivers and STREAMS modules.

USAGE

Drivers and STREAMS modules must not call any kernel routines other than the ones described in this section.

Unless otherwise stated, any kernel utility routine that sleeps will do so such that signals will not interrupt the sleep.

adjmsg (D3)

NAME

adjmsg – trim bytes from a message

SYNOPSIS

```
#include <sys/stream.h>
#include <sys/ddi.h>

int adjmsg(mblk_t *mp, int len);
```

Arguments

mp Pointer to the message to be trimmed.

len The number of bytes to be removed.

DESCRIPTION

adjmsg removes bytes from a message.

Return Values

If the message can be trimmed successfully, 1 is returned. Otherwise, 0 is returned.

USAGE

|*len*| (the absolute value of *len*) specifies how many bytes are to be removed. If *len* is greater than 0, bytes are removed from the head of the message. If *len* is less than 0, bytes are removed from the tail. **adjmsg** fails if |*len*| is greater than the number of bytes in *mp*. If *len* spans more than one message block in the message, the messages blocks must be the same type, or else **adjmsg** will fail.

If *len* is greater than the amount of data in a single message block, that message block is not freed. Rather, it is left linked in the message, and its read and write pointers are set equal to each other, indicating no data present in the block.

Level

Base or Interrupt.

Synchronization Constraints

Does not sleep.

Driver-defined basic locks, read/write locks, and sleep locks may be held across calls to this function.

REFERENCES

msgb(D4)

NOTICES

Availability

SVR4.0, SVR4.1ES, SVR4MP, SVR4.2

Portability

All processors

Interface

Driver-Kernel (STREAMS)

Commitment

Level 1

NAME

`allocb` – allocate a message block

SYNOPSIS

```
#include <sys/types.h>
#include <sys/stream.h>
#include <sys/ddi.h>

mblk_t *allocb(int size, uint_t pri);
```

Arguments

size The number of bytes in the message block.

pri Priority of the request.

DESCRIPTION

`allocb` tries to allocate a STREAMS message block.

Return Values

If successful, `allocb` returns a pointer to the allocated message block of type `M_DATA` (defined in `sys/stream.h`). If a block cannot be allocated, a `NULL` pointer is returned.

USAGE

Buffer allocation fails only when the system is out of memory. If no buffer is available, the `bufcall`(D3) function can help a module recover from an allocation failure.

The *pri* argument is a hint to the allocator indicating how badly the message is needed. `BPRI_LO` should be used for normal data allocations. `BPRI_MED` should be used for other non-critical allocations. `BPRI_HI` should be used for allocations that absolutely must succeed, although success is not guaranteed. Some implementations may choose to ignore this parameter.

The following figure identifies the data structure members that are affected when a message block is allocated.

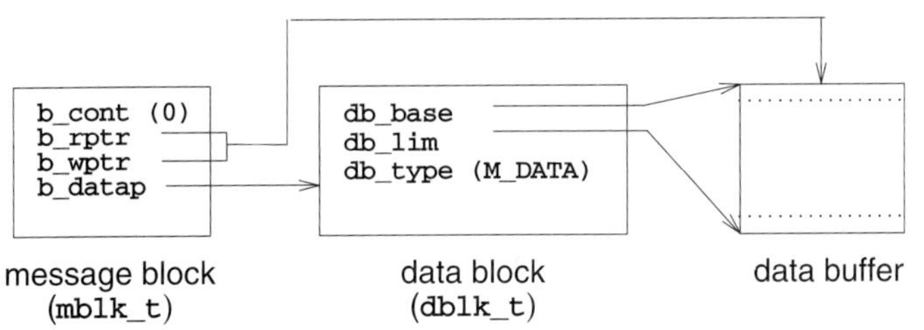

Level

Base or Interrupt.

Synchronization Constraints

Does not sleep.

Driver-defined basic locks, read/write locks, and sleep locks may be held across calls to this function.

Singlethreaded Example

Given a pointer to a queue (*q*) and an error number (*err*), the **send_error** routine sends an **M_ERROR** type message to the stream head.

If a message cannot be allocated, 0 is returned, indicating an allocation failure (line 8). Otherwise, the message type is set to **M_ERROR** (line 9). Line 10 increments the write pointer (**bp->b_wptr**) by the size (one byte) of the data in the message.

A message must be sent up the read side of the stream to arrive at the stream head. To determine whether *q* points to a read queue or a write queue, the **q->q_flag** member is tested to see if **QREADR** is set (line 12). If it is not set, *q* points to a write queue, and on line 13 the **RD**(D3) function is used to find the corresponding read queue. In line 14, the **putnext**(D3) function is used to send the message upstream. Then **send_error** returns 1 indicating success.

```
 1  send_error(q, err)
 2    queue_t *q;
 3    uchar_t err;
 4  {
 5    mblk_t *bp;
 6    long fl=0;

 7    if ((bp = allocb(1, BPRI_HI)) == NULL)
 8          return(0);
 9    bp->b_datap->db_type = M_ERROR;
10    *bp->b_wptr++ = err;
11    (void) strqget(q, QFLAG, 0, &fl);
12    if (fl & QREADR))
13          q = RD(q);
14    putnext(q, bp);
15    return(1);
16  }
```

Multithreaded Example

Given a pointer to a queue (*q*) and an error number (*err*), the **send_error** routine sends an **M_ERROR** type message to the stream head.

If a message cannot be allocated, 0 is returned, indicating an allocation failure (line 7). Otherwise, the message type is set to **M_ERROR** (line 8). Line 9 increments the write pointer (**bp->b_wptr**) by the size (one byte) of the data in the message.

A message must be sent up the read side of the stream to arrive at the stream head. To determine whether *q* points to a read queue or a write queue, the **q->q_flag** member is tested to see if **QREADR** is set (line 10). If it is not set, *q* points to a write queue, and on line 11 the **RD**(D3) function is used to find the corresponding read queue. In line 12, the **putnext**(D3) function is used to send the message upstream. Then **send_error** returns 1 indicating success.

```
 1  send_error(q, err)
 2    queue_t *q;
 3    uchar_t err;
 4  {
```

Commitment
Level 1

bcanput(D3)

NAME

bcanput – test for flow control in a specified priority band

SYNOPSIS

```
#include <sys/types.h>
#include <sys/stream.h>
#include <sys/ddi.h>

int bcanput(queue_t *q, uchar_t pri);
```

Arguments

q Pointer to the message queue.

pri Message priority.

DESCRIPTION

Like the **canput**(D3) function, **bcanput** searches through the stream (starting at *q*) until it finds a queue containing a service routine, or until it reaches the end of the stream. If found, the queue containing the service routine is tested to see if a message of priority *pri* can be enqueued. If the band is full, **bcanput** marks the queue to automatically back-enable the caller's service routine when the amount of data in messages on the queue has reached its low water mark.

Return Values

bcanput returns 1 if a message of priority *pri* can be sent in the stream, or 0 if the priority band is flow-controlled. If **bcanput** reaches the end of the stream without finding a queue with a service routine, then it returns 1.

USAGE

The driver is responsible for both testing a queue with **bcanput** and refraining from placing a message on the queue if **bcanput** fails.

It is possible because of race conditions to test for room using **bcanput** and get an indication that there is room for a message, and then have the queue fill up before subsequently enqueuing the message, causing a violation of flow control. This is not a problem, since the violation of flow control in this case is bounded.

In multithreaded drivers, the *q* argument may not reference **q_next** (for example, an argument of **q->q_next** is erroneous in a multithreaded driver and is disallowed by the DDI/DKI). **bcanputnext(q)** is provided as a multiprocessor-safe equivalent to the common call **bcanput(q->q_next)**, which is no longer allowed [see **canputnext**(D3)].

If *pri* is 0, the **bcanput** call is equivalent to a call to **canput**.

Level

Base or Interrupt.

Synchronization Constraints

Does not sleep.

Driver-defined basic locks, read/write locks, and sleep locks may be held across calls to this function.

The caller cannot have the stream frozen [see **freezestr**(D3)] when calling this function.

REFERENCES

`bcanputnext`(D3), `canput`(D3), `canputnext`(D3), `putbq`(D3), `putnext`(D3)

NOTICES

Availability

SVR4.0, SVR4.1ES, SVR4MP, SVR4.2

Portability

All processors

Interface

Driver-Kernel (STREAMS)

Commitment

Level 1

bcanputnext (D3)

NAME

`bcanputnext` – test for flow control in a specified priority band

SYNOPSIS

```
#include <sys/types.h>
#include <sys/stream.h>
#include <sys/ddi.h>

int bcanputnext(queue_t *q, uchar_t pri);
```

Arguments

q	Pointer to a message queue.
pri	Message priority.

DESCRIPTION

`bcanputnext` searches through the stream (starting at *q->q_next*) until it finds a queue containing a service routine, or until it reaches the end of the stream. If found, the queue containing the service routine is tested to see if a message in priority band *pri* can be enqueued. If the band is full, `bcanputnext` marks the queue to automatically back-enable the caller's service routine when the amount of data in messages on the queue has reached its low water mark.

Return Values

`bcanputnext` returns 1 if a message of priority *pri* can be sent in the stream, or 0 if the priority band is flow-controlled. If `bcanputnext` reaches the end of the stream without finding a queue with a service routine, then it returns 1.

USAGE

The driver writer is responsible for both testing a queue with `bcanputnext` and refraining from placing a message on the queue if `bcanputnext` fails.

It is possible because of race conditions to test for room using `bcanputnext` and get an indication that there is room for a message, and then have the queue fill up before subsequently enqueuing the message, causing a violation of flow control. This is not a problem since the violation of flow control in this case is bounded.

If *pri* is 0, the `bcanputnext` call is equivalent to a call to `canputnext`.

Level

Initialization, Base or Interrupt.

Synchronization Constraints

Does not sleep.

Driver defined basic locks, read/write locks, and sleep locks may be held across calls to this function.

The caller cannot have the stream frozen [see `freezestr`(D3)] when calling this function.

REFERENCES

`bcanput`(D3), `canput`(D3), `canputnext`(D3), `putbq`(D3), `putnext`(D3)

NOTICES

Availability
SVR4MP

Portability
All processors

Interface
Driver-Kernel (STREAMS)

Commitment
Level 1

bcmp (D3)

NAME

bcmp – compare data between two kernel address locations

SYNOPSIS

```
#include <sys/types.h>
#include <sys/ddi.h>

int bcmp(caddr_t m1, caddr_t m2, size_t bcount);
```

Arguments

m1, m2	Starting locations of memory to be compared
bcount	Number of bytes to be compared.

DESCRIPTION

bcmp compares *bcount* bytes starting at kernel address *m1* to *bcount* bytes starting at kernel address *m2*.

Return Values

bcmp returns 0 if they are the same, otherwise 1.

USAGE

The source and destination address ranges must both be within the kernel address space and must be memory resident. No range checking is done. Addresses within user address space are not valid arguments; specifying such an address may cause the driver to corrupt the system in an unpredictable way.

Level

Initialization, Base or Interrupt.

Synchronization Constraints

Does not sleep.

Driver-defined basic locks, read/write locks, and sleep locks may be held across calls to this function.

REFERENCES

bcopy(D3)

NOTICES

Availability

SVR4.0, SVR4.1ES, SVR4MP, SVR4.2

Portability

All processors

Interface

General-purpose utility

Commitment

Level 1

NAME

bcopy – copy data between address locations in the kernel

SYNOPSIS

```
#include <sys/types.h>
#include <sys/ddi.h>

void bcopy(caddr_t from, caddr_t to, size_t bcount);
```

Arguments

from Source address from which the copy is made.

to Destination address to which the copy is made.

bcount Number of bytes to be copied.

DESCRIPTION

bcopy copies *bcount* bytes from one kernel address to another. It chooses the best algorithm based on address alignment and number of bytes to copy.

Return Values

None

USAGE

If the input and output addresses overlap, the function executes, but the results are undefined.

The source and destination address ranges must both be within the kernel address space and must be memory resident. No range checking is done. Since there is no mechanism by which drivers that conform to the rules of the DDI/DKI can obtain and use a kernel address which is not memory resident (an address which is paged out), DDI/DKI conforming drivers can assume that any address to which they have access is memory resident and therefore a valid argument to **bcopy**. Addresses within user address space are not valid arguments, and specifying such an address may cause the driver to corrupt the system in an unpredictable way. For copying between kernel and user space, drivers must use an appropriate function defined for that purpose (for example, **copyin**(D3), **copyout**(D3), **uiomove**(D3), **ureadc**(D3), or **uwritec**(D3)).

Level

Initialization, Base or Interrupt.

Synchronization Constraints

Does not sleep.

Driver-defined basic locks, read/write locks, and sleep locks may be held across calls to this function.

Examples

An I/O request is made for data stored in a RAM disk. If the I/O operation is a read request, data are copied from the RAM disk to a buffer (line 9). If it is a write request, data are copied from a buffer to the RAM disk (line 15). The **bcopy** function is used since both the RAM disk and the buffer are part of the kernel address space.

```
#define RAMDNBLK     1000           /* number of blocks in the RAM disk */
#define RAMDBSIZ     NBPSCTR        /* bytes per block */
char ramdblks[RAMDNBLK][RAMDBSIZ]; /* blocks forming RAM disk */
     ...
if (bp->b_flags & B_READ) {
        /*
         * read request - copy data from RAM disk to system buffer
         */
        bcopy(ramdblks[bp->b_blkno], bp->b_un.b_addr, bp->b_bcount);
} else {
        /*
         * write request - copy data from system buffer to RAM disk
         */
        bcopy(bp->b_un.b_addr, ramdblks[bp->b_blkno], bp->b_bcount);
}
```

REFERENCES

`copyin`(D3), `copyout`(D3), `uiomove`(D3), `ureadc`(D3), `uwritec`(D3)

NOTICES

Availability

SVR4.0, SVR4.1ES, SVR4MP, SVR4.2

Portability

All processors

Interface

General-purpose utility

Commitment

Level 1

NAME

biodone – release buffer after block I/O and wakeup processes

SYNOPSIS

```
#include <sys/types.h>
#include <sys/buf.h>
#include <sys/ddi.h>

void biodone(buf_t *bp);
```

Arguments

bp Pointer to the buffer header structure.

DESCRIPTION

The **biodone** function is called by the driver to indicate that block I/O associated with the buffer header *fp* is complete, and that it can be reused.

Return Values

None

USAGE

biodone is usually called from the driver's **strategy**(D2) routine or I/O completion handler [usually **intr**(D2)].

If the driver (or the kernel) had specified an iodone handler by initializing the **b_iodone** field of the **buf**(D4) structure to the address of a function, that function is called with the single argument, *bp*. Then **biodone** returns.

If an iodone handler had not been specified, **biodone** sets the **B_DONE** flag in the **b_flags** field of the buffer header. Then, if the **B_ASYNC** flag is set, the buffer is released back to the system. If the **B_ASYNC** flag is not set, any processes waiting for the I/O to complete are awakened.

If the buffer was allocated via **getrbuf**(D3), the driver must have specified an iodone handler.

Level

Base or Interrupt.

Synchronization Constraints

Does not sleep.

Driver-defined basic locks, read/write locks, and sleep locks may be held across calls to this function.

Examples

Generally, the first validation test performed by any block device **strategy** routine is a check to verify the bounds of the I/O request. If a **read** request is made for one block beyond the limits of the device (line 8), it will report an end-of-media condition (line 10). Otherwise, if the request is outside the limits of the device, the routine will report an error condition (line 12). In either case, the I/O operation is completed by calling **biodone** (line 14) and the driver returns.

```
1  #define RAMDNBLK  1000          /* Number of blocks in RAM disk */
2  #define RAMDBSIZ   512          /* Number of bytes per block */
3  char ramdblks[RAMDNBLK][RAMDBSIZ]; /* Array containing RAM disk */

4  ramdstrategy(bp)
5    struct buf *bp;
6  {
7    daddr_t blkno = bp->b_blkno;

8    if ((blkno < 0) || (blkno >= RAMDNBLK)) {
9          if ((blkno == RAMDNBLK) && (bp->b_flags & B_READ)) {
10               bp->b_resid = bp->b_bcount;      /* nothing read */
11         } else {
12               bioerror(bp, ENXIO);
13         }
14         biodone(bp);
15         return;
16   }
       . . .
```

On systems where the function **bioerror**(D3) is not available, line 12 could read:

```
bp->b_error = ENXIO;
bp->b_flags |= B_ERROR;
```

REFERENCES

bioerror(D3), **biowait**(D3), **brelse**(D3), **buf**(D4), **freerbuf**(D3), **getrbuf**(D3), **intr**(D2), **strategy**(D2)

NOTICES

Availability

SVR4.0, SVR4.1ES, SVR4MP, SVR4.2

Portability

All processors

Interface

Driver-Kernel

Commitment

Level 1

NAME

bioerror – manipulate error fields within a buffer header

SYNOPSIS

```
#include <sys/types.h>
#include <sys/buf.h>
#include <sys/ddi.h>

void bioerror(buf_t *bp, int errno);
```

Arguments

bp Pointer to the buffer header structure.

errno Error number to be set, or zero to indicate that the error fields within the buffer header should be cleared.

DESCRIPTION

bioerror is used to manipulate the error fields within a buffer header (**buf**(D4) structure).

Return Values

None

USAGE

Driver code (for example, a **strategy**(D2) routine) that wishes to report an I/O error condition associated with the buffer pointed to by *bp* should call **bioerror** with *errno* set to the appropriate error number. This will set the appropriate fields within the buffer header so that higher level code can detect the error and retrieve the error number using **geterror**(D3).

The error fields within the buffer header can be cleared by calling **bioerror** with *errno* set to zero.

On multiprocessor systems, DDI/DKI conforming drivers are no longer permitted to manipulate the error fields of the **buf** structure directly. **bioerror** must be used for this purpose.

Level

Base or Interrupt.

Synchronization Constraints

Does not sleep.

Driver-defined basic locks, read/write locks, and sleep locks may be held across calls to this function.

REFERENCES

buf(D4), **errnos**(D5), **geteblk**(D3), **geterror**(D3), **getrbuf**(D3), **ngeteblk**(D3), **strategy**(D2)

NOTICES

Availability

SVR4MP

Portability

All processors

bioerror (D3)

Interface
Driver-Kernel

Commitment
Level 1

NAME

bioreset – reset a private buffer for reuse after completed I/O

SYNOPSIS

```
#include <sys/buf.h>
#include <sys/ddi.h>

void bioreset(buf_t *bp);
```

Arguments

bp Pointer to the buffer header structure.

DESCRIPTION

The **bioreset** function is called by drivers which have allocated a private buffer for block I/O (via **getrbuf**(D3), for example) and want to use the buffer multiple times. When called, **bioreset** resets the buffer header pointed to by *bp* as follows:

clears the **B_DONE** and **B_ERROR** flags set for the previous I/O operation in the **b_flags** member

clears error codes (if any) returned for the previous I/O operation in the **b_error** member

Return Values

None

USAGE

To reuse a buffer, the driver calls **bioreset** at the end of each I/O operation to reset the buffer's header structure. The reset prepares the buffer for reuse during the next I/O operation. **bioreset** may also be called prior to performing any I/O operation, although this is not required.

The calling driver must "own" the buffer for which the reset is being requested.

I/O must not be in progress when **bioreset** is called.

Level

Initialization or Base.

Synchronization Constraints

Does not sleep.

Driver-defined basic locks, read/write locks, and sleep locks may be held across calls to this function.

REFERENCES

buf(D4), **freerbuf**(D3) **getrbuf**(D3)

NOTICES

Availability

SVR4.2

Portability

All processors

Interface

Driver-Kernel

bioreset(D3)

Commitment

Level 1

NAME

biowait – suspend processes pending completion of block I/O

SYNOPSIS

```
#include <sys/types.h>
#include <sys/buf.h>
#include <sys/ddi.h>

int biowait(buf_t *bp);
```

Arguments

bp Pointer to the buffer header structure.

DESCRIPTION

The **biowait** function suspends process execution during block I/O.

Return Values

If an error occurred during the I/O transfer, the error number is returned. Otherwise, on success, 0 is returned.

USAGE

Block drivers that have allocated their own buffers with **geteblk**(D3), **getrbuf**(D3), or **ngeteblk**(D3) can use **biowait** to suspend the current process execution while waiting for a read or write request to complete.

Drivers using **biowait** must use **biodone**(D3) in their I/O completion handlers to signal **biowait** when the I/O transfer is complete.

Level

Base only.

Synchronization Constraints

Can sleep.

Driver-defined basic locks and read/write locks may not be held across calls to this function.

Driver-defined sleep locks may be held across calls to this function.

REFERENCES

biodone(D3), **buf**(D4), **geteblk**(D3), **getrbuf**(D3), **intr**(D2), **ngeteblk**(D3), **strategy**(D2)

NOTICES

Availability

SVR4.0, SVR4.1ES, SVR4MP, SVR4.2

Portability

All processors

Interface

Driver-Kernel

Commitment

Level 1

bp_mapin (D3)

NAME

bp_mapin – allocate virtual address space for buffer page list

SYNOPSIS

```
#include <sys/types.h>
#include <sys/buf.h>
#include <sys/ddi.h>

void bp_mapin(struct buf *bp);
```

Arguments

bp Pointer to the buffer header structure.

DESCRIPTION

The **bp_mapin** function is used to map virtual address space to a page list maintained by the buffer header [see **buf**(D4)] during a paged-I/O request.

Return Values

None

USAGE

A paged-I/O request is identified by the **B_PAGEIO** flag being set in the **b_flags** field of the buffer header passed to a driver's **strategy**(D2) routine. Before calling **bp_mapin**, the offset of the location in the first page where the I/O is to begin is stored in the **b_un.b_addr** field of the **buf** structure referenced by *bp* (for **strategy** routines, this is done for the driver by the system).

bp_mapin allocates system virtual address space, maps that space to the page list, and returns the new virtual address in the **b_un.b_addr** field of the **buf** structure. This address is the virtual address of the start of the page mappings, plus the offset given by the original value of **bp->b_un.b_addr**. After the I/O completes, the virtual address space can be deallocated using the **bp_mapout**(D3) function.

B_PAGEIO won't be set unless the driver has the **D_NOBRKUP** flag set [see **devflag**(D1)].

Level

Base only.

Synchronization Constraints

This routine may sleep if virtual space is not immediately available.

Driver-defined basic locks and read/write locks may not be held across calls to this function.

Driver-defined sleep locks may be held across calls to this function.

REFERENCES

bp_mapout(D3), **buf**(D4), **devflag**(D1), **strategy**(D2)

NOTICES

Availability

SVR4.0, SVR4.1ES, SVR4MP, SVR4.2

Portability

All processors

Interface
Driver-Kernel

Commitment
Level 1

bp_mapout (D3)

NAME

`bp_mapout` – deallocate virtual address space for buffer page list

SYNOPSIS

```
#include <sys/types.h>
#include <sys/buf.h>
#include <sys/ddi.h>

void bp_mapout(struct buf *bp);
```

Arguments

bp Pointer to the buffer header structure.

DESCRIPTION

The **bp_mapout** function deallocates the system virtual address space associated with a buffer header page list.

Return Values

None

USAGE

The virtual address space must have been allocated by a previous call to **bp_mapin**(D3). Drivers should not reference any virtual addresses in the mapped range after **bp_mapout** has been called.

Level

Base or Interrupt.

Synchronization Constraints

Does not sleep.

Driver-defined basic locks, read/write locks, and sleep locks may be held across calls to this function.

REFERENCES

bp_mapin(D3), **buf**(D4)

NOTICES

Availability

SVR4.0, SVR4.1ES, SVR4MP, SVR4.2

Portability

All processors

Interface

Driver-Kernel

Commitment

Level 1

NAME

brelse – return a buffer to the system's free list

SYNOPSIS

```
#include <sys/types.h>
#include <sys/buf.h>
#include <sys/ddi.h>

void brelse(struct buf *bp);
```

Arguments

bp Pointer to the buffer header structure.

DESCRIPTION

The **brelse** function returns the buffer specified by *bp* to the system's buffer free list. If there were any processes waiting for this specific buffer to become free, or for any buffer to become available on the free list, one is awakened.

Return Values

None

USAGE

The buffer specified by *bp* must have been previously allocated by a call to **geteblk**(D3) or **ngeteblk**(D3). **brelse** may not be called to release a buffer which has been allocated by any other means.

Level

Base or Interrupt.

Synchronization Constraints

Does not sleep.

Driver-defined basic locks, read/write locks, and sleep locks may be held across calls to this function.

REFERENCES

biodone(D3), **biowait**(D3), **buf**(D4), **clrbuf**(D3), **geteblk**(D3), **ngeteblk**(D3)

NOTICES

Availability

SVR4.0, SVR4.1ES, SVR4MP, SVR4.2

Portability

All processors

Interface

Driver-Kernel

Commitment

Level 1

btop(D3)

NAME

`btop` – convert size in bytes to size in pages (round down)

SYNOPSIS

```
#include <sys/types.h>
#include <sys/ddi.h>

ulong_t btop(ulong_t numbytes);
```

Arguments

numbytes Size in bytes to convert to equivalent size in pages.

DESCRIPTION

`btop` returns the number of pages that are contained in the specified number of bytes, with downward rounding if the byte count is not a page multiple.

Return Values

The return value is the number of pages. There are no invalid input values, and therefore no error return values.

USAGE

Level

Initialization, Base or Interrupt.

Synchronization Constraints

Does not sleep.

Driver-defined basic locks, read/write locks, and sleep locks may be held across calls to this function.

Examples

If the page size is 2048, then `btop(4096)` and `btop(4097)` both return 2, and `btop(4095)` returns 1. `btop(0)` returns 0.

REFERENCES

`btopr`(D3), `ptob`(D3)

NOTICES

Availability

SVR4.0, SVR4.1ES, SVR4MP, SVR4.2

Portability

All processors

Interface

Driver-Kernel

Commitment

Level 1

NAME

`btopr` – convert size in bytes to size in pages (round up)

SYNOPSIS

```
#include <sys/types.h>
#include <sys/ddi.h>

ulong_t btopr(ulong_t numbytes);
```

Arguments

numbytes Size in bytes to convert to equivalent size in pages.

DESCRIPTION

`btopr` returns the number of pages that are contained in the specified number of bytes, with upward rounding if the byte count is not a page multiple.

Return Values

The return value is the number of pages. There are no invalid input values, and therefore no error return values.

USAGE

Level

Initialization, Base or Interrupt.

Synchronization Constraints

Does not sleep.

Driver-defined basic locks, read/write locks, and sleep locks may be held across calls to this function.

Examples

If the page size is 2048, then `btopr(4096)` and `btopr(4095)` both return 2, and `btopr(4097)` returns 3. `btopr(0)` returns 0.

REFERENCES

`btop`(D3), `ptob`(D3)

NOTICES

Availability

SVR4.0, SVR4.1ES, SVR4MP, SVR4.2

Portability

All processors

Interface

Driver-Kernel

Commitment

Level 1

bufcall (D3)

NAME

bufcall – call a function when a buffer becomes available

SYNOPSIS

```
#include <sys/types.h>
#include <sys/stream.h>
#include <sys/ddi.h>

toid_t bufcall(uint_t size, int pri, void (*func)(), long arg);
```

Arguments

size Number of bytes in the buffer to be allocated (from the failed **allocb**(D3) request).

pri Priority of the **allocb** allocation request.

func Function or driver routine to be called when a buffer becomes available.

arg Argument to the function to be called when a buffer becomes available.

DESCRIPTION

When a buffer allocation request fails, the function **bufcall** can be used to schedule the routine, *func*, to be called with the argument, *arg*, when a buffer of at least *size* bytes becomes available. **bufcall** serves, in effect, as a timeout call of indeterminate length.

Return Values

On success, **bufcall** returns a non-zero value that identifies the scheduling request. On failure, **bufcall** returns 0.

USAGE

When *func* runs, all interrupts from STREAMS devices will be blocked. On multiprocessor systems, when *func* runs all interrupts from STREAMS devices will be blocked on the processor on which *func* is running. *func* will have no user context and may not call any function that sleeps.

Even when *func* is called, **allocb** can still fail if another module or driver had allocated the memory before *func* was able to call **allocb**.

The *pri* argument is a hint to the allocator indicating how badly the buffer is needed. **BPRI_LO** should be used for normal data allocations. **BPRI_MED** should be used for other non-critical allocations. **BPRI_HI** should be used for allocations that absolutely must succeed, although success is not guaranteed. Some implementations may choose to ignore this argument.

The non-zero identifier returned by **bufcall** may be passed to **unbufcall**(D3) to cancel the request.

Level

Base or Interrupt.

Synchronization Constraints

Does not sleep.

Driver-defined basic locks, read/write locks, and sleep locks may be held across calls to this function.

Singlethreaded Example

The purpose of this service routine [see **srv**(D2)] is to add a header to all **M_DATA** messages. We assume only **M_DATA** messages are added to its queue. Service routines must process all messages on their queues before returning, or arrange to be rescheduled.

While there are messages to be processed (line 19), we check to see if we can send the message on in the stream. If not, we put the message back on the queue (line 21) and return. The STREAMS flow control mechanism will re-enable us later when messages can be sent. If **canput**(D3) succeeded, we try to allocate a buffer large enough to hold the header (line 24). If no buffer is available, the service routine must be rescheduled later, when a buffer is available. We put the original message back on the queue (line 26) and use **bufcall** to attempt the rescheduling (lines 27 and 28). If **bufcall** succeeds, we set the **m_type** field in the module's private data structure to **BUFCALL**. If **bufcall** failed, we use **timeout**(D3) to reschedule us instead (line 30). **modcall** will be called in about a half second [**drv_usectohz(500000)**]. When the rescheduling has been done, we return.

When **modcall** runs, it will set the **m_type** field to zero, indicating that there is no outstanding request. Then the queue's service routine is scheduled to run by calling **qenable**(D3).

If the buffer allocation is successful, we initialize the header (lines 37–39), make the message type **M_PROTO** (line 41), link the **M_DATA** message to it (line 42), and pass it on (line 43).

See **unbufcall**(D3) for the other half of this example.

```
 1  struct hdr {
 2     uint_t h_size;
 3     int    h_version;
 4  };
 5  struct mod {
 6     long   m_id;
 7     char   m_type;
       ...
 8  };
 9  #define TIMEOUT   1
10  #define BUFCALL   2
    ...
11  modsrv(q) /* assume only M_DATA messages enqueued here */
12        queue_t *q;
13  {
14     mblk_t *bp;
15     mblk_t *mp;
16     struct hdr *hp;
17     struct mod *modp;

18     modp = (struct mod *)q->q_ptr;
19     while ((mp = getq(q)) != NULL) {
20            if (!canput(q->q_next)) {
21                   putbq(q, mp);
22                   return;
23            }
24            bp = allocb(sizeof(struct hdr), BPRI_MED);
25            if (bp == NULL) {
```

```
26                    putbq(q, mp);
27                    modp->m_id = bufcall(sizeof(struct hdr), BPRI_MED, modcall,
28                       (long)q);
29                    if (modp->m_id == 0) {
30                       modp->m_id = timeout(modcall, (long)q, drv_usectohz(500000));
31                       modp->m_type = TIMEOUT;
32                    } else {
33                       modp->m_type = BUFCALL;
34                    }
35                    return;
36             }
37             hp = (struct hdr *)bp->b_wptr;
38             hp->h_size = msgdsize(mp);
39             hp->h_version = 1;
40             bp->b_wptr += sizeof(struct hdr);
41             bp->b_datap->db_type = M_PROTO;
42             bp->b_cont = mp;
43             putnext(q, bp);
44      }
45  }
46  modcall(q)
47      queue_t *q;
48  {
49      struct mod *modp;
50      modp = (struct mod *)q->q_ptr;
51      modp->m_type = 0;
52      qenable(q);
53  }
```

Multithreaded Example

The purpose of this service routine [see **srv**(D2)] is to add a header to all **M_DATA** messages. We assume only **M_DATA** messages are added to its queue. Service routines must process all messages on their queues before returning, or arrange to be rescheduled.

While there are messages to be processed (line 21), we check to see if we can send the message on in the stream. If not, we put the message back on the queue (line 23) and return. The STREAMS flow control mechanism will re-enable us later when messages can be sent. If **canputnext**(D3) succeeded, we try to allocate a buffer large enough to hold the header (line 26). If no buffer is available, the service routine must be rescheduled later, when a buffer is available. We put the original message back on the queue (line 28), lock the private data structure, and use **bufcall** to attempt the rescheduling (lines 30 and 31). If **bufcall** succeeds, we set the **m_type** field in the module's private data structure to **BUFCALL**. If **bufcall** failed, we use **itimeout**(D3) to reschedule us instead (line 33). **modcall** will be called in about a half second [**drv_usectohz(500000)**]. When the rescheduling has been done, we unlock the private data structure and return.

When **modcall** runs, it will lock the private data structure and set the **m_type** field to zero, indicating that there is no outstanding request. Then the data structure is unlocked and the queue's service routine is scheduled to run by calling **qenable**(D3) (line 59).

If the buffer allocation is successful, we initialize the header (lines 41–43), make the message type **M_PROTO** (line 45), link the **M_DATA** message to it (line 46), and pass it on (line 47).

See **unbufcall**(D3) for the other half of this example.

```
 1 struct hdr {
 2     uint_t h_size;
 3     int    h_version;
 4 };
 5 struct mod {
 6     toid_t m_id;
 7     char   m_type;
 8     lock_t *m_lock;
       . . .
 9 };
10 #define TIMEOUT  1
11 #define BUFCALL  2
   . . .
12 modsrv(q) /* assume only M_DATA messages enqueued here */
13         queue_t *q;
14 {
15     mblk_t *bp;
16     mblk_t *mp;
17     struct hdr *hp;
18     struct mod *modp;
19     pl_t pl;

20     modp = (struct mod *)q->q_ptr;
21     while ((mp = getq(q)) != NULL) {
22             if (!canputnext(q)) {
23                     putbq(q, mp);
24                     return;
25             }
26             bp = allocb(sizeof(struct hdr), BPRI_MED);
27             if (bp == NULL) {
28                     putbq(q, mp);
29                     pl = LOCK(modp->m_lock, plstr);
30                     modp->m_id = bufcall(sizeof(struct hdr), BPRI_MED, modcall,
31                         (long)q);
32                     if (modp->m_id == 0) {
33                         modp->m_id = itimeout(modcall, q, drv_usectohz(500000), plstr);
34                         modp->m_type = TIMEOUT;
35                     } else {
36                         modp->m_type = BUFCALL;
37                     }
38                     UNLOCK(modp->m_lock, pl);
39                     return;
40             }
41             hp = (struct hdr *)bp->b_wptr;
42             hp->h_size = msgdsize(mp);
43             hp->h_version = 1;
44             bp->b_wptr += sizeof(struct hdr);
45             bp->b_datap->db_type = M_PROTO;
46             bp->b_cont = mp;
47             putnext(q, bp);
```

```
    }
}
modcall(q)
    queue_t *q;
{
    struct mod *modp;
    pl_t pl;

    modp = (struct mod *)q->q_ptr;
    pl = LOCK(modp->m_lock, plstr);
    modp->m_type = 0;
    UNLOCK(modp->m_lock, pl);
    qenable(q);
}
```

REFERENCES

`allocb`(D3), `esballoc`(D3), `esbbcall`(D3), `itimeout`(D3), `timeout`(D3), `unbufcall`(D3)

NOTICES

Availability

SVR4.0, SVR4.1ES, SVR4MP, SVR4.2

Portability

All processors

Interface

Driver-Kernel (STREAMS)

Commitment

Level 1

Future Directions

In more recent SVR4 releases, the `bufcall` function returns a `toid_t` data type. In earlier SVR4 releases, it returns an `int`.

NAME

bzero – clear memory for a given number of bytes

SYNOPSIS

```
#include <sys/types.h>
#include <sys/ddi.h>

void bzero(caddr_t addr, size_t bytes);
```

Arguments

addr Starting virtual address of memory to be cleared.

bytes The number of bytes to clear.

DESCRIPTION

The **bzero** function clears a contiguous portion of memory by filling the memory with zeros. It chooses the best algorithm based on address alignment and number of bytes to clear.

Return Values

None

USAGE

There are no alignment restrictions on *addr*, and no length restrictions on *bytes*, other than the address range specified must be within the kernel address space and must be memory resident. No range checking is done. Since there is no mechanism by which drivers that conform to the rules of the DDI/DKI can obtain and use a kernel address that is not memory resident (an address that is paged out), DDI/DKI conforming drivers can assume that any address to which they have access is memory resident and therefore a valid argument to **bzero**. An address within user address space is not a valid argument, and specifying such an address may cause the driver to corrupt the system in an unpredictable way.

Level

Initialization, Base or Interrupt.

Synchronization Constraints

Does not sleep.

Driver-defined basic locks, read/write locks, and sleep locks may be held across calls to this function.

Examples

In a driver **close**(D2) routine, rather than clear each individual member of its private data structure, the driver could use **bzero** as shown here:

```
bzero((caddr_t)&drv_dat[getminor(dev)], sizeof(struct drvr_data));
```

REFERENCES

bcopy(D3), **clrbuf**(D3), **kmem_zalloc**(D3)

NOTICES

Availability

SVR4.0, SVR4.1ES, SVR4MP, SVR4.2

bzero (D3)

Portability
All processors

Interface
Driver-Kernel

Commitment
Level 1

NAME

canput – test for room in a message queue

SYNOPSIS

```
#include <sys/stream.h>
#include <sys/ddi.h>

int canput(queue_t *q);
```

Arguments

q Pointer to the message queue.

DESCRIPTION

canput tests if there is room for a message in the queue pointed to by *q*. The queue must have a service procedure.

Return Values

canput returns 1 if a message can be placed on the queue. 0 is returned if a message cannot be enqueued because of flow control.

USAGE

The driver is responsible for both testing a queue with canput and refraining from placing a message on the queue if canput fails.

It is possible because of race conditions to test for room using canput and get an indication that there is room for a message, and then have the queue fill up before subsequently enqueuing the message, causing a violation of flow control. This is not a problem, since the violation of flow control in this case is bounded.

In multithreaded drivers, the *q* argument may not reference q_next (for example, an argument of q->q_next is erroneous in a multithreaded driver and is disallowed by the DDI/DKI). canputnext(q) is provided as a multiprocessor-safe equivalent to the common call canput(q->q_next), which is no longer allowed [see canputnext(D3)].

Level

Base or Interrupt.

Synchronization Constraints

Does not sleep.

Driver-defined basic locks, read/write locks, and sleep locks may be held across calls to this function.

The caller cannot have the stream frozen [see freezestr(D3)] when calling this function.

Examples

See bufcall(D3) for an example of canput.

REFERENCES

bcanput(D3), bcanputnext(D3), canputnext(D3), putbq(D3), putnext(D3)

NOTICES

Availability

SVR4.0, SVR4.1ES, SVR4MP, SVR4.2

Portability
All processors

Interface
Driver-Kernel (STREAMS)

Commitment
Level 1

NAME

canputnext – test for flow control in a stream

SYNOPSIS

```
#include <sys/stream.h>
#include <sys/ddi.h>

int canputnext(queue_t *q);
```

Arguments

q Pointer to a message queue.

DESCRIPTION

canputnext searches through the stream (starting at *q->q_next*) until it finds a queue containing a service routine, or until it reaches the end of the stream. If found, the queue containing the service routine is tested to see if there is room for a message in the queue. If the queue is full, **canputnext** marks the queue to automatically back-enable the caller's service routine when the amount of data in messages on the queue has reached its low water mark.

Return Values

canputnext returns 1 if a message can be sent in the stream, or 0 if the stream is flow-controlled. If **canputnext** reaches the end of the stream without finding a queue with a service routine, then it returns 1.

USAGE

The driver is responsible for both testing a queue with **canputnext** and refraining from placing a message on the queue if **canputnext** fails.

It is possible because of race conditions to test for room using **canputnext** and get an indication that there is room for a message, and then have the queue fill up before subsequently enqueuing the message, causing a violation of flow control. This is not a problem since the violation of flow control in this case is bounded.

The *q* argument may not reference **q_next** (for example, an argument of **q->q_next** is erroneous in a multithreaded driver and is disallowed by the DDI/DKI).

Level

Base or Interrupt.

Synchronization Constraints

Does not sleep.

Driver-defined basic locks, read/write locks, and sleep locks may be held across calls to this function.

The caller cannot have the stream frozen [see **freezestr**(D3)] when calling this function.

REFERENCES

bcanput(D3), **bcanputnext**(D3), **canput**(D3), **putbq**(D3), **putnext**(D3)

NOTICES

Availability

SVR4MP

Portability
All processors

Interface
Driver-Kernel (STREAMS)

Commitment
Level 1

NAME

`clrbuf` – erase the contents of a buffer

SYNOPSIS

```
#include <sys/types.h>
#include <sys/buf.h>
#include <sys/ddi.h>

void clrbuf(buf_t *bp);
```

Arguments

bp Pointer to the buffer header structure.

DESCRIPTION

The **clrbuf** function zeros a buffer and sets the **b_resid** member of the **buf**(D4) structure to 0. Zeros are placed in the buffer starting at the address specified by **b_un.b_addr** for a length of **b_bcount** bytes.

Return Values

None

USAGE

If the buffer has the **B_PAGEIO** or the **B_PHYS** flag set in the **b_flags** field, then **clrbuf** should not be called until the proper virtual space has been allocated by a call to **bp_mapin**(D3).

Level

Base or Interrupt.

Synchronization Constraints

Does not sleep.

Driver-defined basic locks, read/write locks, and sleep locks may be held across calls to this function.

REFERENCES

bp_mapin(D3), **buf**(D4)

NOTICES

Availability

SVR4.0, SVR4.1ES, SVR4MP, SVR4.2

Portability

All processors

Interface

Driver-Kernel

Commitment

Level 1

NAME

`cmn_err` – display an error message or panic the system

SYNOPSIS

```
#include <sys/cmn_err.h>
#include <sys/ddi.h>

void cmn_err(int level, char *format, ... /* args */);
```

Arguments

level Indicates the severity of the error condition.

format The message to be displayed.

args The set of arguments passed with the message being displayed.

DESCRIPTION

`cmn_err` displays a specified message on the console and/or stores it in the kernel buffer `putbuf`. `cmn_err` can also panic the system.

Return Values

None

USAGE

level Argument

Valid values for *level* are:

`CE_CONT` Used to continue a previous message or to display an informative message not connected with an error.

`CE_NOTE` Used to display a message preceded with "**NOTICE:** ." This message is used to report system events that do not necessarily require action, but may interest the system administrator. For example, a message saying that a sector on a disk needs to be accessed repeatedly before it can be accessed correctly might be noteworthy.

`CE_WARN` Used to display a message preceded with "**WARNING:** ." This message is used to report system events that require immediate attention, such as those where if an action is not taken, the system may panic. For example, when a peripheral device does not initialize correctly, this level should be used.

`CE_PANIC` Used to display a message preceded with "**PANIC:** ," and panic the system. Drivers should use this level only for debugging or in the case of severe errors that indicate that the system cannot continue to function. This level halts processing.

format Argument

By default, the message is sent both to the system console and to the circular kernel buffer `putbuf`. If the first character in *format* is an exclamation point ("`!`"), the message goes only to `putbuf`. If the first character in *format* is a circumflex ("`^`"), the message goes only to the console. The size of the kernel buffer `putbuf` is defined by the kernel variable `putbufsz`. Driver developers or administrators can read the `putbuf` buffer using appropriate debugging or administrative tools [for example, `crash`(1M)].

`cmn_err` appends `\n` to each *format* string, even when a message is sent to `putbuf`, except when *level* is `CE_CONT`.

Valid conversion specifications are `%s`, `%u`, `%d`, `%o`, and `%x`. The `cmn_err` function is otherwise similar to the `printf`(3S) library subroutine in its interpretation of the *format* string, except that `cmn_err` does not accept length specifications in conversion specifications. For example, `%3d` is invalid and will be treated as a literal string, resulting in a mismatch of arguments.

args Argument

Any argument within the range of supported conversion specifications can be passed.

General Considerations

At times, a driver may encounter error conditions requiring the attention of a system console monitor. These conditions may mean halting the system; however, this must be done with caution. Except during the debugging stage, or in the case of a serious, unrecoverable error, a driver should never stop the system.

The `cmn_err` function with the `CE_CONT` argument can be used by driver developers as a driver code debugging tool. However, using `cmn_err` in this capacity can change system timing characteristics.

Level

Initialization, Base or Interrupt.

Synchronization Constraints

Does not sleep.

If *level* is `CE_PANIC`, then driver-defined basic locks, read/write locks, and sleep locks may not be held across calls to this function. For other levels, locks may be held.

Examples

The `cmn_err` function can record tracing and debugging information only in the `putbuf` buffer (lines 12 and 13) or display problems with a device only on the system console (lines 17 and 18).

```
 1  struct  device {                  /* device registers layout */
       ...
 2     int status;                    /* device status word */
 3  };
 4  extern struct device xx_dev[];    /* physical device registers */
 5  extern int xx_cnt;                /* number of physical devices */
    ...
 6  int
 7  xxopen(dev_t *devp, int flag, int otyp, cred_t *crp)
 8  {
 9     struct device *dp;
10     dp = xx_dev[getminor(*devp)];  /* get dev registers */
11  #ifdef DEBUG                      /* in debugging mode, log function call */
12     cmn_err(CE_NOTE, "!xxopen function call, dev = 0x%x", *devp);
13     cmn_err(CE_CONT, "! flag = 0x%x", flag);
14  #endif
```

```
/* display device power failure on system console */
if ((dp->status & POWER) == OFF)
        cmn_err(CE_WARN, "^xxopen: Power is OFF on device %d port %d",
           getemajor(*devp), geteminor(*devp));
```

REFERENCES

`print`(D2), `printf`(3S)

NOTICES

Availability

SVR4.0, SVR4.1ES, SVR4MP, SVR4.2

Portability

All processors

Interface

Driver-Kernel

Commitment

Level 1

NAME

copyb – copy a message block

SYNOPSIS

```
#include <sys/stream.h>
#include <sys/ddi.h>

mblk_t *copyb(mblk_t *bp);
```

Arguments

bp Pointer to the message block from which data are copied.

DESCRIPTION

copyb allocates a new message block, and copies into it the data from the block pointed to by *bp*. The new block will be at least as large as the block being copied. The **b_rptr** and **b_wptr** members of the message block pointed to by *bp* are used to determine how many bytes to copy.

Return Values

On success, **copyb** returns a pointer to the newly allocated message block containing the copied data. On failure, it returns a **NULL** pointer.

USAGE

Level

Base or Interrupt.

Synchronization Constraints

Does not sleep.

Driver-defined basic locks, read/write locks, and sleep locks may be held across calls to this function.

Singlethreaded Example

This example illustrates how **copyb** can be used during message retransmission. If there are no messages to retransmit, we return (line 18). For each retransmission record in the list, we test to see if the downstream queue is full with the **canput**(D3) function (line 21). If it is full, we skip the current retransmission record and continue searching the list. If it is not full, we use **copyb**(D3) to copy a header message block (line 25), and **dupmsg**(D3) to duplicate the data to be retransmitted (line 28). If either operation fails, we clean up and break out of the loop.

Otherwise, we update the new header block with the correct destination address (line 34), link the message to be retransmitted to it (line 35), and send it downstream (line 36). At the end of the list, we reschedule a **timeout** at the next valid interval (line 39) and return.

```
 1  struct retrns {
 2    mblk_t          *r_mp;        /* message to retransmit */
 3    long             r_address;   /* destination address */
 4    queue_t         *r_outq;      /* output queue */
 5    struct retrns   *r_next;      /* next retransmission */
 6  };
 7  struct protoheader {
 8    long             h_address;   /* destination address */
      ...
 9  };
10  mblk_t *header;
```

```
11  struct retrns *rlist;
    ...
12  retransmit()
13  {
14    mblk_t *bp, *mp;
15    struct retrns *rp;
16    struct protoheader *php;

17    if (!rlist)
18          return;
19    rp = rlist;
20    while (rp) {
21          if (!canput(rp->r_outq->q_next)) {
22                rp = rp->r_next;
23                continue;
24          }
25          bp = copyb(header);
26          if (bp == NULL)
27                break;
28          mp = dupmsg(rp->r_mp);
29          if (mp == NULL) {
30                freeb(bp);
31                break;
32          }
33          php = (struct protoheader *)bp->b_rptr;
34          php->h_address = rp->r_address;
35          bp->bp_cont = mp;
36          putnext(rp->r_outq, bp);
37          rp = rp->r_next;
38    }
39    (void) timeout(retransmit, 0, RETRNS_TIME);
40  }
```

Multithreaded Example

This example illustrates how **copyb** can be used during message retransmission. If there are no messages to retransmit, we return (line 21). Otherwise, we lock the retransmission list (line 23). For each retransmission record in the list, we test to see if either the message has already been retransmitted, or if the downstream queue is full (by calling **canputnext**(D3) on line 26). If either is true, we skip the current retransmission record and continue searching the list. Otherwise, we use **copyb**(D3) to copy a header message block (line 30), and **dupmsg**(D3) to duplicate the data to be retransmitted (line 32).

If either operation fails, we clean up and break out of the loop. Otherwise, we update the new header block with the correct destination address (line 37), link the message to be retransmitted to it (line 38), mark the retransmission record as having sent the message (line 39), unlock the retransmission list (line 40), and send the message downstream (line 41). Then we go back and lock the list again and start searching for more messages to retransmit.

This continues until we are either at the end of the retransmission list, or unable to send a message because of allocation failure. With the list still locked, we clear all the flags for sent messages (lines 44 and 45). Finally, we unlock the list lock and reschedule a **timeout** at the next valid interval (line 47) and return.

Since we are using **itimeout**(D3), **retransmit** will run at the specified processor level, **plstr**.

```
struct retrns {
    mblk_t        *r_mp;           /* message to retransmit */
    long          r_address;       /* destination address */
    queue_t             *r_outq;         /* output queue */
    struct retrns       *r_next;         /* next retransmission */
    uchar_t             r_sent;              /* message sent */
};
struct protoheader {
    long          h_address;       /* destination address */
    ...
};
mblk_t *header;
lock_t *retranslck;
struct retrns *rlist;
...
retransmit()
{
    mblk_t *bp, *mp;
    struct retrns *rp;
    struct protoheader *php;
    pl_t pl;
    if (!rlist)
          return;
loop:
    pl = LOCK(retranslck, plstr);
    rp = rlist;
    while (rp) {
          if (rp->r_sent || !canputnext(rp->r_outq)) {
                rp = rp->r_next;
                continue;
          }
          if ((bp = copyb(header)) == NULL)
                break;
          if ((mp = dupmsg(rp->r_mp)) == NULL) {
                freeb(bp);
                break;
          }
          php = (struct protoheader *)bp->b_rptr;
          php->h_address = rp->r_address;
          bp->bp_cont = mp;
          rp->r_sent = 1;
          UNLOCK(retranslck, pl);
          putnext(rp->r_outq, bp);
          goto loop;
    }
    for (rp = rlist; rp; rp = rp->r_next)
          rp->r_sent = 0;
    UNLOCK(retranslck, pl);
    (void) itimeout(retransmit, 0, RETRNS_TIME, plstr);
}
```

REFERENCES

allocb(D3), **copymsg**(D3), **msgb**(D4)

NOTICES

Availability

SVR4.0, SVR4.1ES, SVR4MP, SVR4.2

Portability

All processors

Interface

Driver-Kernel (STREAMS)

Commitment

Level 1

NAME

copyin – copy data from a user buffer to a driver buffer

SYNOPSIS

```
#include <sys/types.h>
#include <sys/ddi.h>

int copyin(caddr_t userbuf, caddr_t driverbuf, size_t count);
```

Arguments

userbuf User source address from which copy is made.

driverbuf Driver destination address to which copy is made.

count Number of bytes to copy.

DESCRIPTION

copyin copies *count* bytes of data from the user virtual address specified by *userbuf* to the kernel virtual address specified by *driverbuf.*

Return Values

If the copy is successful, 0 is returned. Otherwise, –1 is returned to indicate that the specified user address range is not valid.

USAGE

The driver must ensure that adequate space is allocated for the destination address.

copyin chooses the best algorithm based on address alignment and number of bytes to copy. Although the source and destination addresses are not required to be word aligned, word aligned addresses may result in a more efficient copy.

Drivers usually convert a return value of –1 into an **EFAULT** error.

Level

Base only.

Synchronization Constraints

Can sleep.

Driver-defined basic locks and read/write locks may not be held across calls to this function.

Driver-defined sleep locks may be held across calls to this function.

Warnings

The driver source buffer must be completely within the kernel address space, or the system can panic.

When holding sleep locks across calls to this function, multithreaded drivers must be careful to avoid creating a deadlock. During the data transfer, page fault resolution might result in another I/O to the same device. For example, this could occur if the driver controls the disk drive used as the swap device.

Examples

A driver **ioctl**(D2) routine (line 5) can be used to get or set device attributes or registers. If the specified command is **XX_SETREGS** (line 9), the driver copies user data to the device registers (line 11). If the user address is invalid, an error code is returned.

```
struct  device {  /* device registers layout */
    ...
    int command;  /* device command word */
};
extern struct device xx_dev[]; /* physical device registers */
...
xxioctl(dev_t dev, int cmd, void *arg, int mode, cred_t *crp, int *rvp)
{
    struct device *dp;
    switch (cmd) {
    case XX_SETREGS:      /* copy user program data to device registers */
            dp = &xx_dev[getminor(dev)];
            if (copyin(arg, (caddr_t)dp, sizeof(struct device)))
                    return (EFAULT);
            break;
```

REFERENCES

`bcopy`(D3), `copyout`(D3), `uiomove`(D3), `ureadc`(D3), `uwritec`(D3)

NOTICES

Availability

SVR4.0, SVR4.1ES, SVR4MP, SVR4.2

Portability

All processors

Interface

Driver-Kernel

Commitment

Level 1

NAME

copymsg – copy a message

SYNOPSIS

```
#include <sys/stream.h>
#include <sys/ddi.h>

mblk_t *copymsg(mblk_t *mp);
```

Arguments

mp Pointer to the message to be copied.

DESCRIPTION

copymsg forms a new message by allocating new message blocks, copies the contents of the message referred to by *mp* (using the **copyb**(D3) function), and returns a pointer to the new message.

Return Values

On success, **copymsg** returns a pointer to the new message. On failure, it returns a `NULL` pointer.

USAGE

Level

Base or Interrupt.

Synchronization Constraints

Does not sleep.

Driver-defined basic locks, read/write locks, and sleep locks may be held across calls to this function.

Examples

The routine `lctouc` converts all the lower case ASCII characters in the message to upper case. If the reference count is greater than one (line 8), then the message is shared, and must be copied before changing the contents of the data buffer. If the call to **copymsg** fails (line 9), we return **NULL** (line 10). Otherwise, we free the original message (line 11). If the reference count was equal to one, the message can be modified. For each character (line 16) in each message block (line 15), if it is a lower case letter, we convert it to an upper case letter (line 18). When done, we return a pointer to the converted message (line 21).

```
 1  mblk_t *lctouc(mp)
 2    mblk_t *mp;
 3  {
 4    mblk_t *cmp;
 5    mblk_t *tmp;
 6    uchar_t *cp;
 7
 8    if (mp->b_datap->db_ref > 1) {
 9          if ((cmp = copymsg(mp)) == NULL)
10                return(NULL);
11          freemsg(mp);
12    } else {
13          cmp = mp;
14    }
15    for (tmp = cmp; tmp; tmp = tmp->b_next) {
16          for (cp = tmp->b_rptr; cp < tmp->b_wptr; cp++) {
```

```
                        if ((*cp <= 'z') && (*cp >= 'a'))
                                *cp -= 0x20;
                }
        }
        return(cmp);
}
```

REFERENCES

`allocb`(D3), `copyb`(D3), `msgb`(D4)

NOTICES

Availability

SVR4.0, SVR4.1ES, SVR4MP, SVR4.2

Portability

All processors

Interface

Driver-Kernel (STREAMS)

Commitment

Level 1

NAME

`copyout` – copy data from a driver buffer to a user buffer

SYNOPSIS

```
#include <sys/types.h>
#include <sys/ddi.h>

int copyout(caddr_t driverbuf, caddr_t userbuf, size_t count);
```

Arguments

driverbuf Driver source address from which copy is made.

userbuf User destination address to which copy is made.

count Number of bytes to copy.

DESCRIPTION

copyout copies *count* bytes of data from the kernel virtual address specified by *driverbuf* to the user virtual address specified by *userbuf*.

Return Values

On success, **copyout** returns 0. On failure, it returns –1 to indicate that the specified user address range is not valid.

USAGE

copyout chooses the best algorithm based on address alignment and number of bytes to copy. Although the source and destination addresses are not required to be word aligned, word aligned addresses may result in a more efficient copy.

Drivers usually convert a return value of –1 into an **EFAULT** error.

Level

Base only.

Synchronization Constraints

Can sleep.

Driver-defined basic locks and read/write locks may not be held across calls to this function.

Driver-defined sleep locks may be held across calls to this function.

Warnings

The driver source buffer must be completely within the kernel address space, or the system can panic.

When holding sleep locks across calls to this function, drivers must be careful to avoid creating a deadlock. During the data transfer, page fault resolution might result in another I/O to the same device. For example, this could occur if the driver controls the disk drive used as the swap device.

Examples

A driver **ioctl**(D2) routine (line 5) can be used to get or set device attributes or registers. If the specified command is **XX_GETREGS** (line 9), the driver copies the current device register values to a user data area (line 11). If the user address is invalid, an error code is returned.

```
struct  device {                  /* device registers layout */
...
   int status;                    /* device status word */
};
extern struct device xx_dev[];    /* physical device registers */
...
xxioctl(dev_t dev, int cmd, void *arg, int mode, cred_t *crp, int *rvp)
{
  struct device *dp;
  switch (cmd) {
  case XX_GETREGS:        /* copy device registers to user program */
        dp = &xx_dev[getminor(dev)];
        if (copyout((caddr_t)dp, arg, sizeof(struct device)))
              return (EFAULT);
        break;
```

REFERENCES

bcopy(D3), **copyin**(D3), **uiomove**(D3), **ureadc**(D3), **uwritec**(D3)

NOTICES

Availability

SVR4.0, SVR4.1ES, SVR4MP, SVR4.2

Portability

All processors

Interface

Driver-Kernel

Commitment

Level 1

NAME

datamsg – test whether a message is a data message

SYNOPSIS

```
#include <sys/types.h>
#include <sys/stream.h>
#include <sys/ddi.h>

int datamsg(uchar_t type);
```

Arguments

type The type of message to be tested.

DESCRIPTION

The **datamsg** function tests the type of message to determine if it is a data message type (**M_DATA**, **M_DELAY**, **M_PROTO**, or **M_PCPROTO**).

Return Values

datamsg returns 1 if the message is a data message and 0 if the message is any other type.

USAGE

The **db_type** field of the **datab** structure contains the message type. This field may be accessed through the message block using **mp->b_datap->db_type**.

Level

Base or Interrupt.

Synchronization Constraints

Does not sleep.

Driver-defined basic locks, read/write locks, and sleep locks may be held across calls to this function.

Examples

The **put**(D2) routine enqueues all data messages for handling by the **srv**(D2) (service) routine. All non-data messages are handled in the **put** routine.

```
xxxput(q, mp)
  queue_t *q;
  mblk_t *mp;
{
  if (datamsg(mp->b_datap->db_type)) {
        putq(q, mp);
        return;
  }
  switch (mp->b_datap->db_type) {
  case M_FLUSH:
  ...
  }
}
```

REFERENCES

allocb(D3), **datab**(D4), **messages**(D5), **msgb**(D4)

NOTICES

Availability

SVR4.0, SVR4.1ES, SVR4MP, SVR4.2

Portability

All processors

Interface

Driver-Kernel (STREAMS)

Commitment

Level 1

NAME

`delay` – delay process execution for a specified number of clock ticks

SYNOPSIS

`void delay(long` *ticks*`);`

Arguments

ticks The number of clock ticks to delay.

DESCRIPTION

delay causes the caller to sleep for the amount of time specified by *ticks*, which is in units of clock ticks. The exact length of the delay is not guaranteed but it will not be less than *ticks -1* clock ticks.

Return Values

None

USAGE

The length of a clock tick can vary across different implementations and therefore drivers should not include any hard-coded assumptions about the length of a tick. The **drv_usectohz**(D3) and **drv_hztousec**(D3) functions can be used, as necessary, to convert between clock ticks and microseconds (implementation independent units).

The **delay** function calls **timeout**(D3) [or, for multithreaded drivers, **itimeout**(D3)] to schedule a wakeup after the specified amount of time has elapsed. **delay** then goes to sleep until **timeout** (or **itimeout**) wakes up the sleeping process.

Level

Base only.

Synchronization Constraints

Can sleep.

Driver-defined basic locks and read/write locks may not be held across calls to this function.

Driver-defined sleep locks may be held across calls to this function, but this is discouraged because it can adversely affect performance by forcing any other processes contending for the lock to sleep for the duration of the delay.

REFERENCES

drv_hztousec(D3), **drv_usectohz**(D3), **drv_usecwait**(D3), **itimeout**(D3), **sleep**(D3), **timeout**(D3), **untimeout**(D3), **wakeup**(D3)

NOTICES

Availability

SVR4.0, SVR4.1ES, SVR4MP, SVR4.2

Portability

All processors

Interface

Driver-Kernel

delay (D3)

Commitment

Level 1

NAME

`dma_disable` – disable recognition of hardware requests on a DMA channel

SYNOPSIS

```
#include <sys/dma.h>
#include <sys/ddi.h>

void dma_disable(int chan);
```

Arguments

chan Channel to be disabled.

DESCRIPTION

`dma_disable` disables recognition of hardware requests on the DMA channel *chan*. The channel is then released and made available for other use.

Return Values

None.

USAGE

The caller must ensure that it is acting on behalf of the channel owner, and that it makes sense to release the channel.

The caller must ensure that the channel is in use for hardware-initiated DMA transfers and not software-initiated transfers.

Level

Initialization, Base or Interrupt.

Synchronization Constraints

Does not sleep.

Driver-defined basic locks, read/write locks, and sleep locks may be held across calls to this function.

REFERENCES

`dma_enable`(D3), `dma_prog`(D3), `dma_cb`(D4)

NOTICES

Availability

SVR4.0, SVR4.1ES, SVR4MP, SVR4.2

Portability

AT-compatible architectures

Interface

Driver-Hardware

Commitment

Level 2 effective August 31, 1992

dma_enable (D3)

NAME

`dma_enable` – enable recognition of hardware requests on a DMA channel

SYNOPSIS

```
#include <sys/dma.h>
#include <sys/ddi.h>

void dma_enable(int chan);
```

Arguments

chan Channel to be enabled.

DESCRIPTION

`dma_enable` enables recognition of hardware requests on the DMA channel *chan*.

Return Values

None.

USAGE

The channel should have been programmed previously by **dma_prog**(D3).

Level

Initialization, Base or Interrupt.

Synchronization Constraints

Does not sleep.

Driver-defined basic locks, read/write locks, and sleep locks may be held across calls to this function.

REFERENCES

`dma_disable`(D3), **dma_prog**(D3), **dma_cb**(D4)

NOTICES

Availability

SVR4.0, SVR4.1ES, SVR4MP, SVR4.2

Portability

AT-compatible architectures

Interface

Driver-Hardware

Commitment

Level 2 effective August 31, 1992

NAME

`dma_free_buf` – free a previously allocated DMA buffer descriptor

SYNOPSIS

```
#include <sys/dma.h>
#include <sys/ddi.h>

void dma_free_buf(struct dma_buf *dmabufptr);
```

Arguments

dmabufptr Address of the allocated DMA buffer descriptor to be returned.

DESCRIPTION

`dma_free_buf` frees a DMA buffer descriptor.

Return Values

None.

USAGE

The *dmabufptr* argument must specify the address of a DMA buffer descriptor previously allocated by **`dma_get_buf`**(D3).

Level

Initialization, Base or Interrupt.

Synchronization Constraints

Does not sleep.

Driver-defined basic locks, read/write locks, and sleep locks may be held across calls to this function.

REFERENCES

`dma_get_buf`(D3), `dma_buf`(D4)

NOTICES

Availability

SVR4.0, SVR4.1ES, SVR4MP, SVR4.2

Portability

AT-compatible architectures

Interface

Driver-Hardware

Commitment

Level 2 effective August 31, 1992

dma_free_cb (D3)

NAME

dma_free_cb – free a previously allocated DMA command block

SYNOPSIS

```
#include <sys/dma.h>
#include <sys/ddi.h>

void dma_free_cb(struct dma_cb *dmacbptr);
```

Arguments

dmacbptr Address of the allocated DMA command block to be returned.

DESCRIPTION

dma_free_cb frees a DMA command block.

Return Values

None.

USAGE

The *dmacbptr* argument must specify the address of a DMA command block previously allocated by dma_get_cb(D3).

Level

Initialization, Base or Interrupt.

Synchronization Constraints

Does not sleep.

Driver-defined basic locks, read/write locks, and sleep locks may be held across calls to this function.

REFERENCES

dma_get_cb(D3), dma_cb(D4)

NOTICES

Availability

SVR4.0, SVR4.1ES, SVR4MP, SVR4.2

Portability

AT-compatible architectures

Interface

Driver-Hardware

Commitment

Level 2 effective August 31, 1992

NAME

dma_get_best_mode – determine best transfer mode for DMA command

SYNOPSIS

```
#include <sys/types.h>
#include <sys/dma.h>
#include <sys/ddi.h>

uchar_t dma_get_best_mode(struct dma_cb *dmacbptr);
```

Arguments

dmacbptr Pointer to a DMA command block.

DESCRIPTION

dma_get_best_mode determines the best DMA transfer mode to use with the DMA operation specified in the command block whose address is given by *dmacbptr*.

Return Values

dma_get_best_mode returns a value that specifies the transfer mode. This value should be used to set the **cycles** field of the **dma_cb**(D4) structure.

USAGE

Prior to the call to **dma_get_best_mode**, all fields of the command block should have been initialized except for **cycles**. The **cycles** field should be initialized using the return value from **dma_get_best_mode**.

Level

Initialization, Base or Interrupt.

Synchronization Constraints

Does not sleep.

Driver-defined basic locks, read/write locks, and sleep locks may be held across calls to this function.

REFERENCES

dma_cb(D4)

NOTICES

Availability

SVR4.0, SVR4.1ES, SVR4MP, SVR4.2

Portability

AT-compatible architectures

Interface

Driver-Hardware

Commitment

Level 2 effective August 31, 1992

dma_get_buf(D3)

NAME

`dma_get_buf` – allocate a DMA buffer descriptor

SYNOPSIS

```
#include <sys/types.h>
#include <sys/dma.h>
#include <sys/ddi.h>

struct dma_buf *dma_get_buf(uchar_t mode);
```

Arguments

mode Specifies whether the caller is willing to sleep waiting for memory.

DESCRIPTION

`dma_get_buf` allocates memory for a DMA command block structure [see `dma_buf`(D4)], zeroes it out, and returns a pointer to the structure.

Return Values

`dma_get_buf` returns a pointer to the allocated DMA control block. If **`DMA_NOSLEEP`** is specified and memory for a **`dma_buf`** is not immediately available, `dma_get_buf` returns a **`NULL`** pointer.

USAGE

If *mode* is set to **`DMA_SLEEP`**, the caller will sleep if necessary until the memory for a **`dma_buf`** is available. If *mode* is set to **`DMA_NOSLEEP`**, the caller will not sleep, but `dma_get_buf` will return **`NULL`** if memory for a **`dma_buf`** is not immediately available.

Level

Base only if *mode* is set to **`DMA_SLEEP`**.

Initialization, Base or Interrupt if *mode* is set to **`DMA_NOSLEEP`**.

Synchronization Constraints

May sleep if *mode* is set to **`DMA_SLEEP`**.

Driver-defined basic locks, read/write locks, and sleep locks may be held across calls to this function.

REFERENCES

`dma_free_buf`(D3), `dma_buf`(D4)

NOTICES

Availability

SVR4.0, SVR4.1ES, SVR4MP, SVR4.2

Portability

AT-compatible architectures

Interface

Driver-Hardware

Commitment

Level 2 effective August 31, 1992

NAME

dma_get_cb – allocate a DMA command block

SYNOPSIS

```
#include <sys/types.h>
#include <sys/dma.h>
#include <sys/ddi.h>

struct dma_cb *dma_get_cb(uchar_t mode);
```

Arguments

mode Specifies whether the caller is willing to sleep waiting for memory.

DESCRIPTION

dma_get_cb allocates memory for a DMA command block structure [see dma_cb(D4)], zeroes it out, and returns a pointer to the structure.

Return Values

dma_get_cb returns a pointer to the allocated DMA control block. If DMA_NOSLEEP is specified and memory for a dma_cb is not immediately available, dma_get_cb returns a NULL pointer.

USAGE

If *mode* is set to DMA_SLEEP, the caller will sleep if necessary until the memory for a dma_cb is available. If *mode* is set to DMA_NOSLEEP, the caller will not sleep, but dma_get_cb will return NULL if memory for a dma_cb is not immediately available.

Level

Base only if *mode* is set to DMA_SLEEP.

Initialization, Base or Interrupt if *mode* is set to DMA_NOSLEEP.

Synchronization Constraints

May sleep if *mode* is set to DMA_SLEEP.

Driver-defined basic locks, read/write locks, and sleep locks may be held across calls to this function.

REFERENCES

dma_free_cb(D3), dma_cb(D4)

NOTICES

Availability

SVR4.0, SVR4.1ES, SVR4MP, SVR4.2

Portability

AT-compatible architectures

Interface

Driver-Hardware

Commitment

Level 2 effective August 31, 1992

dma_pageio (D3)

NAME

dma_pageio – break up an I/O request into manageable units

SYNOPSIS

```
#include <sys/buf.h>
#include <sys/ddi.h>

void dma_pageio(void (*strat)(), buf_t *bp);
```

Arguments

strat Address of the **strategy**(D2) routine to call to complete the I/O transfer.

bp Pointer to the buffer header structure.

DESCRIPTION

dma_pageio breaks up a data transfer request from **physiock**(D3) into units of contiguous memory. This function enhances the capabilities of the direct memory access controller (DMAC).

Return Values

None

USAGE

When the transfer completes, any allocated buffers are freed.

The interrupt priority level is not maintained across calls to **dma_pageio**.

Level

Base only.

Synchronization Constraints

Can sleep.

Driver-defined basic locks and read/write locks may not be held across calls to this function.

Driver-defined sleep locks may be held across calls to this function.

Examples

The following example shows how **dma_pageio** is used when reading or writing disk data. The driver's **read**(D2) and **write**(D2) entry points use **physiock** to check the validity of the I/O and perform the data transfer. The **strategy**(D2) routine passed to **physiock** just calls **dma_pageio** to perform the data transfer one page at a time.

```
struct dsize {
  daddr_t nblocks;   /* number of blocks in disk partition */
  int cyloff;        /* starting cylinder # of partition */
} my_sizes[2] = {
  20448, 21,         /* partition 0 = cyl 21-305 */
  21888, 1           /* partition 1 = cyl  1-305 */
};

int
my_read(dev, uiop, crp)
  dev_t dev;
  uio_t *uiop;
  cred_t *crp;
{
  int nblks;
```

```
	nblks = my_sizes[getminor(dev)].nblocks;
	return(physiock(my_breakup, 0, dev, B_READ, nblks, uiop));
}

int
my_write(dev, uiop, crp)
	dev_t dev;
	uio_t *uiop;
	cred_t *crp;
{
	int nblks;

	nblks = my_sizes[getminor(dev)].nblocks;
	return(physiock(my_breakup, 0, dev, B_WRITE, nblks, uiop));
}

static void
my_breakup(bp)
	buf_t *bp;
{
	dma_pageio(my_strategy, bp);
}
```

REFERENCES

`buf`(D4), `physiock`(D3), `read`(D2), `strategy`(D2), `write`(D2)

NOTICES

Availability

SVR4.0, SVR4.1ES, SVR4MP, SVR4.2

Portability

All processors

Interface

Driver-Hardware

Commitment

Level 1

dma_prog (D3)

NAME

dma_prog – program a DMA operation for a subsequent hardware request

SYNOPSIS

```
#include <sys/types.h>
#include <sys/dma.h>
#include <sys/ddi.h>

int dma_prog(struct dma_cb *dmacbptr, int chan, uchar_t mode);
```

Arguments

dmacbptr Pointer to the DMA command block specifying the DMA operation.

chan DMA channel over which the operation is to take place.

mode Specifies whether the caller is willing to sleep waiting to allocate desired DMA channel.

DESCRIPTION

dma_prog programs the DMA channel *chan* for the operation specified by the DMA command block whose address is given by *dmacbptr*.

Return Values

dma_prog returns the value **TRUE** upon successful completion and returns the value **FALSE** otherwise.

USAGE

dma_prog does not initiate the DMA transfer. Instead, the transfer will be initiated by a subsequent request from hardware. The hardware request will be recognized only if the channel has been enabled via **dma_enable**(D3) following the call to **dma_prog**.

In order to program the operation, **dma_prog** requires exclusive use of the specified DMA channel. The caller may specify, via the *mode* argument, whether or not **dma_prog** should sleep waiting for a busy channel to become available. If the specified channel is in use, and *mode* is set to **DMA_SLEEP**, then **dma_prog** will sleep until the channel becomes available for its use. Otherwise, if **DMA_NOSLEEP** is specified and the requested channel is not immediately available, **dma_prog** will not program the channel, but will simply return a value of **FALSE**.

Level

Base only if *mode* is set to **DMA_SLEEP**.

Initialization, Base or Interrupt if *mode* is set to **DMA_NOSLEEP**.

Synchronization Constraints

May sleep if *mode* is set to **DMA_SLEEP**.

Driver-defined basic locks, read/write locks, and sleep locks may be held across calls to this function.

REFERENCES

dma_disable(D3), **dma_enable**(D3), **dma_cb**(D4)

NOTICES

Availability

SVR4.0, SVR4.1ES, SVR4MP, SVR4.2

Portability

AT-compatible architectures

Interface

Driver-Hardware

Commitment

Level 2 effective August 31, 1992

dma_stop (D3)

NAME

dma_stop – stop software-initiated DMA operation on a channel and release it

SYNOPSIS

```
#include <sys/dma.h>
#include <sys/ddi.h>

void dma_stop(int chan);
```

Arguments

chan Channel on which DMA operation is to be stopped.

DESCRIPTION

dma_stop stops a software-initiated DMA operation in progress on the channel *chan*. The channel is then released and made available for other use.

Return Values

None.

USAGE

The caller must ensure that it is acting on behalf of the channel owner, and that it makes sense to release the channel.

The caller must ensure that the channel is currently in use for software-initiated DMA transfers rather than hardware-initiated transfers.

Level

Initialization, Base or Interrupt.

Synchronization Constraints

Does not sleep.

Driver-defined basic locks, read/write locks, and sleep locks may be held across calls to this function.

REFERENCES

dma_swsetup(D3), **dma_swstart**(D3), **dma_cb**(D4)

NOTICES

Availability

SVR4.0, SVR4.1ES, SVR4MP, SVR4.2

Portability

AT-compatible architectures

Interface

Driver-Hardware

Commitment

Level 2 effective August 31, 1992

NAME

dma_swstart – initiate a DMA operation via software request

SYNOPSIS

```
#include <sys/types.h>
#include <sys/dma.h>
#include <sys/ddi.h>

void dma_swstart(struct dma_cb *dmacbptr, int chan, uchar_t mode);
```

Arguments

dmacbptr Pointer to a DMA command block specifying the DMA operation.

chan Channel over which the operation is to take place.

mode Specifies whether the caller should sleep waiting for the operation to complete.

DESCRIPTION

dma_swstart initiates a DMA operation previously programmed by **dma_swsetup**(D3).

Return Values

None.

USAGE

If *mode* is set to **DMA_NOSLEEP**, then **dma_swstart** simply starts the operation but does not wait for the operation to complete and instead returns to the caller immediately. If *mode* is set to **DMA_SLEEP**, then **dma_swstart** starts the operation and then waits for the operation to complete, and returns to the caller after the operation has finished.

The operation being initiated must have already been programmed on the specified channel by **dma_swsetup**.

Level

Base only if *mode* is set to **DMA_SLEEP**.

Initialization, Base or Interrupt if *mode* is set to **DMA_NOSLEEP**.

Synchronization Constraints

May sleep if *mode* is set to **DMA_SLEEP**.

Driver-defined basic locks, read/write locks, and sleep locks may be held across calls to this function.

REFERENCES

dma_stop(D3), **dma_swsetup**(D3), **dma_cb**(D4)

NOTICES

Availability

SVR4.0, SVR4.1ES, SVR4MP, SVR4.2

Portability

AT-compatible architectures

dma_swstart (D3)

Interface
Driver-Hardware

Commitment
Level 2 effective August 31, 1992

NAME

dma_swsetup – program a DMA operation for a subsequent software request

SYNOPSIS

```
#include <sys/types.h>
#include <sys/dma.h>
#include <sys/ddi.h>

int dma_swsetup(struct dma_cb *dmacbptr, int chan, uchar_t mode);
```

Arguments

dmacbptr Pointer to the DMA command block specifying the DMA operation.

chan DMA channel over which the operation is to take place.

mode Specifies whether the caller is willing to sleep waiting to allocate desired DMA channel.

DESCRIPTION

dma_swsetup programs the DMA channel *chan* for the operation specified by the DMA command block whose address is given by *dmacbptr*.

Return Values

dma_swsetup returns the value **TRUE** on success and returns the value **FALSE** otherwise.

USAGE

dma_swsetup does not initiate the DMA transfer. Instead, the transfer will be initiated by a subsequent request initiated via software by **dma_swstart**(D3). If **dma_swsetup** programs the operation successfully, it then calls the procedure specified by the **proc** field of the **dma_cb**(D4) structure. It passes as an argument the value in the **procparms** field. If **proc** is set to **NULL**, then no routine is called.

To program the operation, **dma_swsetup** requires exclusive use of the specified DMA channel. The caller may specify, via the *mode* argument, whether **dma_swsetup** should sleep waiting for a busy channel to become available. If the specified channel is in use and *mode* is set to **DMA_SLEEP**, then **dma_swsetup** will sleep until the channel becomes available for its use. Otherwise, if **DMA_NOSLEEP** is specified and the requested channel is not immediately available, **dma_swsetup** will not program the channel, but will simply return a value of **FALSE**.

Level

Base only if either (1) *mode* is set to **DMA_SLEEP** or (2) the routine specified by the **proc** field of the **dma_cb** structure sleeps.

Initialization, Base or Interrupt otherwise.

Synchronization Constraints

May sleep if *mode* is set to **DMA_SLEEP** or if the routine specified by the **proc** field of the **dma_cb** structure sleeps.

Driver-defined basic locks, read/write locks, and sleep locks may be held across calls to this function.

REFERENCES

dma_swstart(D3), **dma_stop**(D3), **dma_cb**(D4)

NOTICES

Availability

SVR4.0, SVR4.1ES, SVR4MP, SVR4.2

Portability

AT-compatible architectures

Interface

Driver-Hardware

Commitment

Level 2 effective August 31, 1992

NAME

drv_gethardware – retrieve hardware information

SYNOPSIS

```
#include <sys/types.h>
#include <sys/ddi.h>
#include <sys/ddi_i386at.h>

int drv_gethardware(ulong_t parm, void *value_p);
```

Arguments

parm The hardware information to be obtained.

value_p A pointer to the data space into which the value of the parameter specified by *parm* is to be copied.

DESCRIPTION

drv_gethardware returns the value of the parameter specified by *parm* in the location pointed to by *value_p*.

Return Values

On success, **drv_gethardware** returns 0. On failure, **drv_gethardware** returns –1 to indicate that *parm* specified an invalid parameter.

USAGE

It is the responsibility of the driver to correctly declare the data space needed to hold the information returned.

Valid values for *parm* are:

PROC_INFO

Retrieve processor identification information. *value_p* should point to a structure of type **struct cpuparms**. The **cpuparms** structure is defined as:

```
struct cpuparms {
        ulong_t cpu_id;          /* CPU identification */
        ulong_t cpu_step;        /* Step (revision) number */
        ulong_t cpu_resrvd[2];   /* RESERVED for future expansion */
};

/* Valid values for cpu_id */

#define CPU_UNK   0
#define CPU_i386  1
#define CPU_i486  2
#define CPU_i586  3
#define CPU_i686  4
#define CPU_i786  5

/* Valid values for cpu_step */

#define STEP_UNK  0
#define STEP_B1   1             /* if cpu_id == CPU_i386 */
```

IOBUS_TYPE

Retrieve the bus type. Valid values are **BUS_ISA**, **BUS_EISA**, and **BUS_MCA**.

`TOTAL_MEM`
Retrieve the size of memory (in bytes).

`DMA_SIZE`
Retrieve the number of bits available for DMA addressing.

`BOOT_DEV`
Retrieve which device the system was booted from. *value_p* should point to a structure of type **struct bootdev**. The **bootdev** structure is defined as:

```
struct bootdev {
        ulong_t    bdv_type;           /* Type of the boot device */
        ulong_t    bdv_unit;           /* Unit number of the boot device */
        ulong_t    bdv_resrvd[2];      /* RESERVED for future expansion */
};

/* Valid values for bdv_type */

#define BOOT_FLOPPY    1
#define BOOT_DISK      2
#define BOOT_CDROM     3
#define BOOT_NETWORK   4
```

`HD_PARMS`
Retrieve a pointer to the parameters for a specified hard disk. *value_p* should point to a structure of type **struct hdparms**. The driver must specify the hard disk by setting the **hp_unit** field of the **hdparms** structure pointed to by *value_p* to the unit number of the hard disk prior to calling **drv_gethardware**. The **hdparms** structure is defined as:

```
struct hdparms {
        ulong_t    hp_unit;            /* Hard disk unit number */
        ulong_t    hp_ncyls;           /* Number of cylinders (0 == no disk) */
        ulong_t    hp_nheads;          /* Number of heads */
        ulong_t    hp_nsects;          /* Number of sectors per track */
        ulong_t    hp_resrvd[3];       /* RESERVED for future expansion */
};
```

Level
Initialization, Base or Interrupt.

Synchronization Constraints
Does not sleep.

Driver-defined basic locks, read/write locks, and sleep locks may be held across calls to this function.

NOTICES

Availability
SVR4.2

Portability
Intel386, Intel486, Intel860

Interface
Driver-Hardware

UCRED Retrieve a pointer to the credential structure describing the current user credentials for the current process. The value returned in **value_p* is of type **(cred_t *)** and the only valid use of the value is as an argument to **drv_priv**(D3). Since this value is associated with the current process, the caller must have process context (that is, must be at base level) when attempting to retrieve this value. Also, this value should only be used in the context of the process in which it was retrieved.

Level

Base only when using the **UPROCP** or **UCRED** argument values.

Initialization, Base or Interrupt when using the **LBOLT** or **TIME** argument values.

Synchronization Constraints

Does not sleep.

Driver-defined basic locks, read/write locks, and sleep locks may be held across calls to this function.

REFERENCES

drv_hztousec(D3), **drv_priv**(D3), **drv_usectohz**(D3), **vtop**(D3)

NOTICES

Availability

SVR4.0, SVR4.1ES, SVR4MP, SVR4.2

Portability

All processors

Interface

Driver-Kernel

Commitment

Level 2 effective August 31, 1992

Future Directions

In more recent SVR4 releases, the *value_p* argument returns a **void**. In earlier SVR4 releases, it returns a **ulong_t** data type.

drv_hztousec (D3)

NAME

drv_hztousec – convert clock ticks to microseconds

SYNOPSIS

```
#include <sys/types.h>
#include <sys/ddi.h>

clock_t drv_hztousec(clock_t ticks);
```

Arguments

ticks The number of clock ticks to convert to equivalent microseconds.

DESCRIPTION

drv_hztousec converts the length of time expressed by *ticks*, which is in units of clock ticks, into units of microseconds.

Return Values

drv_hztousec returns the number of microseconds equivalent to the *ticks* argument. No error value is returned. If the microsecond equivalent to *ticks* is too large to be represented as a **clock_t**, then the maximum **clock_t** value is returned.

USAGE

Several functions either take time values expressed in clock ticks as arguments [**timeout**(D3), **timeout**(D3), **delay**(D3)] or return time values expressed in clock ticks [**drv_getparm**(D3)]. The length of a clock tick can vary across different implementations, and therefore drivers should not include any hard-coded assumptions about the length of a tick. **drv_hztousec** and the complementary function **drv_usectohz**(D3) can be used, as necessary, to convert between clock ticks and microseconds.

Note that the time value returned by **drv_getparm** with an **LBOLT** argument will frequently be too large to represent in microseconds as a **clock_t**. When using **drv_getparm** together with **drv_hztousec** to time operations, drivers can help avoid overflow by converting the difference between return values from successive calls to **drv_getparm** instead of trying to convert the return values themselves.

Level

Initialization, Base or Interrupt.

Synchronization Constraints

Does not sleep.

Driver-defined basic locks, read/write locks, and sleep locks may be held across calls to this function.

REFERENCES

delay(D3), **drv_getparm**(D3), **drv_usectohz**(D3), **itimeout**(D3) **timeout**(D3)

NOTICES

Availability

SVR4.0, SVR4.1ES, SVR4MP, SVR4.2

Portability

All processors

Interface
Driver-Kernel

Commitment
Level 1

drv_priv (D3)

NAME

drv_priv – determine whether credentials are privileged

SYNOPSIS

```
int drv_priv(cred_t *crp);
```

Arguments

crp Pointer to the user credential structure.

DESCRIPTION

The **drv_priv** function determines whether the credentials specified by the credential structure pointed to by *crp* identify a privileged process.

Return Values

drv_prv returns 0 if the specified credentials identify a privileged process and **EPERM** otherwise.

USAGE

This function should only be used when file access modes and special minor device numbers are insufficient to provide the necessary protection for the driver operation being performed. Calls to **drv_priv** should replace all calls to **suser** and any explicit checks for effective user ID equal to zero in driver code.

A credential structure pointer is passed into various driver entry point functions [**open**(D2), **close**(D2), **read**(D2), **write**(D2), and **ioctl**(D2)] and can also be obtained by calling **drv_getparm**(D3) from base level driver code.

Level

Base or Interrupt.

Synchronization Constraints

Does not sleep.

Driver-defined basic locks, read/write locks, and sleep locks may be held across calls to this function.

Warnings

The only valid use for a credential structure pointer is as an argument to **drv_priv**. The contents of a credential structure are not defined by the DDI/DKI and a driver may not examine the contents of the structure directly.

NOTICES

Availability

SVR4.0, SVR4.1ES, SVR4MP, SVR4.2

Portability

All processors

Interface

Driver-Kernel

Commitment

Level 1

NAME

`drv_setparm` – set kernel state information

SYNOPSIS

```
#include <sys/types.h>
#include <sys/ddi.h>

int drv_setparm(ulong_t parm, ulong_t value);
```

Arguments

parm The kernel parameter to be updated.

value The value to be added to the parameter.

DESCRIPTION

`drv_setparm` verifies that *parm* corresponds to a kernel parameter that may be modified. If the value of *parm* corresponds to a parameter that may not be modified, –1 is returned. Otherwise, the parameter is incremented by *value*.

Return Values

If the function is successful, 0 is returned. Otherwise, –1 is returned to indicate that *parm* specified an invalid parameter.

USAGE

No checking is performed to determine the validity of *value*. It is the driver's responsibility to guarantee the correctness of *value*.

Valid values for *parm* are:

`SYSCANC` Add *value* to `sysinfo.canch`. `sysinfo.canch` is a count of the number of characters received from a terminal device after the characters have been processed to remove special characters such as *break* or *backspace*.

`SYSMINT` Add *value* to `sysinfo.mdmint`. `sysinfo.mdmint` is a count of the number of modem interrupts received.

`SYSOUTC` Add *value* to `sysinfo.outch`. `sysinfo.outch` is a count of the number of characters output to a terminal device.

`SYSRAWC` Add *value* to `sysinfo.rawc`. `sysinfo.rawc` is a count of the number of characters received from a terminal device, before canonical processing has occurred.

`SYSRINT` Add *value* to `sysinfo.rcvint`. `sysinfo.rcvint` is a count of the number of interrupts generated by data ready to be received from a terminal device.

`SYSXINT` Add *value* to `sysinfo.xmtint`. `sysinfo.xmtint` is a count of the number of interrupts generated by data ready to be transmitted to a terminal device.

Level

Base or Interrupt.

Synchronization Constraints

Does not sleep.

Driver-defined basic locks, read/write locks, and sleep locks may be held across calls to this function.

REFERENCES

`drv_getparm`(D3)

NOTICES

Availability

SVR4.0, SVR4.1ES, SVR4MP, SVR4.2

Portability

All processors

Interface

Driver-Kernel

Commitment

Level 2 effective August 31, 1992

NAME

drv_usectohz – convert microseconds to clock ticks

SYNOPSIS

```
#include <sys/types.h>
#include <sys/ddi.h>

clock_t drv_usectohz(clock_t microsecs);
```

Arguments

microsecs The number of microseconds to convert to equivalent clock ticks.

DESCRIPTION

drv_usectohz converts the length of time expressed by *microsecs*, which is in units of microseconds, into units of clock ticks.

Return Values

The value returned is the smallest number of clock ticks that represent a time interval equal to or greater than the *microsecs* argument. No error value is returned. If the number of ticks equivalent to the *microsecs* argument is too large to be represented as a **clock_t**, then the maximum **clock_t** value will be returned.

USAGE

Several functions either take time values expressed in clock ticks as arguments [**timeout**(D3), **timeout**(D3), **delay**(D3)] or return time values expressed in clock ticks [**drv_getparm**(D3)]. The length of a clock tick can vary across different implementations, and therefore drivers should not include any hard-coded assumptions about the length of a tick. **drv_usectohz** and the complementary function **drv_hztousec**(D3) can be used, as necessary, to convert between microseconds and clock ticks.

Level

Initialization, Base or Interrupt.

Synchronization Constraints

Does not sleep.

Driver-defined basic locks, read/write locks, and sleep locks may be held across calls to this function.

REFERENCES

delay(D3), **drv_getparm**(D3), **drv_hztousec**(D3), **itimeout**(D3) **timeout**(D3)

NOTICES

Availability

SVR4.0, SVR4.1ES, SVR4MP, SVR4.2

Portability

All processors

Interface

Driver-Kernel

Commitment

Level 1

drv_usecwait (D3)

NAME

`drv_usecwait` – busy-wait for specified interval

SYNOPSIS

```
#include <sys/types.h>
#include <sys/ddi.h>

void drv_usecwait(clock_t microsecs);
```

Arguments

microsecs The number of microseconds to busy-wait.

DESCRIPTION

`drv_usecwait` causes the caller to busy-wait for at least the number of microseconds specified by *microsecs*. The amount of time spent busy-waiting may be greater than the time specified by *microsecs* but will not be less.

Return Values

None

USAGE

`drv_usecwait` should only be used to wait for short periods of time (less than a clock tick) or when it is necessary to wait without sleeping (for example, at interrupt level). When the desired delay is at least as long as clock tick and it is possible to sleep, the **`delay`**(D3) function should be used instead since it will not waste processor time busy-waiting as **`drv_usecwait`** does.

Because excessive busy-waiting is wasteful the driver should only make calls to `drv_usecwait` as needed, and only for as much time as needed. **`drv_usecwait`** does not raise the interrupt priority level; if the driver wishes to block interrupts for the duration of the wait, it is the driver's responsibility to set the priority level before the call and restore it to its original value afterward.

Level

Initialization, Base or Interrupt.

Synchronization Constraints

Does not sleep.

Driver-defined basic locks, read/write locks, and sleep locks may be held across calls to this function.

Warnings

Busy-waiting can increase the preemption latency experienced by high priority processes. Since short and bounded preemption latency can be critical in a real time environment, drivers intended for use in such an environment should not use this interface or should limit the length of the wait to an appropriately short length of time.

REFERENCES

`delay`(D3), **`drv_hztousec`**(D3), **`drv_usectohz`**(D3), **`itimeout`**(D3), **`timeout`**(D3), **`untimeout`**(D3)

NOTICES

Availability
SVR4.0, SVR4.1ES, SVR4MP, SVR4.2

Portability
All processors

Interface
Driver-Kernel

Commitment
Level 1

dtimeout (D3)

NAME

`dtimeout` – execute a function on a specified processor after a specified length of time

SYNOPSIS

```
#include <sys/types.h>
#include <sys/ddi.h>

toid_t dtimeout(void (*fn)(), void *arg, long ticks, pl_t pl,
                processorid_t processor);
```

Arguments

fn	Function to execute on the specified processor when the time increment expires.
arg	Argument to the function.
ticks	Number of clock ticks to wait before the function is called.
pl	The interrupt priority level at which the function will be called.
processor	Processor on which the function must execute.

DESCRIPTION

`dtimeout` causes the function specified by *fn* to be called after the time interval specified by *ticks*, on the processor specified by *processor*, at the interrupt priority level specified by *pl*. *arg* will be passed as the only argument to function *fn*. The `dtimeout` call returns immediately without waiting for the specified function to execute.

Return Values

If the function specified by *fn* is successfully scheduled, `dtimeout` returns a non-zero identifier that can be passed to `untimeout` to cancel the request. If the function could not be scheduled on the specified processor, `dtimeout` returns a value of 0.

USAGE

This directed timeout capability provides a form of dynamic processor binding for driver code.

Drivers should be careful to cancel any pending `dtimeout` functions that access data structures before these structures are de-initialized or deallocated.

fn Argument

The function specified by *fn* must neither sleep, reference process context, nor lower the interrupt priority level below *pl*.

After the time interval has expired, *fn* only runs if the processor is at base level. Otherwise, *fn* is deferred until some time in the near future.

If `dtimeout` is called holding a lock that is contended for by *fn*, the caller must hold the lock at a processor level greater than the base processor level.

ticks Argument

The length of time before the function is called is not guaranteed to be exactly equal to the requested time, but will be at least *ticks–1* clock ticks in length.

A *ticks* argument of 0 has the same effect as a *ticks* argument of 1. Both will result in an approximate wait of between 0 and 1 tick (possibly longer).

pl Argument

pl must specify a priority level greater than or equal to *pltimeout*; thus, *plbase* cannot be used. See **LOCK_ALLOC**(D3) for a list of values for *pl*.

Level

Base or Interrupt.

Synchronization Constraints

Does not sleep.

Driver-defined basic locks, read/write locks, and sleep locks may be held across calls to this function.

REFERENCES

`itimeout`(D3), `LOCK_ALLOC`(D3), `untimeout`(D3)

NOTICES

Availability

SVR4MP

Portability

All processors

Interface

Driver-Kernel

Commitment

Level 1

dupb (D3)

NAME

`dupb` – duplicate a message block

SYNOPSIS

```
#include <sys/stream.h>
#include <sys/ddi.h>

mblk_t *dupb(mblk_t *bp);
```

Arguments

bp Pointer to the message block to be duplicated.

DESCRIPTION

dupb creates a new message block structure to reference the message block pointed to by *bp*. Unlike **copyb**(D3), **dupb** does not copy the information in the data block, but creates a new structure to point to it.

Return Values

On success, **dupb** returns a pointer to the new message block. On failure, it returns a `NULL` pointer.

USAGE

The following figure shows how the **db_ref** field of the data block structure has been changed from 1 to 2, reflecting the increase in the number of references to the data block. The new message block contains the same information as the first. Note that **b_rptr** and **b_wptr** are copied from *bp*, and that **db_ref** is incremented.

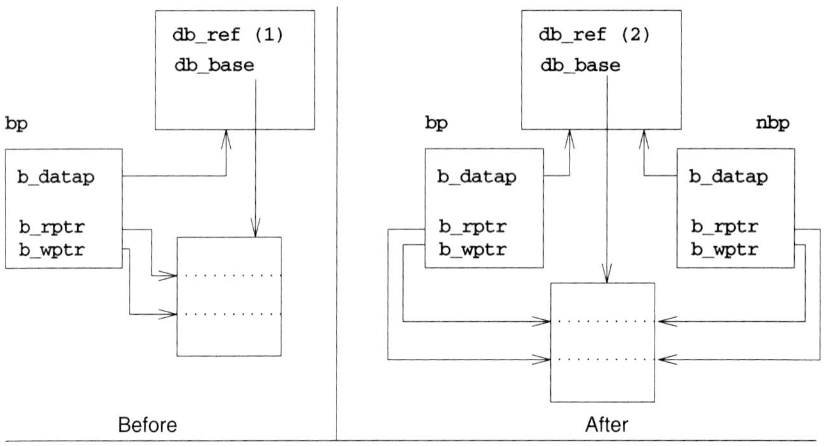

`nbp=dupb(bp);`

Level

Base or Interrupt.

Synchronization Constraints

Does not sleep.

Driver-defined basic locks, read/write locks, and sleep locks may be held across calls to this function.

REFERENCES

copyb(D3), **dupmsg**(D3), **datab**(D4), **msgb**(D4)

NOTICES

Availability

SVR4.0, SVR4.1ES, SVR4MP, SVR4.2

Portability

All processors

Interface

Driver-Kernel (STREAMS)

Commitment

Level 1

dupmsg (D3)

NAME

dupmsg – duplicate a message

SYNOPSIS

```
#include <sys/stream.h>
#include <sys/ddi.h>

mblk_t *dupmsg(mblk_t *mp);
```

Arguments

mp Pointer to the message.

DESCRIPTION

dupmsg forms a new message by duplicating the message blocks in the message pointed to by *mp* and linking them via their **b_cont** pointers.

Return Values

On success, **dupmsg** returns a pointer to the new message. On failure, it returns a **NULL** pointer.

USAGE

Level

Base or Interrupt.

Synchronization Constraints

Does not sleep.

Driver-defined basic locks, read/write locks, and sleep locks may be held across calls to this function.

Examples

See the **copyb**(D3) manual page for an example of **dupmsg**.

REFERENCES

copyb(D3), **copymsg**(D3), **dupb**(D3), **datab**(D4), **msgb**(D4)

NOTICES

Availability

SVR4.0, SVR4.1ES, SVR4MP, SVR4.2

Portability

All processors

Interface

Driver-Kernel (STREAMS)

Commitment

Level 1

NAME

enableok – allow a queue to be serviced

SYNOPSIS

```
#include <sys/stream.h>
#include <sys/ddi.h>

void enableok(queue_t *q);
```

Arguments

q Pointer to the queue.

DESCRIPTION

The **enableok** function allows the service routine of the queue pointed to by *q* to be rescheduled for service. It cancels the effect of a previous use of the **noenable**(D3) function on *q*.

Return Values

None

USAGE

Level

Base or Interrupt.

Synchronization Constraints

Does not sleep.

Driver-defined basic locks, read/write locks, and sleep locks may be held across calls to this function.

The caller cannot have the stream frozen [see **freezestr**(D3)] when calling this function.

Examples

The **qrestart** routine uses two STREAMS functions to re-enable a queue that has been disabled. The **enableok** function removes the restriction that prevented the queue from being scheduled when a message was enqueued. Then, if there are messages on the queue, it is scheduled by calling **qenable**(D3).

```
void
qrestart(q)
   queue_t *q;
{
   enableok(q);
   if (q->q_first)
         qenable(q);
}
```

REFERENCES

noenable(D3), **qenable**(D3), **queue**(D4), **srv**(D2)

NOTICES

Availability

SVR4.0, SVR4.1ES, SVR4MP, SVR4.2

Portability
All processors

Interface
Driver-Kernel (STREAMS)

Commitment
Level 1

NAME

esballoc – allocate a message block using an externally-supplied buffer

SYNOPSIS

```
#include <sys/types.h>
#include <sys/stream.h>
#include <sys/ddi.h>

mblk_t *esballoc(uchar_t *base, int size, int pri, frtn_t *fr_rtnp);
```

Arguments

base Address of driver-supplied data buffer.

size Number of bytes in data buffer.

pri Priority of allocation request (used to allocate the message and data blocks).

fr_rtnp Pointer to the free-routine data structure.

DESCRIPTION

esballoc creates a STREAMS message and attaches a driver-supplied data buffer in place of a STREAMS data buffer. It allocates a message and data block header only. The driver-supplied data buffer, pointed to by *base*, is used as the data buffer for the message.

When **freeb**(D3) is called to free the message, on the last reference to the message, the driver's free-routine, specified by the **free_func** field in the **free_rtn**(D4) structure, is called with one argument, specified by the **free_arg** field, to free the data buffer.

Return Values

On success, a pointer to the newly allocated message block is returned. On failure, **NULL** is returned.

USAGE

Instead of requiring a specific number of arguments, the **free_arg** field is defined of type **char ***. This way, the driver can pass a pointer to a structure if more than one argument is needed.

When the **free_func** function runs, interrupts from all STREAMS devices will be blocked. It has no user context and may not call any routine that sleeps. The function may not access any dynamically allocated data structures that might no longer exist when it runs.

The *pri* argument is a hint to the allocator indicating how badly the message block is needed. **BPRI_LO** should be used for normal data allocations. **BPRI_MED** should be used for other non-critical allocations. **BPRI_HI** should be used for allocations that absolutely must succeed, although success is not guaranteed. Some implementations may choose to ignore this argument.

Level

Base or Interrupt.

Synchronization Constraints

Does not sleep.

Driver-defined basic locks, read/write locks, and sleep locks may be held across calls to this function.

REFERENCES

allocb(D3), **esbbcall**(D3), **freeb**(D3), **free_rtn**(D4)

NOTICES

Availability

SVR4.0, SVR4.1ES, SVR4MP, SVR4.2

Portability

All processors

Interface

Driver-Kernel (STREAMS)

Commitment

Level 1

NAME

esbbcall – call a function when an externally-supplied buffer can be allocated

SYNOPSIS

```
#include <sys/types.h>
#include <sys/stream.h>
#include <sys/ddi.h>

toid_t esbbcall(int pri, void (*func)(), long arg);
```

Arguments

pri Priority of the **esballoc**(D3) allocation request.

func Function to be called when a buffer becomes available.

arg Argument to the function to be called when a buffer becomes available.

DESCRIPTION

If **esballoc**(D3) is unable to allocate a message block header and a data block header to go with its externally supplied data buffer, the function **esbbcall** can be used to schedule the routine *func*, to be called with the argument *arg* when memory becomes available. **esbbcall**, like **bufcall**(D3), serves, in effect, as a timeout call of indeterminate length.

Return Values

On success, **esbbcall** returns a non-zero value that identifies the scheduling request. On failure, **esbbcall** returns 0.

USAGE

When *func* runs, all interrupts from STREAMS devices will be blocked. On mutiprocessor systems, the interrupts will be blocked only on the processor on which *func* is running. *func* will have no user context and may not call any function that sleeps.

Even when *func* is called, **esballoc** can still fail if another module or driver had allocated the memory before *func* was able to call **allocb**.

The *pri* argument is a hint to the allocator indicating how badly the buffer is needed. **BPRI_LO** should be used for normal data allocations. **BPRI_MED** should be used for other non-critical allocations. **BPRI_HI** should be used for allocations that absolutely must succeed, although success is not guaranteed. Some implementations may choose to ignore this argument.

The non-zero identifier returned by **esballoc** may be passed to **unbufcall**(D3) to cancel the request.

Level

Base or Interrupt.

Synchronization Constraints

Does not sleep.

Driver-defined basic locks, read/write locks, and sleep locks may be held across calls to this function.

REFERENCES

allocb(D3), bufcall(D3), esballoc(D3), itimeout(D3), timeout(D3), unbufcall(D3)

NOTICES

Availability

SVR4.0, SVR4.1ES, SVR4MP, SVR4.2

Portability

All processors

Interface

Driver-Kernel (STREAMS)

Commitment

Level 1

Future Directions

In more recent SVR4 releases, the `esbbcall` function returns a `toid_t` data type. In earlier SVR4 releases, it returns an `int`.

NAME

`etoimajor` – convert external to internal major device number

SYNOPSIS

```
#include <sys/types.h>
#include <sys/ddi.h>

int etoimajor(major_t emaj);
```

Arguments

emaj External major number.

DESCRIPTION

`etoimajor` converts the external major number *emaj* to an internal major number.

Return Values

`etoimajor` returns the internal major number or **`NODEV`** if the external major number is invalid.

USAGE

See **`getemajor`**(D3) for a description of external and internal major numbers.

Level

Initialization, Base or Interrupt.

Synchronization Constraints

Does not sleep.

Driver-defined basic locks, read/write locks, and sleep locks may be held across calls to this function.

REFERENCES

`getemajor`(D3), `geteminor`(D3), `getmajor`(D3), `getminor`(D3), `itoemajor`(D3), `makedevice`(D3)

NOTICES

Availability

SVR4.0, SVR4.1ES, SVR4MP, SVR4.2

Portability

All processors

Interface

Driver-Kernel

Commitment

Level 1

flush (D3)

NAME

`flush` – flush on-chip data cache

SYNOPSIS

```
void flush()
```

```
void flush1(addr_t vaddr)
```

Arguments

vaddr Virtual address of the line in the data cache to be flushed.

DESCRIPTION

The **`flush`** function flushes the entire on-chip data cache by forcing modified data to external memory.

The **`flush1`** function flushes modified data from the data-cache line residing at the location addressed by **`addr_t`** *vaddr* only.

Return Values

None

USAGE

The **`flush`** and **`flush1`** functions are used to maintain data consistency in DMA operations on Intel i860 computers.

The i860XR microprocessor has an on-chip write-back data cache, composed of a two-way, set-associative memory of 8K bytes, with 32-byte blocks. The i860XP microprocessor has an on-chip write-back cache, composed of four-way, set-associative memory of 16K bytes, with 32-byte lines. The i860XP microprocessor also supports a MESI cache protocol to maintain cache consistency in multiprocessor and multimaster systems.

Level

Base or Interrupt.

Synchronization Constraints

Can sleep.

Driver-defined basic locks, read/write locks, and sleep locks may be held across calls to this function.

NOTICES

Availability

SVR4MP

Portability

Intel860

Interface

Driver-Hardware

Commitment

Level 1

NAME

`flushband` – flush messages in a specified priority band

SYNOPSIS

```
#include <sys/types.h>
#include <sys/stream.h>
#include <sys/ddi.h>

void flushband(queue_t *q, uchar_t pri, int flag);
```

Arguments

q	Pointer to the queue.
pri	Priority band of messages to be flushed.
flag	Determines messages to flush.

DESCRIPTION

The **flushband** function flushes messages associated with the priority band specified by *pri*. If *pri* is `0`, only normal and high priority messages are flushed. Otherwise, messages are flushed from the band *pri* according to the value of *flag*.

If the band's count falls below the low water mark and someone wants to write to the band, the nearest upstream or downstream service procedure is enabled.

Return Values

None

USAGE

Valid values for *flag* are:

FLUSHDATA	Flush only data messages (types **M_DATA**, **M_DELAY**, **M_PROTO**, and **M_PCPROTO**).
FLUSHALL	Flush all messages.

Level

Base or Interrupt.

Synchronization Constraints

Does not sleep.

Driver-defined basic locks, read/write locks, and sleep locks may be held across calls to this function.

The caller cannot have the stream frozen [see **freezestr**(D3)] when calling this function.

Examples

See **put**(D2) for an example of **flushband**.

REFERENCES

flushq(D3), **put**(D2), **queue**(D4)

NOTICES

Availability

SVR4.0, SVR4.1ES, SVR4MP, SVR4.2

flushband (D3)

Portability
All processors

Interface
Driver-Kernel (STREAMS)

Commitment
Level 1

NAME

flushq – flush messages on a queue

SYNOPSIS

```
#include <sys/stream.h>
#include <sys/ddi.h>

void flushq(queue_t *q, int flag);
```

Arguments

q Pointer to the queue to be flushed.

flag Determines messages to flush.

DESCRIPTION

flushq frees messages on a queue by calling **freemsg**(D3) for each message. If the queue's count falls below the low water mark and someone wants to write to the queue, the nearest upstream or downstream service procedure is enabled.

Return Values

None

USAGE

Valid values for *flag* are:

FLUSHDATA	Flush only data messages (types **M_DATA**, **M_DELAY**, **M_PROTO**, and **M_PCPROTO**).
FLUSHALL	Flush all messages.

Level

Base or Interrupt.

Synchronization Constraints

Does not sleep.

Driver-defined basic locks, read/write locks, and sleep locks may be held across calls to this function.

The caller cannot have the stream frozen [see **freezestr**(D3)] when calling this function.

Examples

See **put**(D2) for an example of **flushq**.

REFERENCES

flushband(D3), **freemsg**(D3), **put**(D2), **putq**(D3), **queue**(D4)

NOTICES

Availability

SVR4.0, SVR4.1ES, SVR4MP, SVR4.2

Portability

All processors

Interface

Driver-Kernel (STREAMS)

flushq(D3)

Commitment
Level 1

NAME

freeb – free a message block

SYNOPSIS

```
#include <sys/stream.h>
#include <sys/ddi.h>

void freeb(mblk_t *bp);
```

Arguments

bp Pointer to the message block to be deallocated.

DESCRIPTION

freeb deallocates a message block. If the reference count of the **db_ref** member of the **datab**(D4) structure is greater than 1, **freeb** decrements the count and returns. Otherwise, if **db_ref** equals 1, it deallocates the message block and the corresponding data block and buffer.

If the data buffer to be freed was allocated with **esballoc**(D3), the driver is notified that the attached data buffer needs to be freed by calling the free-routine [see **free_rtn**(D4)] associated with the data buffer. Once this is accomplished, **freeb** releases the STREAMS resources associated with the buffer.

Return Values

None

USAGE

Level

Base or Interrupt.

Synchronization Constraints

Does not sleep.

Driver-defined basic locks, read/write locks, and sleep locks may be held across calls to this function.

Examples

See **copyb**(D3) for an example of **freeb**.

REFERENCES

allocb(D3), **dupb**(D3), **esballoc**(D3), **datab**(D4), **free_rtn**(D4), **msgb**(D4)

NOTICES

Availability

SVR4.0, SVR4.1ES, SVR4MP, SVR4.2

Portability

All processors

Interface

Driver-Kernel (STREAMS)

Commitment

Level 1

freemsg (D3)

NAME

`freemsg` – free a message

SYNOPSIS

```
#include <sys/stream.h>
#include <sys/ddi.h>

void freemsg(mblk_t *mp);
```

Arguments

mp Pointer to the message to be deallocated.

DESCRIPTION

`freemsg` frees all message blocks, data blocks, and data buffers associated with the message pointed to by *mp*. `freemsg` walks down the `b_cont` list [see `msgb`(D4)], calling `freeb`(D3) for every message block in the message.

Return Values

None

USAGE

Level

Base or Interrupt.

Synchronization Constraints

Does not sleep.

Driver-defined basic locks, read/write locks, and sleep locks may be held across calls to this function.

Examples

See `copymsg`(D3) for an example of `freemsg`.

REFERENCES

`freeb`(D3), `msgb`(D4)

NOTICES

Availability

SVR4.0, SVR4.1ES, SVR4MP, SVR4.2

Portability

All processors

Interface

Driver-Kernel (STREAMS)

Commitment

Level 1

NAME

freerbuf – free a raw buffer header

SYNOPSIS

```
#include <sys/buf.h>
#include <sys/ddi.h>

void freerbuf(buf_t *bp);
```

Arguments

bp Pointer to a previously allocated buffer header structure.

DESCRIPTION

freerbuf frees a raw buffer header previously allocated by **getrbuf**(D3).

Return Values

None

USAGE

freerbuf may not be used on a buffer header obtained through an interface other than **getrbuf**.

freerbuf is typically called from a driver's **biodone** (D3) routine, as specified in the **b_iodone** field of the **buf**(D4) structure.

Level

Base or Interrupt.

Synchronization Constraints

Does not sleep.

Driver-defined basic locks, read/write locks, and sleep locks may be held across calls to this function.

REFERENCES

biodone(D3), **bioreset**(D3), **biowait**(D3), **buf**(D4), **getrbuf**(D3)

NOTICES

Availability

SVR4.0, SVR4.1ES, SVR4MP, SVR4.2

Portability

All processors

Interface

Driver-Kernel

Commitment

Level 1

freezestr (D3)

NAME

`freezestr` – freeze the state of a stream

SYNOPSIS

```
#include <sys/types.h>
#include <sys/stream.h>
#include <sys/ddi.h>

pl_t freezestr(queue_t *q);
```

Arguments

q Pointer to a message queue.

DESCRIPTION

`freezestr` sets the interrupt priority level to `plstr` (if the current level is lower than `plstr` and the implementation requires that interrupts be blocked while the stream is frozen) and freezes the state of the stream containing the queue specified by *q*. Freezing the stream prevents any further entries into open, close, put, and service procedures on the stream and prevents any messages from being placed on or taken off any queues in the stream (except by the caller of `freezestr`).

Freezing the stream does not automatically stop all functions that are running within the stream; functions will continue to run until they attempt to perform some operation which changes the state of the stream, at which point they will be forced to wait for the stream to be unfrozen by a call to `unfreezestr`(D3).

Return Values

`freezestr` returns the previous interrupt priority level which is typically used in a subsequent call to `unfreezestr`.

USAGE

Drivers and modules must freeze the stream while they manipulate its queues directly. This includes searching the queues and for the duration of any calls to `insq`(D3), `rmvq`(D3), `strqset`(D3), and `strqget`(D3).

Level

Base or Interrupt.

Synchronization Constraints

Does not sleep.

Driver-defined basic locks, read/write locks, and sleep locks may be held across calls to this function.

Warnings

`freezestr` should be used sparingly as it is rarely necessary to freeze a stream (most modules do not need to manipulate their queues directly) and freezing a stream can have a significant negative effect on performance.

Calling `freezestr` to freeze a stream that is already frozen by the caller will result in deadlock.

Examples

See `insq`(D3) for an example of `freezestr`.

REFERENCES

`unfreezestr`(D3)

NOTICES

Availability

SVR4MP

Portability

All processors

Interface

Driver-Kernel (STREAMS)

Commitment

Level 1

geteblk (D3)

NAME

`geteblk` – get an empty buffer

SYNOPSIS

```
#include <sys/types.h>
#include <sys/buf.h>
#include <sys/ddi.h>

buf_t *geteblk(void);
```

DESCRIPTION

geteblk retrieves a buffer [see **buf**(D4)] from the buffer cache and returns a pointer to the buffer header. If a buffer is not available, **geteblk** sleeps until one is available.

Return Values

A pointer to the buffer header structure is returned.

USAGE

When the driver **strategy**(D2) routine receives a buffer header from the kernel, all the necessary members are already initialized. However, when a driver allocates buffers for its own use, it must set up some of the members before calling its **strategy** routine.

The following list describes the state of these members when the buffer header is received from **geteblk**:

`b_flags`	is set to indicate the transfer is from the user's buffer to the kernel. The driver must set the **B_READ** flag if the transfer is from the kernel to the user's buffer.
`b_edev`	is set to **NODEV** and must be initialized by the driver.
`b_bcount`	is set to 1024.
`b_un.b_addr`	is set to the buffer's virtual address.
`b_blkno`	is not initialized by **geteblk**, and must be initialized by the driver

Typically, block drivers do not allocate buffers. The buffer is allocated by the kernel, and the associated buffer header is used as an argument to the driver **strategy** routine. However, to implement some special features, such as **ioctl**(D2) commands that perform I/O, the driver may need its own buffer space. The driver can get the buffer space from the system by using **geteblk** or **ngeteblk**(D3). If the driver chooses to use its own memory for the buffer, it can allocate a buffer header only using **getrbuf**(D3).

Buffers allocated via **geteblk** must be freed using either **brelse**(D3) or **biodone**(D3).

Level

Base only.

Synchronization Constraints

Can sleep.

Driver-defined basic locks and read/write locks may not be held across calls to this function.

Driver-defined sleep locks may be held across calls to this function.

REFERENCES

biodone(D3), **biowait**(D3), **brelse**(D3), **buf**(D4), **ngeteblk**(D3)

NOTICES

Availability

SVR4.0, SVR4.1ES, SVR4MP, SVR4.2

Portability

All processors

Interface

Driver-Kernel

Commitment

Level 1

getemajor (D3)

NAME

`getemajor` – get external major device number

SYNOPSIS

```
#include <sys/types.h>
#include <sys/ddi.h>

major_t getemajor(dev_t dev);
```

Arguments

dev External device number.

DESCRIPTION

`getemajor` returns the external major number given a device number, *dev*.

Return Values

The external major number.

USAGE

External major numbers are visible to the user. Internal major numbers are only visible in the kernel. Since, on some architectures, the range of major numbers may be large and sparsely populated, the kernel keeps a mapping between external and internal major numbers to save space.

All driver entry points are passed device numbers using external major numbers.

Usually, a driver with more than one external major number will have only one internal major number. However, some system implementations map one-to-one between external and internal major numbers. Here, the internal major number is the same as the external major number and the driver may have more than one internal major number.

Level

Initialization, Base or Interrupt.

Synchronization Constraints

Does not sleep.

Driver-defined basic locks, read/write locks, and sleep locks may be held across calls to this function.

REFERENCES

etoimajor(D3), **geteminor**(D3), **getmajor**(D3), **getminor**(D3), **makedevice**(D3)

NOTICES

Availability

SVR4.0, SVR4.1ES, SVR4MP, SVR4.2

Portability

All processors

Interface

Driver-Kernel

Commitment

Level 1

NAME

`geteminor` – get external minor device number

SYNOPSIS

```
#include <sys/types.h>
#include <sys/ddi.h>

minor_t geteminor(dev_t dev);
```

Arguments

dev External device number.

DESCRIPTION

`geteminor` returns the external minor number given a device number, *dev*.

Return Values

The external minor number.

USAGE

External minor numbers are visible to the user. Internal minor numbers are only visible in the kernel. Since, on some architectures, a driver can support more than one external major device that maps to the same internal major device, the kernel keeps a mapping between external minor numbers and internal minor numbers to allow drivers to index arrays more easily. For example, a driver may support two devices, each with five minor numbers. The user may see each set of minor numbers numbered from zero to four, but the driver sees them as one set of minor numbers numbered from zero to nine.

All driver entry points are passed device numbers using external minor numbers.

Systems that map external major device numbers one-to-one with internal major numbers also map external minor numbers one-to-one with internal minor numbers.

Level

Initialization, Base or Interrupt.

Synchronization Constraints

Does not sleep.

Driver-defined basic locks, read/write locks, and sleep locks may be held across calls to this function.

REFERENCES

`etoimajor`(D3), `getemajor`(D3), `getmajor`(D3), `getminor`(D3), `makedevice`(D3)

NOTICES

Availability

SVR4.0, SVR4.1ES, SVR4MP, SVR4.2

Portability

All processors

Interface

Driver-Kernel

geteminor (D3)

Commitment

Level 1

NAME

geterror – retrieve error number from a buffer header

SYNOPSIS

```
#include <sys/buf.h>
#include <sys/ddi.h>

int geterror(struct buf *bp);
```

Arguments

bp Pointer to the buffer header.

DESCRIPTION

geterror is called to retrieve the error number from the error field of a buffer header (**buf**(D4) structure).

Return Values

An error number indicating the error condition of the I/O request is returned. If the I/O request completed successfully, 0 is returned.

USAGE

Level

Base or Interrupt.

Synchronization Constraints

Does not sleep.

Driver-defined basic locks, read/write locks, and sleep locks may be held across calls to this function.

REFERENCES

buf(D4), **errnos**(D5)

NOTICES

Availability

SVR4.0, SVR4.1ES, SVR4MP, SVR4.2

Portability

All processors

Interface

Driver-Kernel

Commitment

Level 1

getmajor (D3)

NAME

`getmajor` – get internal major device number

SYNOPSIS

```
#include <sys/types.h>
#include <sys/ddi.h>

major_t getmajor(dev_t dev);
```

Arguments

dev Device number.

DESCRIPTION

The `getmajor` function extracts the internal major number from a device number.

Return Values

The internal major number.

USAGE

No validity checking is performed. If *dev* is invalid, an invalid number is returned.

See `getemajor`(D3) for an explanation of external and internal major numbers.

Level

Initialization, Base or Interrupt.

Synchronization Constraints

Does not sleep.

Driver-defined basic locks, read/write locks, and sleep locks may be held across calls to this function.

REFERENCES

`etoimajor`(D3), `getemajor`(D3), `geteminor`(D3), `getminor`(D3), `makedevice`(D3)

NOTICES

Availability

SVR4.0, SVR4.1ES, SVR4MP, SVR4.2

Portability

All processors

Interface

Driver-Kernel

Commitment

Level 1

NAME

`getminor` – get internal minor device number

SYNOPSIS

```
#include <sys/types.h>
#include <sys/ddi.h>

minor_t getminor(dev_t dev);
```

Arguments

dev Device number.

DESCRIPTION

The **getminor** function extracts the internal minor number from a device number.

Return Values

The internal minor number.

USAGE

No validity checking is performed. If *dev* is invalid, an invalid number is returned.

See **getemajor**(D3) for an explanation of external and internal major numbers.

Level

Initialization, Base or Interrupt.

Synchronization Constraints

Does not sleep.

Driver-defined basic locks, read/write locks, and sleep locks may be held across calls to this function.

REFERENCES

etoimajor(D3), **getemajor**(D3), **geteminor**(D3), **getmajor**(D3), **makedevice**(D3)

NOTICES

Availability

SVR4.0, SVR4.1ES, SVR4MP, SVR4.2

Portability

All processors

Interface

Driver-Kernel

Commitment

Level 1

getnextpg (D3)

NAME

getnextpg – get next page pointer

SYNOPSIS

```
#include <sys/types.h>
#include <vm/page.h>
#include <sys/buf.h>
#include <sys/ddi.h>

page_t *getnextpg(buf_t *bp, page_t *pp);
```

Arguments

bp Pointer to the buffer header structure.

pp Pointer to the previous page structure returned.

DESCRIPTION

getnextpg returns a pointer to the next page in a buffer header's page list [see **buf**(D4)] during a paged-I/O request. A paged-I/O request is identified by the **B_PAGEIO** flag being set in the **b_flags** field of the buffer header passed to a driver's **strategy**(D2) routine.

Given a buffer header, *bp*, and a pointer to the page, *pp*, returned from the previous call to **getnextpg**, the next page is returned. If *pp* is **NULL**, the first page in the page list is returned.

Return Values

On success, a pointer to the next page structure in the page list is returned. If the end of the list is reached, **NULL** is returned.

USAGE

B_PAGEIO won't be set unless the driver has the **D_NOBRKUP** flag set [see **devflag**(D1).]

Level

Base or Interrupt.

Synchronization Constraints

Does not sleep.

Driver-defined basic locks, read/write locks, and sleep locks may be held across calls to this function.

REFERENCES

bp_mapin(D3), **bp_mapout**(D3), **buf**(D4), **devflag**(D1), **pptophys**(D3), **strategy**(D2)

NOTICES

Availability

SVR4MP

Portability

All processors

Interface

Driver-Kernel

Commitment

Level 1

getq (D3)

NAME

`getq` – get the next message from a queue

SYNOPSIS

```
#include <sys/stream.h>
#include <sys/ddi.h>

mblk_t *getq(queue_t *q);
```

Arguments

q Pointer to the queue from which the message is to be retrieved.

DESCRIPTION

`getq` gets the next available message from the top of the queue pointed to by *q*. It handles flow control, restarting I/O that was blocked as needed.

Return Values

If there is a message to retrieve, **getq** returns a pointer to it. If no message is queued, **getq** returns a **NULL** pointer.

USAGE

`getq` is typically used by service routines [see **srv**(D2)] to retrieve queued messages.

Level

Base or Interrupt.

Synchronization Constraints

Does not sleep.

Driver-defined basic locks, read/write locks, and sleep locks may be held across calls to this function.

The caller cannot have the stream frozen [see **freezestr**(D3)] when calling this function.

Examples

See **srv**(D2) for an example of **getq**.

REFERENCES

bcanput(D3), **canput**(D3), **putbq**(D3), **putq**(D3), **qenable**(D3), **rmvq**(D3), **srv**(D2)

NOTICES

Availability

SVR4.0, SVR4.1ES, SVR4MP, SVR4.2

Portability

All processors

Interface

Driver-Kernel (STREAMS)

Commitment

Level 1

NAME

getrbuf – get a raw buffer header

SYNOPSIS

```
#include <sys/buf.h>
#include <sys/kmem.h>
#include <sys/ddi.h>

buf_t *getrbuf(long flag);
```

Arguments

flag Indicates whether the caller should sleep for free space.

DESCRIPTION

getrbuf allocates the space for a buffer header [see **buf**(D4)]. If *flag* is set to **KM_SLEEP**, the caller will sleep if necessary until memory is available. If *flag* is set to **KM_NOSLEEP**, the caller will not sleep, but **getrbuf** will return **NULL** if memory is not immediately available.

Return Values

Upon successful completion, **getrbuf** returns a pointer to the allocated buffer header. If **KM_NOSLEEP** is specified and sufficient memory is not immediately available, **getrbuf** returns a **NULL** pointer.

USAGE

getrbuf is used when a block driver is performing raw I/O (character interface) and needs to set up a buffer header that is not associated with a system-provided data buffer. The driver provides its own memory for the data buffer.

After allocating the buffer header, the caller must set the **b_iodone** field to the address of an iodone handler to be invoked when the I/O is complete [see **biodone**(D3)]. The caller must also initialize the following fields:

b_flags Must be modified to indicate the direction of data transfer. Initially, it is set to indicate the transfer is from the user's buffer to the kernel. The driver must set the **B_READ** flag if the transfer is from the kernel to the user's buffer.

b_edev Must be initialized to the proper device number.

b_bcount Must be set to the number of bytes to transfer.

b_un.b_addr Must be set to the virtual address of the caller-supplied buffer.

b_blkno Must be set to the block number to be accessed.

b_resid Must be set to the same value as **b_bcount**.

b_bufsize Can be used to remember the size of the data buffer associated with the buffer header.

Typically, block drivers do not allocate buffers. The buffer is allocated by the kernel and the associated buffer header is used as an argument to the driver **strategy** routine. However, to implement some special features, such as **ioctl**(D2) commands that perform I/O, the driver may need its own buffer space. The driver can get the buffer space from the system by using **geteblk**(D3) or **ngeteblk**(D3). Or the driver can choose to use its own memory for the buffer and only allocate a buffer header with **getrbuf**.

Level

Base only if *flag* is set to **KM_SLEEP**.

Base or Interrupt if *flag* is set to **KM_NOSLEEP**.

Synchronization Constraints

May sleep if *flag* is set to **KM_SLEEP**.

Driver-defined basic locks and read/write locks may be held across calls to this function if *flag* is **KM_NOSLEEP**, but may not be held if *flag* is **KM_SLEEP**.

Driver-defined sleep locks may be held across calls to this function regardless of the value of *flag*.

REFERENCES

`biodone`(D3), `bioreset`(D3), `biowait`(D3), `buf`(D4), `freerbuf`(D3)

NOTICES

Availability

SVR4.0, SVR4.1ES, SVR4MP, SVR4.2

Portability

All processors

Interface

Driver-Kernel

Commitment

Level 1

NAME

`hat_getkpfnum` – get physical page ID for kernel virtual address

SYNOPSIS

```
#include <sys/vm.h>
#include <sys/types.h>
#include <sys/ddi.h>

uint_t hat_getkpfnum(caddr_t addr);
```

Arguments

addr The kernel virtual address for which the physical page ID is to be returned.

DESCRIPTION

`hat_getkpfnum` returns the physical page ID corresponding to the virtual address *addr*.

Return Values

If *addr* is valid, the corresponding physical page ID is returned. Otherwise, `NOPAGE` is returned.

USAGE

This routine can be used to obtain a physical page ID suitable to be used as the return value of the driver's `mmap`(D2) entry point.

A physical page ID is a machine-specific token that uniquely identifies a page of physical memory in the system (either system memory or device memory.) No assumptions should be made about the format of a physical page ID.

Level

Base or Interrupt.

Synchronization Constraints

Does not sleep.

REFERENCES

`hat_getppfnum`(D3), `mmap`(D2)

NOTICES

Availability

SVR4.0, SVR4.1ES, SVR4.2

Portability

All processors

Interface

Driver-Kernel

Commitment

Level 2 effective October 8, 1991

Future Directions

In SVR4MP, `hat_getkpfnum` is replaced by `kvtoppid`(D3).

hat_getppfnum (D3)

NAME

`hat_getppfnum` – get physical page ID for physical address

SYNOPSIS

```
#include <sys/types.h>
#include <sys/vm.h>
#include <sys/ddi.h>

uint_t hat_getppfnum(paddr_t addr, uint_t pspace);
```

Arguments

addr The physical address for which the physical page ID is to be returned.

pspace The physical address space to which *addr* belongs.

DESCRIPTION

`hat_getppfnum` returns the physical page ID corresponding to the physical address *addr*.

Return Values

If *addr* and *pspace* are valid, the corresponding physical page ID is returned. Otherwise, **NOPAGE** is returned.

USAGE

This routine can be used to obtain a physical page ID suitable to be used as the return value of the driver's **mmap**(D2) entry point.

Some systems have multiple physical address spaces (different buses, and so on). For these systems, *pspace* indicates the address space to which *addr* belongs. For all systems, **PSPACE_MAINSTORE** is defined as the address space that includes mainstore system memory. Other values are implementation-defined.

A physical page ID is a machine-specific token that uniquely identifies a page of physical memory in the system (either system memory or device memory.) No assumptions should be made about the format of a physical page ID.

Level

Base or Interrupt.

Synchronization Constraints

Does not sleep.

REFERENCES

`hat_getkpfnum`(D3), **mmap**(D2)

NOTICES

Availability

SVR4.0, SVR4.1ES, SVR4.2

Portability

All processors

Interface

Driver-Kernel

Commitment

Level 2 effective October 8, 1991

Future Directions

In SVR4MP, **hat_getppfnum** is replaced by **phystoppid**(D3).

inb (D3)

NAME

`inb` – read a byte from an 8 bit I/O port

SYNOPSIS

```
#include <sys/types.h>
#include <sys/ddi.h>

uchar_t inb(int port);
```

Arguments

port A valid 8 bit I/O port.

DESCRIPTION

The **inb** function provides a C language interface to the machine instruction that reads a byte from an 8 bit I/O port using the I/O address space, instead of the memory address space.

Return Values

Returns the value of the byte read from the I/O port.

USAGE

This function may not be meaningful on all implementations because some implementations may not support I/O-mapped I/O (direct I/O instructions). On Intel860 systems, I/O is mapped to memory (memory-mapped I/O). Therefore, on Intel860 systems, a *port* is not really an I/O port, but rather a memory pointer that points to the memory-mapped I/O location. The *port* argument is similar to a token that can represent a 16-bit address for the I/O port for Intel386 systems or a 32-bit memory address for Intel860 systems.

Level

Initialization, Base or Interrupt.

Synchronization Constraints

Does not sleep.

Driver-defined basic locks, read/write locks, and sleep locks may be held across calls to this function.

REFERENCES

inl(D3), **inw**(D3), **outb**(D3), **outl**(D3), **outw**(D3), **repinsb**(D3), **repinsd**(D3), **repinsw**(D3), **repoutsb**(D3), **repoutsd**(D3), **repoutsw**(D3)

NOTICES

Availability

SVR4.0, SVR4.1ES, SVR4MP, SVR4.2

Portability

Intel386, Intel486, Intel860

Interface

Driver-Hardware

Commitment

Level 1

NAME

`inl` – read a 32 bit word from a 32 bit I/O port

SYNOPSIS

```
#include <sys/types.h>
#include <sys/ddi.h>

ulong_t inl(int port);
```

Arguments

port A valid 32 bit I/O port.

DESCRIPTION

The **inl** function provides a C language interface to the machine instruction that reads a 32 bit word from a 32 bit I/O port using the I/O address space, instead of the memory address space.

Return Values

Returns the value of the 32 bit word read from the I/O port.

USAGE

This function may not be meaningful on all implementations because some implementations may not support I/O-mapped I/O (direct I/O instructions). On Intel860 systems, I/O is mapped to memory (memory-mapped I/O). Therefore, on Intel860 systems, a *port* is not really an I/O port, but rather a memory pointer that points to the memory-mapped I/O location. The *port* argument is similar to a token that can represent a 16-bit address for the I/O port for Intel386 systems or a 32-bit memory address for Intel860 systems.

Level

Initialization, Base or Interrupt.

Synchronization Constraints

Does not sleep.

Driver-defined basic locks, read/write locks, and sleep locks may be held across calls to this function.

REFERENCES

inb(D3), **inw**(D3), **outb**(D3), **outl**(D3), **outw**(D3), **repinsb**(D3), **repinsd**(D3), **repinsw**(D3), **repoutsb**(D3), **repoutsd**(D3), **repoutsw**(D3)

NOTICES

Availability

SVR4.0, SVR4.1ES, SVR4MP, SVR4.2

Portability

Intel386, Intel486, Intel860

Interface

Driver-Hardware

Commitment

Level 1

insq (D3)

NAME

insq – insert a message into a queue

SYNOPSIS

```
#include <sys/stream.h>
#include <sys/ddi.h>

int insq(queue_t *q, mblk_t *emp, mblk_t *nmp);
```

Arguments

q Pointer to the queue containing message *emp*.

emp Pointer to the existing message before which the new message is to be inserted.

nmp Pointer to the new message to be inserted.

DESCRIPTION

insq inserts a message into a queue. The message to be inserted, *nmp*, is placed in the queue pointed to by *q*, immediately before the message, *emp*. If *emp* is **NULL**, the new message is placed at the end of the queue. All flow control parameters are updated. The service procedure is scheduled to run unless disabled by a previous call to **noenable**(D3).

Return Values

If *nmp* was successfully enqueued, **insq** returns 1. Otherwise, **insq** returns 0.

USAGE

Messages are ordered in the queue based on their priority, as described in **srv**(D2). If an attempt is made to insert a message out of order in the queue, then *nmp* is not enqueued.

The insertion can fail if there is not enough memory to allocate the accounting data structures used with messages whose priority bands are greater than zero.

If *emp* is non-**NULL**, it must point to a message in the queue pointed to by *q*, or a system panic could result.

Level

Base or Interrupt.

Synchronization Constraints

Does not sleep.

Driver-defined basic locks, read/write locks, and sleep locks may be held across calls to this function.

The caller must have the stream frozen [see **freezestr**(D3)] when calling this function.

Singlethreaded Example

This routine illustrates the use of **insq** to insert a message into the middle of a queue. This routine can be used to strip all the **M_PROTO** headers off all messages on a queue. We traverse the list of messages on the queue, looking for **M_PROTO** messages (line 9). When one is found, we remove it from the queue using **rmvq**(D3) (line 10). If there is no data portion to the message (line 11), we free the entire message using **freemsg**(D3). Otherwise, for every **M_PROTO** message block in the message, we strip the **M_PROTO** block off using **unlinkb**(D3) (line 15) and free the message block using **freeb**(D3). When the header has been stripped, the data portion of the message is inserted back into the queue where it was originally found (line 19).

```
 1  void
 2  striproto(q)
 3    queue_t *q;
 4  {
 5    mblk_t *emp, *nmp, *mp;

 6    mp = q->q_first;
 7    while (mp) {
 8          emp = mp->b_next;
 9          if (mp->b_datap->db_type == M_PROTO) {
10                rmvq(q, mp);
11                if (msgdsize(mp) == 0) {
12                      freemsg(mp);
13                } else {
14                      while (mp->b_datap->db_type == M_PROTO) {
15                            nmp = unlinkb(mp);
16                            freeb(mp);
17                            mp = nmp;
18                      }
19                      insq(q, emp, mp);
20                }
21          }
22          mp = emp;
23    }
24  }
```

Multithreaded Example

This routine illustrates the use of **insq** to insert a message into the middle of a queue. This routine can be used to strip all the **M_PROTO** headers off all messages on a queue. First, we freeze the stream (line 7) so the state of the queue does not change while we are searching it. Then we traverse the list of messages on the queue, looking for **M_PROTO** messages (line 11). When one is found, we remove it from the queue using **rmvq**(D3) (line 12). If there is no data portion of the message (line 13), we free the entire message using **freemsg**(D3). Otherwise, for every **M_PROTO** message block in the message, we strip the **M_PROTO** block off using **unlinkb**(D3) (line 17) and free the message block using **freeb**(D3). When the header has been stripped, the data portion of the message is inserted back into the queue where it was originally found (line 21). Finally, when we are done searching the queue, we unfreeze the stream (line 26).

```
 1  void
 2  striproto(q)
 3    queue_t *q;
 4  {
 5    mblk_t *emp, *nmp, *mp;
 6    pl_t pl;

 7    pl = freezestr(q);
 8    strqget(q, QFIRST, 0, &mp);
 9    while (mp) {
10          emp = mp->b_next;
```

```
        if (mp->b_datap->db_type == M_PROTO) {
            rmvq(q, mp);
            if (msgdsize(mp) == 0) {
                freemsg(mp);
            } else {
                while (mp->b_datap->db_type == M_PROTO) {
                    nmp = unlinkb(mp);
                    freeb(mp);
                    mp = nmp;
                }
                insq(q, emp, mp);
            }
        }
        mp = emp;
    }
    unfreezestr(q, pl);
}
```

REFERENCES

freezestr(D3), **getq**(D3), **putbq**(D3), **putq**(D3), **rmvq**(D3), **srv**(D2) **unfreezestr**(D3),

NOTICES

Availability

SVR4.0, SVR4.1ES, SVR4MP, SVR4.2

Portability

All processors

Interface

Driver-Kernel (STREAMS)

Commitment

Level 1

NAME

inw – read a 16 bit short word from a 16 bit I/O port

SYNOPSIS

```
#include <sys/types.h>
#include <sys/ddi.h>

ushort_t inw(int port);
```

Arguments

port A valid 16 bit I/O port.

DESCRIPTION

The **inw** function provides a C language interface to the machine instruction that reads a 16 bit short word from a 16 bit I/O port using the I/O address space, instead of the memory address space.

Return Values

Returns the value of the 16 bit short word read from the I/O port.

USAGE

This function may not be meaningful on all implementations because some implementations may not support I/O-mapped I/O (direct I/O instructions). On Intel860 systems, I/O is mapped to memory (memory-mapped I/O). Therefore, on Intel860 systems, a *port* is not really an I/O port, but rather a memory pointer that points to the memory-mapped I/O location. The *port* argument is similar to a token that can represent a 16-bit address for the I/O port for Intel386 systems or a 32-bit memory address for Intel860 systems.

Level

Initialization, Base or Interrupt.

Synchronization Constraints

Does not sleep.

Driver-defined basic locks, read/write locks, and sleep locks may be held across calls to this function.

REFERENCES

inb(D3), **inl**(D3), **outb**(D3), **outl**(D3), **outw**(D3), **repinsb**(D3), **repinsd**(D3), **repinsw**(D3), **repoutsb**(D3), **repoutsd**(D3), **repoutsw**(D3)

NOTICES

Availability

SVR4.0, SVR4.1ES, SVR4MP, SVR4.2

Portability

Intel386, Intel486, Intel860

Interface

Driver-Hardware

Commitment

Level 1

itimeout (D3)

NAME

`itimeout` – execute a function after a specified length of time

SYNOPSIS

```
#include <sys/types.h>
#include <sys/ddi.h>

toid_t itimeout(void (*func)(), void *arg, long ticks, pl_t pl);
```

Arguments

func	Function to execute when the time increment expires.
arg	Argument to the function.
ticks	Number of clock ticks to wait before the function is called.
pl	The interrupt priority level at which the function will be called.

DESCRIPTION

`itimeout` causes the function specified by *func* to be called after the time interval specified by *ticks*, at the interrupt priority level specified by *pl*. *arg* will be passed as the only argument to function *func*. The `itimeout` call returns immediately without waiting for the specified function to execute.

Return Values

If the function specified by *func* is successfully scheduled, `itimeout` returns a non-zero identifier that can be passed to `untimeout` to cancel the request. If the function could not be scheduled, `itimeout` returns a value of 0.

USAGE

pl must specify a priority level greater than or equal to *pltimeout*; thus, *plbase* cannot be used. See `LOCK_ALLOC`(D3) for a list of values for *pl*.

The length of time before the function is called is not guaranteed to be exactly equal to the requested time, but will be at least *ticks–1* clock ticks in length.

The function specified by *func* must neither sleep, reference process context, nor lower the interrupt priority level below *pl*.

After the time interval has expired, *func* only runs if the processor is at base level. Otherwise, *func* is deferred until some time in the near future.

If `itimeout` is called holding a lock that is contended for by *func*, the caller must hold the lock at a processor level greater than the base processor level.

A *ticks* argument of 0 has the same effect as a *ticks* argument of 1. Both will result in an approximate wait of between 0 and 1 tick (possibly longer).

Drivers should be careful to cancel any pending `itimeout` functions that access data structures before these structures are de-initialized or deallocated.

Level

Base or Interrupt.

Synchronization Constraints

Does not sleep.

Driver-defined basic locks, read/write locks, and sleep locks may be held across calls to this function.

Examples

See `copyb`(D3) for an example of `itimeout`.

REFERENCES

`dtimeout`(D3), `LOCK_ALLOC`(D3), `untimeout`(D3)

NOTICES

Availability

SVR4MP

Portability

All processors

Interface

Driver-Kernel

Commitment

Level 1

itoemajor (D3)

NAME

`itoemajor` – convert internal to external major device number

SYNOPSIS

```
#include <sys/types.h>
#include <sys/ddi.h>

int itoemajor(major_t imaj, int prevemaj);
```

Arguments

imaj Internal major number.

prevemaj Most recently obtained external major number (or **NODEV**, if this is the first time the function has been called).

DESCRIPTION

`itoemajor` converts the internal major number *imaj* to the external major number. The external-to-internal major number mapping can be many-to-one, and so any internal major number may correspond to more than one external major number.

Return Values

External major number, or **NODEV**, if all have been searched.

USAGE

By repeatedly invoking this function and passing the most recent external major number obtained, the driver can obtain all possible external major number values.

See `getemajor`(D3) for an explanation of external and internal major numbers.

Level

Initialization, Base or Interrupt.

Synchronization Constraints

Does not sleep.

Driver-defined basic locks, read/write locks, and sleep locks may be held across calls to this function.

REFERENCES

`etoimajor`(D3), `getemajor`(D3), `geteminor`(D3), `getmajor`(D3), `getminor`(D3), `makedevice`(D3)

NOTICES

Availability

SVR4.0, SVR4.1ES, SVR4MP, SVR4.2

Portability

All processors

Interface

Driver-Kernel

Commitment

Level 1

NAME

`kmem_alloc` – allocate space from kernel free memory

SYNOPSIS

```
#include <sys/types.h>
#include <sys/kmem.h>
#include <sys/ddi.h>

void *kmem_alloc(size_t size, int flag);
```

Arguments

size Number of bytes to allocate.

flag Specifies whether the caller is willing to sleep waiting for memory.

DESCRIPTION

`kmem_alloc` allocates *size* bytes of kernel memory and returns a pointer to the allocated memory. If *flag* is set to `KM_SLEEP`, the caller will sleep if necessary until the specified amount of memory is available. If *flag* is set to `KM_NOSLEEP`, the caller will not sleep, but `kmem_alloc` will return `NULL` if the specified amount of memory is not immediately available.

Return Values

Upon successful completion, `kmem_alloc` returns a pointer to the allocated memory. If `KM_NOSLEEP` is specified and sufficient memory is not immediately available, `kmem_alloc` returns a `NULL` pointer. If *size* is set to `0`, `kmem_alloc` returns `NULL` regardless of the value of *flag*.

USAGE

Kernel memory is a limited resource and should be used judiciously. Memory allocated using `kmem_alloc` should be freed as soon as possible. Drivers should not use local freelists for memory or similar schemes that cause the memory to be held for longer than necessary.

Since holding memory allocated using `kmem_alloc` for extended periods of time (e.g allocating memory at system startup and never freeing it) can have an adverse effect on overall memory usage and system performance, memory needed for such extended periods should be statically allocated whenever possible.

The address returned by a successful call to `kmem_alloc` is word-aligned.

Level

Base only if *flag* is set to `KM_SLEEP`.

Initialization, Base or Interrupt if *flag* is set to `KM_NOSLEEP`.

Synchronization Constraints

May sleep if *flag* is set to `KM_SLEEP`.

Driver-defined basic locks and read/write locks may be held across calls to this function if *flag* is `KM_NOSLEEP`, but may not be held if *flag* is `KM_SLEEP`.

Driver-defined sleep locks may be held across calls to this function regardless of the value of *flag*.

REFERENCES

`kmem_free`(D3), `kmem_zalloc`(D3)

NOTICES

Availability

SVR4.0, SVR4.1ES, SVR4MP, SVR4.2

Portability

All processors

Interface

Driver-Kernel

Commitment

Level 1

NAME

`kmem_free` – free previously allocated kernel memory

SYNOPSIS

```
#include <sys/types.h>
#include <sys/kmem.h>
#include <sys/ddi.h>

void kmem_free(void *addr, size_t size);
```

Arguments

addr Address of the allocated memory to be returned.

size Number of bytes to free.

DESCRIPTION

`kmem_free` returns *size* bytes of previously allocated kernel memory.

Return Values

None

USAGE

The *addr* argument must specify the same address that was returned by the corresponding call to `kmem_alloc`(D3) or `kmem_zalloc`(D3) which allocated the memory.

The *size* argument must specify the same number of bytes as was allocated by the corresponding call to `kmem_alloc` or `kmem_zalloc`.

Together, the *addr* and *size* arguments must specify exactly one complete area of memory that was allocated by a call to `kmem_alloc` or `kmem_zalloc` (that is, the memory cannot be freed piecemeal).

Level

Initialization, Base or Interrupt.

Synchronization Constraints

Does not sleep.

Driver-defined basic locks, read/write locks, and sleep locks may be held across calls to this function.

REFERENCES

`kmem_alloc`(D3), `kmem_zalloc`(D3)

NOTICES

Availability

SVR4.0, SVR4.1ES, SVR4MP, SVR4.2

Portability

All processors

Interface

Driver-Kernel

Commitment

Level 1

kmem_zalloc (D3)

NAME

`kmem_zalloc` – allocate and clear space from kernel free memory

SYNOPSIS

```
#include <sys/types.h>
#include <sys/kmem.h>
#include <sys/ddi.h>
```

`void *kmem_zalloc(size_t` *size*`, int` *flag*`);`

Arguments

size	Number of bytes to allocate.
flag	Specifies whether the caller is willing to sleep waiting for memory.

DESCRIPTION

`kmem_zalloc` allocates *size* bytes of kernel memory, clears the memory by filling it with zeros, and returns a pointer to the allocated memory. If *flag* is set to `KM_SLEEP`, the caller will sleep if necessary until the specified amount of memory is available. If *flag* is set to `KM_NOSLEEP`, the caller will not sleep, but `kmem_zalloc` will return `NULL` if the specified amount of memory is not immediately available.

Return Values

Upon successful completion, `kmem_zalloc` returns a pointer to the allocated memory. If `KM_NOSLEEP` is specified and sufficient memory is not immediately available, `kmem_zalloc` returns a `NULL` pointer. If *size* is set to `0`, `kmem_zalloc` returns `NULL` regardless of the value of *flag*.

USAGE

Kernel memory is a limited resource and should be used judiciously. Memory allocated using `kmem_zalloc` should be freed as soon as possible. Drivers should not use local freelists for memory or similar schemes that cause the memory to be held for longer than necessary.

Since holding memory allocated using `kmem_zalloc` for extended periods of time (e.g allocating memory at system startup and never freeing it) can have an adverse effect on overall memory usage and system performance, memory needed for such extended periods should be statically allocated whenever possible.

The address returned by a successful call to `kmem_zalloc` is word-aligned.

Level

Initialization or Base if *flag* is set to `KM_SLEEP`.

Initialization, Base or Interrupt if *flag* is set to `KM_NOSLEEP`.

Synchronization Constraints

May sleep if *flag* is set to `KM_SLEEP`.

Driver-defined basic locks, read/write locks, and sleep locks may be held across calls to this function if *flag* is `KM_NOSLEEP`, but may not be held if *flag* is `KM_SLEEP`.

Driver-defined sleep locks may be held across calls to this function regardless of the value of *flag*.

REFERENCES

`kmem_alloc`(D3), `kmem_free`(D3)

NOTICES

Availability

SVR4.0, SVR4.1ES, SVR4MP, SVR4.2

Portability

All processors

Interface

Driver-Kernel

Commitment

Level 1

kvtoppid (D3)

NAME

`kvtoppid` – get physical page ID for kernel virtual address

SYNOPSIS

```
#include <sys/types.h>
#include <sys/vmparam.h>
#include <sys/ddi.h>

ppid_t kvtoppid(caddr_t addr);
```

Arguments

addr The kernel virtual address for which the physical page ID is to be returned.

DESCRIPTION

kvtoppid returns the physical page ID corresponding to the virtual address *addr*.

Return Values

If *addr* is valid, the corresponding physical page ID is returned. Otherwise, **NOPAGE** is returned.

USAGE

This routine can be used to obtain a physical page ID suitable to be used as the return value of the driver's **mmap**(D2) entry point.

A physical page ID is a machine-specific token that uniquely identifies a page of physical memory in the system (either system memory or device memory). No assumptions should be made about the format of a physical page ID.

Level

Base or Interrupt.

Synchronization Constraints

Does not sleep.

Driver-defined basic locks, read/write locks, and sleep locks may be held across calls to this function.

REFERENCES

mmap(D2), **intro**(D3), **phystoppid**(D3)

NOTICES

Availability

SVR4MP

Portability

All processors

Interface

Driver-Kernel

Commitment

Level 1

NAME

`linkb` – concatenate two message blocks

SYNOPSIS

```
#include <sys/stream.h>
#include <sys/ddi.h>

void linkb(mblk_t *mp1, mblk_t *mp2);
```

Arguments

mp1 Pointer to the message to which *mp2* is to be added.

mp2 Pointer to the message to be added.

DESCRIPTION

`linkb` appends the message *mp2* to the tail of message *mp1*. The continuation pointer (`b_cont`) of the last message block in the first message is set to point to the second message:

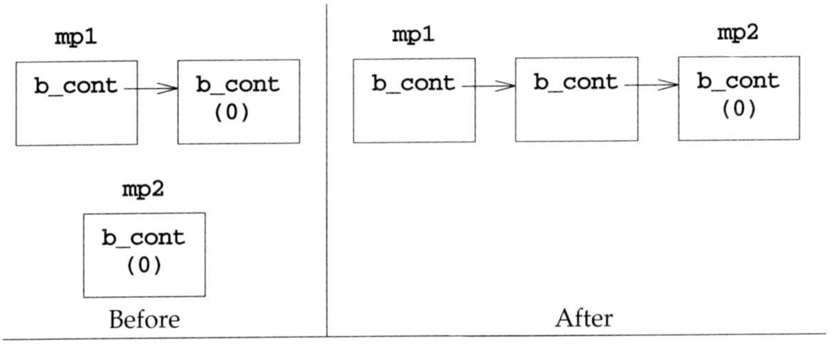

`linkb(mp1, mp2);`

Return Values

None.

USAGE

Level

Base or Interrupt.

Synchronization Constraints

Does not sleep.

Driver-defined basic locks, read/write locks, and sleep locks may be held across calls to this function.

REFERENCES

`msgb`(D4), `unlinkb`(D3)

NOTICES

Availability

SVR4.0, SVR4.1ES, SVR4MP, SVR4.2

Portability
All processors

Interface
Driver-Kernel (STREAMS)

Commitment
Level 1

NAME

LOCK – acquire a basic lock

SYNOPSIS

```
#include <sys/types.h>
#include <sys/ksynch.h>
#include <sys/ddi.h>

pl_t LOCK(lock_t *lockp, pl_t pl);
```

Arguments

lockp Pointer to the basic lock to be acquired.

pl The interrupt priority level to be set while the lock is held by the caller.

DESCRIPTION

LOCK sets the interrupt priority level in accordance with the value specified by *pl* (if required by the implementation) and acquires the lock specified by *lockp*. If the lock is not immediately available, the caller will wait until the lock is available. It is implementation defined whether the caller will block during the wait. Some implementations may cause the caller to spin for the duration of the wait, while on others the caller may block at some point.

Return Values

Upon acquiring the lock, **LOCK** returns the previous interrupt priority level (**plbase** – **plhi**).

USAGE

Because some implementations require that interrupts that might attempt to acquire the lock be blocked on the processor on which the lock is held, portable drivers must specify a *pl* value that is sufficient to block out any interrupt handler that might attempt to acquire this lock. See the description of the *min_pl* argument to **LOCK_ALLOC**(D3) for additional discussion and a list of the valid values for *pl*. Implementations which do not require that the interrupt priority level be raised during lock acquisition may choose to ignore this argument.

Level

Base or Interrupt.

Synchronization Constraints

Driver-defined sleep locks may be held across calls to this function.

Driver-defined basic locks and read/write locks may be held across calls to this function subject to the hierarchy and recursion restrictions described below.

Warnings

Basic locks are not recursive. A call to **LOCK** attempting to acquire a lock that is currently held by the calling context will result in deadlock.

Calls to **LOCK** should honor the ordering defined by the lock hierarchy [see **LOCK_ALLOC**(D3)] in order to avoid deadlock.

When called from interrupt level, the *pl* argument must not specify a priority level below the level at which the interrupt handler is running.

LOCK(D3)

REFERENCES

LOCK_ALLOC(D3), LOCK_DEALLOC(D3), TRYLOCK(D3), UNLOCK(D3)

NOTICES

Availability

SVR4MP

Portability

All processors

Interface

Driver-Kernel

Commitment

Level 1

NAME

LOCK_ALLOC – allocate and initialize a basic lock

SYNOPSIS

```
#include <sys/types.h>
#include <sys/kmem.h>
#include <sys/ksynch.h>
#include <sys/ddi.h>

lock_t *LOCK_ALLOC(uchar_t hierarchy, pl_t min_pl, lkinfo_t *lkinfop,
      int flag);
```

Arguments

hierarchy Hierarchy value which asserts the order in which this lock will be acquired relative to other basic and read/write locks.

min_pl Minimum priority level argument which asserts the minimum priority level that will be passed in with any attempt to acquire this lock [see LOCK(D3)].

lkinfop Pointer to a **lkinfo** structure. The **lk_name** member of the **lkinfo** structure points to a character string defining a name that will be associated with the lock for the purpose of statistics gathering.

flag Specifies whether the caller is willing to sleep waiting for memory.

DESCRIPTION

LOCK_ALLOC dynamically allocates and initializes an instance of a basic lock. The lock is initialized to the unlocked state.

If *flag* is set to KM_SLEEP, the caller will sleep if necessary until sufficient memory is available. If *flag* is set to KM_NOSLEEP, the caller will not sleep, but LOCK_ALLOC will return NULL if sufficient memory is not immediately available.

Return Values

Upon successful completion, LOCK_ALLOC returns a pointer to the newly allocated lock. If KM_NOSLEEP is specified and sufficient memory is not immediately available, LOCK_ALLOC returns a NULL pointer.

USAGE

hierarchy Argument

Implementations of lock testing may differ in whether they assume a separate range of *hierarchy* values for each interrupt priority level or a single range that spans all interrupt priority levels. In order to be portable across different implementations, drivers which may acquire locks at more than one interrupt priority level should define the *hierarchy* among those locks such that the *hierarchy* is strictly increasing with increasing priority level (e.g. if M is the maximum *hierarchy* value defined for any lock that may be acquired at priority level N, then M + 1 should be the minimum hierarchy value defined for any lock that may be acquired at any priority level greater than N).

This assertion is enforced by the system when the driver is compiled with the DEBUG and _LOCKTEST compilation options defined. *hierarchy* must be within the range 1 through 32 inclusive and must be chosen such that locks are normally acquired in order of increasing *hierarchy* number. In other words, when acquiring a basic lock using any function other than TRYLOCK(D3), the lock being acquired must have a *hierarchy* value that is strictly greater than the *hierarchy* values associated with all locks currently held by the calling context.

min_pl Argument

This assertion may be enforced by the system when the driver is compiled with the **DEBUG** and **_LOCKTEST** compilation options defined. Implementations which do not require that the interrupt priority level be raised during lock acquisition may choose not to enforce the *min_pl* assertion, even when the appropriate compilation options have been defined. The valid values for this argument are as follows:

plbase	Block no interrupts
pltimeout	Block functions scheduled by itimeout and dtimeout
pldisk	Block disk device interrupts
plstr	Block STREAMS interrupts
plhi	Block all interrupts

The notion of a *min_pl* assumes a defined order of priority levels. The following partial order is defined:

plbase < pltimeout <= pldisk,plstr <= plhi

The ordering of **pldisk** and **plstr** relative to each other is not defined.

Setting a given priority level will block interrupts associated with that level as well as any levels that are defined to be less than or equal to the specified level. In order to be portable a driver should not acquire locks at different priority levels where the relative order of those priority levels is not defined above.

The *min_pl* argument should specify a priority level that would be sufficient to block out any interrupt handler that might attempt to acquire this lock. In addition, potential deadlock problems involving multiple locks should be considered when defining the *min_pl* value. For example, if the normal order of acquisition of locks A and B (as defined by the lock hierarchy) is to acquire A first and then B, lock B should never be acquired at a priority level less than the *min_pl* for lock A. Therefore, the *min_pl* for lock B should be greater than or equal to the *min_pl* for lock A.

Note that the specification of *min_pl* with a **LOCK_ALLOC** call does not actually cause any interrupts to be blocked upon lock acquisition, it simply asserts that subsequent **LOCK** calls to acquire this lock will pass in a priority level at least as great as *min_pl*.

lkinfop Argument

The name should begin with the driver prefix and should be unique to the lock or group of locks for which the driver wishes to collect a uniquely identifiable set of statistics (i.e. if a given name is shared by a group of locks, the statistics of individual locks within the group will not be uniquely identifiable). There are no flags defined within the **lk_flags** member of the **lkinfo** structure for use with **LOCK_ALLOC**.

The *lkinfop* pointer is recorded in a statistics buffer along with the lock statistics when the driver is compiled with the **DEBUG** and **_MPSTATS** compilation options defined. A given **lkinfo** structure may be shared among multiple basic locks and read/write locks but a **lkinfo** structure may not be shared between a basic lock and a sleep lock. The caller must ensure that the **lk_flags** and **lk_pad** members of the **lkinfo** structure are zeroed out before passing it to **LOCK_ALLOC**.

flag Argument

Under the **_MPSTATS** compilation option, if **KM_NOSLEEP** is specified and sufficient memory can be immediately allocated for the lock itself but not for an accompanying statistics buffer, **LOCK_ALLOC** will return a pointer to the allocated lock but individual statistics will not be collected for the lock.

Level

Base only if *flag* is set to **KM_SLEEP**.

Initialization, Base or Interrupt if *flag* is set to **KM_NOSLEEP**.

Synchronization Constraints

May sleep if flag is set to **KM_SLEEP**.

Driver-defined basic locks and read/write locks may be held across calls to this function if *flag* is **KM_NOSLEEP** but may not be held if *flag* is **KM_SLEEP**.

Driver-defined sleep locks may be held across calls to this function regardless of the value of *flag*.

REFERENCES

LOCK(D3), **LOCK_DEALLOC**(D3), **TRYLOCK**(D3), **UNLOCK**(D3)

NOTICES

Availability

SVR4MP

Portability

All processors

Interface

Driver-Kernel

Commitment

Level 1

LOCK_DEALLOC(D3)

NAME

LOCK_DEALLOC – deallocate an instance of a basic lock

SYNOPSIS

```
#include <sys/types.h>
#include <sys/ksynch.h>
#include <sys/ddi.h>

void LOCK_DEALLOC(lock_t *lockp);
```

Arguments

lockp Pointer to the basic lock to be deallocated.

DESCRIPTION

LOCK_DEALLOC deallocates the basic lock specified by *lockp*.

Return Values

None.

USAGE

Attempting to deallocate a lock that is currently locked or is being waited for is an error and will result in undefined behavior.

Level

Base or Interrupt.

Synchronization Constraints

Does not sleep.

Driver-defined basic locks (other than the one being deallocated), read/write locks, and sleep locks may be held across calls to this function.

REFERENCES

LOCK(D3), LOCK_ALLOC(D3), TRYLOCK(D3), UNLOCK(D3)

NOTICES

Availability

SVR4MP

Portability

All processors

Interface

Driver-Kernel

Commitment

Level 1

NAME

makedevice – make device number from major and minor numbers

SYNOPSIS

```
#include <sys/types.h>
#include <sys/ddi.h>

dev_t makedevice(major_t majnum, minor_t minnum);
```

Arguments

majnum Major number.

minnum Minor number.

DESCRIPTION

The **makedevice** function creates a device number from major and minor device numbers.

Return Values

The device number, containing both the major number and the minor number, is returned. No validation of the major or minor numbers is performed.

USAGE

makedevice should be used to create device numbers so that the driver will port easily to releases that treat device numbers differently.

Level

Initialization, Base or Interrupt.

Synchronization Constraints

Does not sleep.

Driver-defined basic locks, read/write locks, and sleep locks may be held across calls to this function.

Singlethreaded Example

In the following example, **makedevice** is used to create the device number selected during a clone open. If the **CLONEOPEN** flag is set (line 9), we search through the list of minor devices looking for one that is available (lines 10–11). If we find an unused minor, we break off the search, create a new device number, and store it in the memory location pointed to by **devp** (line 15). If no unused minor was found, we return the error **ENXIO**.

```
1   xxxopen(q, devp, oflag, sflag, crp)
2       queue_t *q;
3       dev_t *dev;
4       int oflag;
5       int sflag;
6       cred_t *crp;
7   {
8       minor_t minnum;
9       if (sflag == CLONEOPEN) {
10              for (minnum = 0; minnum < XXXMAXMIN; minnum++)
11                      if (!INUSE(minnum))
12                              break;
13              if (minnum >= XXXMAXMIN)
14                      return(ENXIO);
15              *devp = makedevice(getemajor(*devp), minnum);
16      }
```

. . .

Multithreaded Example

In the following example, **makedevice** is used to create the device number selected during a clone open. If the **CLONEOPEN** flag is set (line 11), we lock the list of minor devices (line 12) and search through the list, looking for a minor device that is available (lines 13–14). If we find an unused minor, we break off the search, mark the minor as being in use (line 20), unlock the list, create a new device number, and store it in the memory location pointed to by **devp** (line 22). If no unused minor was found, we unlock the list and return the error **ENXIO**.

```
1  xxxopen(q, devp, oflag, sflag, crp)
2      queue_t *q;
3      dev_t *dev;
4      int oflag;
5      int sflag;
6      cred_t *crp;
7  {
8      minor_t minnum;
9      pl_t pl;
10     extern lock_t *xxxminlock;

11     if (sflag == CLONEOPEN) {
12             pl = LOCK(xxxminlock, plstr);
13             for (minnum = 0; minnum < XXXMAXMIN; minnum++)
14                     if (!INUSE(minnum))
15                             break;
16             if (minnum >= XXXMAXMIN) {
17                     UNLOCK(xxxminlock, pl);
18                     return(ENXIO);
19             } else {
20                     SETINUSE(minnum);
21                     UNLOCK(xxxminlock, pl);
22                     *devp = makedevice(getemajor(*devp), minnum);
23             }
24     }
        . . .
```

REFERENCES

getemajor(D3), **geteminor**(D3), **getmajor**(D3), **getminor**(D3)

NOTICES

Availability

SVR4.0, SVR4.1ES, SVR4MP, SVR4.2

Portability

All processors

Interface

Driver-Kernel

Commitment

Level 1

NAME

`max` – return the larger of two integers

SYNOPSIS

```
#include <sys/ddi.h>

int max(int int1, int int2);
```

Arguments

int1, int2 The integers to be compared.

DESCRIPTION

`max` compares two integers and returns the larger of two.

Return Values

The larger of the two integers.

USAGE

If the *int1* and *int2* arguments are not of the specified type the results are undefined.

This interface may be implemented in a way that causes the arguments to be evaluated multiple times, so callers should beware of side effects.

Level

Initialization, Base or Interrupt.

Synchronization Constraints

Does not sleep.

Driver-defined basic locks, read/write locks, and sleep locks may be held across calls to this function.

REFERENCES

`min`(D3)

NOTICES

Availability

SVR4.0, SVR4.1ES, SVR4MP, SVR4.2

Portability

All processors

Interface

General-purpose utility

Commitment

Level 1

min (D3)

NAME

`min` – return the lesser of two integers

SYNOPSIS

```
#include <sys/ddi.h>

int min(int int1, int int2);
```

Arguments

int1, int2 The integers to be compared.

DESCRIPTION

`min` compares two integers and returns the lesser of the two.

Return Values

The lesser of the two integers.

USAGE

If the *int1* and *int2* arguments are not of the specified type the results are undefined.

This interface may be implemented in a way that causes the arguments to be evaluated multiple times, so callers should beware of side effects.

Level

Initialization, Base or Interrupt.

Synchronization Constraints

Does not sleep.

Driver-defined basic locks, read/write locks, and sleep locks may be held across calls to this function.

REFERENCES

`max`(D3)

NOTICES

Availability

SVR4.0, SVR4.1ES, SVR4MP, SVR4.2

Portability

All processors

Interface

General-purpose utility

Commitment

Level 1

NAME

`mod_drvattach` – install interrupts for a loadable device driver

SYNOPSIS

```
#include <sys/moddefs.h>
#include <sys/ddi.h>

void mod_drvattach(void *iip);
```

Arguments

iip Pointer to the driver's *prefix*`attach_info` structure.

DESCRIPTION

`mod_drvattach` is called from a loadable driver's `_load`(D2) routine. It installs and enables interrupts for a driver being dynamically loaded into a running system.

USAGE

The *prefix*`attach_info` structure is defined and initialized by the kernel configuration tools at the time the driver is configured into the system. The definition of the `attach_info` structure is not included in the DDI/DKI, and can change across releases. It should be treated as a "black box" by the driver; none of its fields may be referenced.

Return Values

None

Level

Base only.

Synchronization Constraints

Can sleep.

Driver-defined basic locks and read/write locks may not be held across calls to this function.

Driver-defined sleep locks may be held across calls to this function.

Examples

See `_load`(D2) for an example of `mod_drvattach`.

REFERENCES

`_load`(D2), `mod_drvdetach`(D3)

NOTICES

Availability

SVR4.2

Portability

All processors

Interface

Driver-Kernel

Commitment

Level 1

mod_drvdetach (D3)

NAME

`mod_drvdetach` – remove interrupts for a loadable device driver

SYNOPSIS

```
#include <sys/moddefs.h>
#include <sys/ddi.h>

void mod_drvdetach(void *iip);
```

Arguments

iip Pointer to the driver's *prefix*`attach_info` structure.

DESCRIPTION

`mod_drvdetach` is called from a loadable driver's `_unload`(D2) routine. It disables and removes interrupts for a driver being dynamically unloaded from a running system.

USAGE

The *prefix*`attach_info` structure is defined and initialized by the kernel configuration tools at the time the driver is configured into the system. The definition of the `attach_info` structure is not included in the DDI/DKI, and can change across releases. It should be treated as a "black box" by the driver; none of its fields may be referenced.

Return Values

None

Level

Base only.

Synchronization Constraints

Does not sleep.

Driver-defined basic locks and read/write locks may not be held across calls to this function.

Driver-defined sleep locks may be held across calls to this function.

Examples

See `_load`(D2) for an example of `mod_drvdetach`.

REFERENCES

`_unload`(D2), `mod_drvattach`(D3)

NOTICES

Availability

SVR4.2

Portability

All processors

Interface

Driver-Kernel

Commitment

Level 1

NAME

`msgdsize` – return number of bytes of data in a message

SYNOPSIS

```
#include <sys/stream.h>
#include <sys/ddi.h>

int msgdsize(mblk_t *mp);
```

Arguments

mp Pointer to the message to be evaluated.

DESCRIPTION

msgdsize counts the number of bytes of data in the message pointed to by *mp*. Only bytes included in message blocks of type **M_DATA** are included in the count.

Return Values

The number of bytes of data in the message.

USAGE

Level

Base or Interrupt.

Synchronization Constraints

Does not sleep.

Driver-defined basic locks, read/write locks, and sleep locks may be held across calls to this function.

Examples

See **insq**(D3) for an example of **msgdsize**.

REFERENCES

msgb(D4)

NOTICES

Availability

SVR4.0, SVR4.1ES, SVR4MP, SVR4.2

Portability

All processors

Interface

Driver-Kernel (STREAMS)

Commitment

Level 1

msgpullup (D3)

NAME

`msgpullup` – concatenate bytes in a message

SYNOPSIS

```
#include <sys/stream.h>
#include <sys/ddi.h>

mblk_t *msgpullup(mblk_t *mp, int len);
```

Arguments

mp Pointer to the message whose blocks are to be concatenated.

len Number of bytes to concatenate.

DESCRIPTION

`msgpullup` concatenates and aligns the first *len* data bytes of the message pointed to by *mp*, copying the data into a new message. All message blocks that remain in the original message once *len* bytes have been concatenated and aligned (including any partial message blocks) are copied and linked to the end of the new message, so that the length of the new message is equal to the length of the original message.

The original message is unaltered. If *len* equals –1, all data are concatenated. If *len* bytes of the same message type cannot be found, `msgpullup` fails and returns `NULL`.

Return Values

On success, `msgpullup` returns a pointer to the new message. On failure, `msgpullup` returns `NULL`.

USAGE

Level

Base or Interrupt.

Synchronization Constraints

Does not sleep.

Driver-defined basic locks, read/write locks, and sleep locks may be held across calls to this function.

REFERENCES

`allocb`(D3), `msgb`(D4)

NOTICES

Availability

SVR4MP

Portability

All processors

Interface

Driver-Kernel (STREAMS)

Commitment

Level 1

NAME

`putctl` – send a control message to a queue

SYNOPSIS

```
#include <sys/stream.h>
#include <sys/ddi.h>

int putctl(queue_t *q, int type);
```

Arguments

q Pointer to the queue to which the message is to be sent.

type Message type (must be a control type).

DESCRIPTION

putctl tests the *type* argument to make sure a data type has not been specified, and then attempts to allocate a message block. **putctl** fails if *type* is **M_DATA**, **M_PROTO**, or **M_PCPROTO**, or if a message block cannot be allocated. If successful, **putctl** calls the **put**(D2) routine of the queue pointed to by *q*, passing it the allocated message.

Return Values

On success, 1 is returned. Otherwise, if *type* is a data type, or if a message block cannot be allocated, 0 is returned.

USAGE

In multithreaded drivers, the *q* argument may not reference **q_next** (for example, an argument of **q->q_next** is erroneous in a multithreaded driver and is disallowed by the DDI/DKI). **putnextctl(q, type)** is provided as a multiprocessor-safe equivalent to the common call **putctl(q->q_next, type)**, which is no longer allowed.

Level

Base or Interrupt.

Synchronization Constraints

Does not sleep.

Driver-defined basic locks, read/write locks, and sleep locks may not be held across calls to this function.

The caller cannot have the stream frozen [see **freezestr**(D3)] when calling this function.

Examples

The **send_ctl** routine is used to pass control messages downstream. **M_BREAK** messages are handled with **putctl** (line 9). **putctl1** (line 11) is used for **M_DELAY** messages, so that *param* can be used to specify the length of the delay. If an invalid message type is detected, **send_ctl** returns 0, indicating failure (line 13).

```
1  int
2  send_ctl(wrq, type, param)
3    queue_t *wrq;
4    uchar_t type;
5    uchar_t param;
6  {
7    switch (type) {
8    case M_BREAK:
9          return(putctl(wrq->q_next, M_BREAK));
```

```
    case M_DELAY:
        return(putctl1(wrq->q_next, M_DELAY, param));
    default:
        return(0);
    }
}
```

REFERENCES

put(D2), put(D3), putctl1(D3), putnextctl(D3), putnextctl1(D3)

NOTICES

Availability

SVR4.0, SVR4.1ES, SVR4MP, SVR4.2

Portability

All processors

Interface

Driver-Kernel (STREAMS)

Commitment

Level 1

NAME

`putctl1` – send a control message with a one-byte parameter to a queue

SYNOPSIS

```
#include <sys/stream.h>
#include <sys/ddi.h>

int putctl1(queue_t *q, int type, int param);
```

Arguments

q Pointer to the queue to which the message is to be sent.

type Message type (must be a control type).

param One-byte parameter.

DESCRIPTION

putctl1, like **putctl**(D3), tests the *type* argument to make sure a data type has not been specified, and attempts to allocate a message block. The *param* parameter can be used, for example, to specify the signal number when an **M_PCSIG** message is being sent. **putctl1** fails if **type** is **M_DATA**, **M_PROTO**, or **M_PCPROTO**, or if a message block cannot be allocated. If successful, **putctl1** calls the **put**(D2) routine of the queue pointed to by *q*, passing it the allocated message.

Return Values

On success, 1 is returned. Otherwise, if *type* is a data type, or if a message block cannot be allocated, 0 is returned.

USAGE

In multithreaded drivers, the *q* argument to **putctl1** and **putnextctl1**(D3) may not reference **q_next** (for example, an argument of **q->q_next** is erroneous in a multithreaded driver and is disallowed by the DDI/DKI). **putnextctl1(q, type)** is provided as a multiprocessor-safe equivalent to the common call **putctl1(q->q_next, type)**, which is no longer allowed.

Level

Base or Interrupt.

Synchronization Constraints

Does not sleep.

Driver-defined basic locks, read/write locks, and sleep locks may not be held across calls to this function.

The caller cannot have the stream frozen [see **freezestr**(D3)] when calling this function.

Examples

See **putctl**(D3) for an example of **putctl1**.

REFERENCES

put(D2), **put**(D3), **putctl**(D3), **putnextctl**(D3), **putnextctl1**(D3)

NOTICES

Availability

SVR4.0, SVR4.1ES, SVR4MP, SVR4.2

Portability
All processors

Interface
Driver-Kernel (STREAMS)

Commitment
Level 1

NAME

`putnext` – send a message to the next queue

SYNOPSIS

```
#include <sys/stream.h>
#include <sys/ddi.h>

int putnext(queue_t *q, mblk_t *mp);
```

Arguments

q	Pointer to the queue from which the message *mp* will be sent.
mp	Pointer to the message to be passed.

DESCRIPTION

The **putnext** function is used to pass a message to the **put**(D2) routine of the next queue (*q–>q_next*) in the stream.

Return Values

Ignored

USAGE

Level

Base or Interrupt.

Synchronization Constraints

Does not sleep.

Driver-defined basic locks, read/write locks, and sleep locks may not be held across calls to this function.

The caller cannot have the stream frozen [see **freezestr**(D3)] when calling this function.

Examples

See **allocb**(D3) for an example of **putnext**.

REFERENCES

put(D2)

NOTICES

Availability

SVR4.0, SVR4.1ES, SVR4MP, SVR4.2

Portability

All processors

Interface

Driver-Kernel (STREAMS)

Commitment

Level 1

putnextctl (D3)

NAME

putnextctl – send a control message to a queue

SYNOPSIS

#include <sys/stream.h>
#include <sys/ddi.h>

int putnextctl(queue_t ***q*****, int** ***type*****);**

Arguments

q	Pointer to the queue from which the message is to be sent.
type	Message type (must be a control type).

DESCRIPTION

putnextctl tests the *type* argument to make sure a data type has not been specified, and then attempts to allocate a message block. **putnextctl** fails if *type* is **M_DATA**, **M_PROTO**, or **M_PCPROTO**, or if a message block cannot be allocated. If successful, **putnextctl** calls the **put**(D2) procedure of the queue pointed to by *q->q_next*, passing it the allocated message.

Return Values

Upon successful completion, **putnextctl** returns 1. If *type* is a data type, or if a message block cannot be allocated, 0 is returned.

USAGE

In multithreaded drivers, the *q* argument to **putctl**(D3) and **putnextctl** may not reference **q_next** (for example, an argument of **q->q_next** is erroneous in a multithreaded driver and is disallowed by the DDI/DKI). **putnextctl(q, type)** is provided as a multiprocessor-safe equivalent to the common call **putctl(q->q_next, type)**, which is no longer allowed.

Level

Base or Interrupt.

Synchronization Constraints

Does not sleep.

Driver-defined basic locks, read/write locks, and sleep locks may not be held across calls to this function.

The caller cannot have the stream frozen [see **freezestr**(D3)] when calling this function.

Examples

The **send_ctl** routine is used to pass control messages downstream. **M_BREAK** messages are handled with **putnextctl** (line 9). **putnextctl1** (line 11) is used for **M_DELAY** messages, so that *param* can be used to specify the length of the delay. If an invalid message type is detected, **send_ctl** returns 0, indicating failure (line 13).

```
1  int
2  send_ctl(wrq, type, param)
3     queue_t *wrq;
4     uchar_t type;
5     uchar_t param;
6  {
7     switch (type) {
```

```
	case M_BREAK:
		return(putnextctl(wrq, M_BREAK));
	case M_DELAY:
		return(putnextctl1(wrq, M_DELAY, param));
	default:
		return(0);
	}
}
```

REFERENCES

`put`(D2), `put`(D3), `putctl`(D3), `putctl1`(D3), `putnextctl1`(D3)

NOTICES

Availability

SVR4MP

Portability

All processors

Interface

Driver-Kernel (STREAMS)

Commitment

Level 1

putnextctl1 (D3)

NAME

`putnextctl1` – send a control message with a one byte parameter to a queue

SYNOPSIS

```
#include <sys/stream.h>
#include <sys/ddi.h>

int putnextctl1(queue_t *q, int type, int param);
```

Arguments

q	Pointer to the queue from which the message is to be sent.
type	Message type (must be a control type).
param	One byte parameter.

DESCRIPTION

`putnextctl1` tests the *type* argument to make sure a data type has not been specified, and then attempts to allocate a message block. `putnextctl1` fails if *type* is `M_DATA`, `M_PROTO`, or `M_PCPROTO`, or if a message block cannot be allocated. If successful, `putnextctl` calls the `put`(D2) procedure of the queue pointed to by *q->q_next*, passing it the allocated message with the one byte parameter specified by *param*.

Return Values

Upon successful completion, `putnextctl1` returns 1. If *type* is a data type, or if a message block cannot be allocated, 0 is returned.

USAGE

In multithreaded drivers, the *q* argument to `putctl1`(D3) and `putnextctl1` may not reference `q_next` (for example, an argument of `q->q_next` is erroneous in a multithreaded driver and is disallowed by the DDI/DKI). `putnextctl1(q, type)` is provided as a multiprocessor-safe equivalent to the common call `putctl1(q->q_next, type)`, which is no longer allowed.

Level

Base or Interrupt.

Synchronization Constraints

Does not sleep.

Driver-defined basic locks, read/write locks, and sleep locks may not be held across calls to this function.

The caller cannot have the stream frozen [see `freezestr`(D3)] when calling this function.

Examples

See `putnextctl`(D3) for an example of `putnextctl1`.

REFERENCES

`put`(D2), `put`(D3), `putctl`(D3), `putctl1`(D3), `putnextctl`(D3)

NOTICES

Availability

SVR4MP

Portability
All processors

Interface
Driver-Kernel (STREAMS)

Commitment
Level 1

putq (D3)

NAME

putq – put a message on a queue

SYNOPSIS

```
#include <sys/stream.h>
#include <sys/ddi.h>

int putq(queue_t *q, mblk_t *bp);
```

Arguments

q Pointer to the queue.

bp Pointer to the message.

DESCRIPTION

putq is used to put messages on a queue after the **put**(D2) routine has finished processing the message. The message is placed after any other messages of the same priority, and flow control parameters are updated. The queue's service routine is scheduled if it has not been disabled by a previous call to **noenable**(D3), or if the message being enqueued has greater than normal priority (that is, it is not in band zero).

Return Values

putq returns 1 on success and 0 on failure.

USAGE

putq can fail if there is not enough memory to allocate the accounting data structures used with messages whose priority bands are greater than zero.

Level

Base or Interrupt.

Synchronization Constraints

Does not sleep.

Driver-defined basic locks, read/write locks, and sleep locks may be held across calls to this function.

The caller cannot have the stream frozen [see **freezestr**(D3)] when calling this function.

Examples

See **datamsg**(D3) for an example of **putq**.

REFERENCES

getq(D3), **insq**(D3), **msgb**(D4), **put**(D2), **putbq**(D3), **queue**(D4), **rmvq**(D3), **srv**(D2)

NOTICES

Availability

SVR4.0, SVR4.1ES, SVR4MP, SVR4.2

Portability

All processors

Interface

Driver-Kernel (STREAMS)

Commitment
Level 1

qenable (D3)

NAME

`qenable` – schedule a queue's service routine to be run

SYNOPSIS

```
#include <sys/stream.h>
#include <sys/ddi.h>

void qenable(queue_t *q);
```

Arguments

q	Pointer to the queue.

DESCRIPTION

`qenable` puts the queue pointed to by *q* on the linked list of those whose service routines are ready to be called by the STREAMS scheduler.

Return Values

None

USAGE

`qenable` works regardless of whether the service routine has been disabled by a prior call to **`noenable`**(D3).

Level

Base or Interrupt.

Synchronization Constraints

Does not sleep.

Driver-defined basic locks, read/write locks, and sleep locks may be held across calls to this function.

The caller cannot have the stream frozen [see **`freezestr`**(D3)] when calling this function.

Examples

See **`enableok`**(D3) for an example of `qenable`.

REFERENCES

`enableok`(D3), **`noenable`**(D3), **`queue`**(D4), **`srv`**(D2)

NOTICES

Availability

SVR4.0, SVR4.1ES, SVR4MP, SVR4.2

Portability

All processors

Interface

Driver-Kernel (STREAMS)

Commitment

Level 1

NAME

`qprocsoff` – disable put and service routines

SYNOPSIS

```
#include <sys/stream.h>
#include <sys/ddi.h>

void qprocsoff(queue_t *rq);
```

Arguments

rq Pointer to a read queue.

DESCRIPTION

`qprocsoff` disables the put and service routines of the driver or module whose read queue is pointed to by *rq*. It removes the queue's service routines from the list of service routines to be run and waits until any concurrent **put** or service routines are finished. When the routines are disabled in a module, messages flow around the module as if it were not present in the stream.

Return Values

None

USAGE

`qprocsoff` must be called by the **close**(D2) routine of a driver or module before deallocating any resources on which the driver/module's put and service routines depend.

Level

Base only.

Synchronization Constraints

Can sleep.

Driver-defined basic locks and read/write locks may not be held across calls to this function.

Driver-defined sleep locks may be held across calls to this function.

The caller cannot have the stream frozen [see **freezestr**(D3)] when calling this function.

Examples

See `unbufcall`(D3) for an example of `qprocsoff`.

REFERENCES

`close`(D2), `put`(D2), `srv`(D2), `qprocson`(D3)

NOTICES

Availability

SVR4MP

Portability

All processors

Interface

Driver-Kernel (STREAMS)

qprocsoff (D3)

Commitment

Level 1

NAME

qprocson – enable put and service routines

SYNOPSIS

```
#include <sys/stream.h>
#include <sys/ddi.h>

void qprocson(queue_t *rq);
```

Arguments

rq Pointer to a read queue.

DESCRIPTION

qprocson enables the put and service routines of the driver or module whose read queue is pointed to by *rq*. Prior to the call to **qprocson**, the put and service routines of a newly pushed module or newly opened driver are disabled. When the routines are diabled in a module, messages flow around the module as if it were not present in the stream.

Return Values

None

USAGE

qprocson must be called by the first open of a module or driver after allocation and initialization of any resources on which the put and service routines depend.

Level

Base only.

Synchronization Constraints

Can sleep.

Driver-defined basic locks and read/write locks may not be held across calls to this function.

Driver-defined sleep locks may be held across calls to this function.

The caller cannot have the stream frozen [see **freezestr**(D3)] when calling this function.

REFERENCES

open(D2), **put**(D2), **srv**(D2), **qprocsoff**(D3)

NOTICES

Availability

SVR4MP

Portability

All processors

Interface

Driver-Kernel (STREAMS)

Commitment

Level 1

qreply (D3)

NAME

qreply – send a message in the opposite direction in a stream

SYNOPSIS

```
#include <sys/stream.h>
#include <sys/ddi.h>

void qreply(queue_t *q, mblk_t *bp);
```

Arguments

q Pointer to the queue from which the message is being sent.

bp Pointer to the message to be sent in the opposite direction.

DESCRIPTION

qreply sends a message in the opposite direction from that which *q* is pointing. It calls the **OTHERQ**(D3) function to find *q*'s partner, and passes the message by calling the **put**(D2) routine of the next queue in the stream after *q*'s partner.

Return Values

None

USAGE

Level

Base or Interrupt.

Synchronization Constraints

Does not sleep.

Driver-defined basic locks, read/write locks, and sleep locks may not be held across calls to this function.

The caller cannot have the stream frozen [see **freezestr**(D3)] when calling this function.

Examples

See **put**(D2) for an example of **qreply**.

REFERENCES

OTHERQ(D3), **put**(D2), **putnext**(D3)

NOTICES

Availability

SVR4.0, SVR4.1ES, SVR4MP, SVR4.2

Portability

All processors

Interface

Driver-Kernel (STREAMS)

Commitment

Level 1

NAME

`qsize` – find the number of messages on a queue

SYNOPSIS

```
#include <sys/stream.h>
#include <sys/ddi.h>

int qsize(queue_t *q);
```

Arguments

q Pointer to the queue to be evaluated.

DESCRIPTION

`qsize` evaluates the queue pointed to by *q* and returns the number of messages it contains.

Return Values

If there are no message on the queue, `qsize` returns 0. Otherwise, it returns the number of messages on the queue.

USAGE

Level

Base or Interrupt.

Synchronization Constraints

Does not sleep.

Driver-defined basic locks, read/write locks, and sleep locks may be held across calls to this function.

The caller cannot have the stream frozen [see **freezestr**(D3)] when calling this function.

REFERENCES

msgb(D4), **queue**(D4)

NOTICES

Availability

SVR4.0, SVR4.1ES, SVR4MP, SVR4.2

Portability

All processors

Interface

Driver-Kernel (STREAMS)

Commitment

Level 1

RD(D3)

NAME

RD – get a pointer to the read queue

SYNOPSIS

```
#include <sys/stream.h>
#include <sys/ddi.h>

queue_t *RD(queue_t *q);
```

Arguments

q Pointer to the queue whose read queue is to be returned.

DESCRIPTION

The **RD** function accepts a queue pointer as an argument and returns a pointer to the read queue of the same module or driver.

Return Values

The pointer to the read queue.

USAGE

Note that when **RD** is passed a read queue pointer as an argument, it returns a pointer to this read queue.

Level

Base or Interrupt.

Synchronization Constraints

Does not sleep.

Driver-defined basic locks, read/write locks, and sleep locks may be held across calls to this function.

Examples

See the `put`(D2) function page for an example of **RD**.

REFERENCES

OTHERQ(D3), **WR**(D3)

NOTICES

Availability

SVR4.0, SVR4.1ES, SVR4MP, SVR4.2

Portability

All processors

Interface

Driver-Kernel (STREAMS)

Commitment

Level 1

NAME

rdma_filter – filter transfers to use only DMA-able memory

SYNOPSIS

```
#include <sys/types.h>
#include <sys/buf.h>
#include <sys/ddi.h>

void rdma_filter(void (*strat)(), buf_t *bp);
```

Arguments

strat Address of the driver's strategy routine.

bp Pointer to the **buf**(D4) structure describing the I/O request.

DESCRIPTION

rdma_filter ensures that DMA transfers only occur to DMA-able memory. On systems with restrictions on DMA-able memory, **rdma_filter** calls the function specified by *strat*, passing a buffer that is guaranteed to be DMA-able. On systems without restrictions on DMA-able memory, **rdma_filter** simply calls the *strat* function passing on the buffer without modification.

Return Values

None. Any errors will be marked in the buffer header structure.

USAGE

rdma_filter can be used as an alternative to the **D_DMA** device flag [see **devflag**(D1)]. When the **devflag D_DMA** flag is set, all I/O requests to the device are filtered before calling the device's **strategy** routine. By using **rdma_filter** instead of the **D_DMA** device flag, drivers can achieve a higher degree of control over the sometimes expensive conversions to DMA-able memory.

Drivers that use **rdma_filter** should not set the **D_DMA** device flag.

Level

Base only.

Synchronization Constraints

Can sleep.

Driver-defined basic locks and read/write locks may not be held across calls to this function.

Driver-defined sleep locks may be held across calls to this function.

REFERENCES

buf(D4), **devflag**(D1), **strategy**(D2)

NOTICES

Availability

SVR4.2

Portability

All processors

Interface

Driver-Kernel

rdma_filter (D3)

Commitment

Level 1

NAME

repinsd – read 32 bit words from I/O port to buffer

SYNOPSIS

```
#include <sys/types.h>
#include <sys/ddi.h>

void repinsd(int port, ulong_t *addr, int cnt);
```

Arguments

port A valid 32 bit I/O port.

addr The address of the buffer where data is stored after *cn* port.

cnt The number of 32 bit words to be read from the I/O pc

DESCRIPTION

The **repinsd** function provides a C language interface to the ma that read a string of 32 bit words from a 32 bit I/O port using space, instead of the memory address space. The data from *cnt* port is stored in the data buffer pointed to by *addr*.

Return Values

None

USAGE

The data buffer should be at least *cnt* 32 bit words in length.

This function may not be meaningful on all implementations bec mentations may not support I/O-mapped I/O (direct I/O Intel860 systems, I/O is mapped to memory (memory-mapped I/ Intel860 systems, a *port* is not really an I/O port, but rather a me points to the memory-mapped I/O location. The *port* argument is that can represent a 16-bit address for the I/O port for Intel386 s memory address for Intel860 systems.

Level

Base or Interrupt.

Synchronization Constraints

Does not sleep.

Driver-defined basic locks, read/write locks, and sleep locks m calls to this function.

REFERENCES

inb(D3), **inl**(D3), **inw**(D3), **outb**(D3), **outl**(D3), **outw**(D3), **repin** **repinsw**(D3), **repoutsb**(D3), **repoutsd**(D3), **repoutsw**(D3)

NOTICES

Availability

SVR4.0, SVR4.1ES, SVR4MP, SVR4.2

Portability

Intel386, Intel486, Intel860

NAME

repinsb – read bytes from I/O port to buffer

SYNOPSIS

```
#include <sys/types.h>
#include <sys/ddi.h>

void repinsb(int port, uchar_t *addr, int cnt);
```

Arguments

port A valid 8 bit I/O port.

addr The address of the buffer where data is stored after *cnt* reads of the I/O port.

cnt The number of bytes to be read from the I/O port.

DESCRIPTION

The **repinsb** function provides a C language interface to the machine instructions that read a string of bytes from an 8 bit I/O port using the I/O address space, instead of the memory address space. The data from *cnt* reads of the I/O port is stored in the data buffer pointed to by *addr*.

Return Values

None

USAGE

The data buffer should be at least *cnt* bytes in length.

This function may not be meaningful on all implementations because some implementations may not support I/O-mapped I/O (direct I/O instructions). On Intel860 systems, I/O is mapped to memory (memory-mapped I/O). Therefore, on Intel860 systems, a *port* is not really an I/O port, but rather a memory pointer that points to the memory-mapped I/O location. The *port* argument is similar to a token that can represent a 16-bit address for the I/O port for Intel386 systems or a 32-bit memory address for Intel860 systems.

Level

Initialization, Base or Interrupt.

Synchronization Constraints

Does not sleep.

Driver-defined basic locks, read/write locks, and sleep locks may be held across calls to this function.

REFERENCES

inb(D3), **inl**(D3), **inw**(D3), **outb**(D3), **outl**(D3), **outw**(D3), **repinsd**(D3), **repinsw**(D3), **repoutsb**(D3), **repoutsd**(D3), **repoutsw**(D3)

NOTICES

Availability

SVR4.0, SVR4.1ES, SVR4MP, SVR4.2

Portability

Intel386, Intel486, Intel860

repinsb (D3)

Interface
Driver-Hardware

Commitment
Level 1

repinsd (D3)

Interface
Driver-Hardware

Commitment
Level 1

NAME

repinsw – read 16 bit words from I/O port to buffer

SYNOPSIS

```
#include <sys/types.h>
#include <sys/ddi.h>

void repinsw(int port, ushort_t *addr, int cnt);
```

Arguments

port — A valid 16 bit I/O port.

addr — The address of the buffer where data is stored after *cnt* reads of the I/O port.

cnt — The number of 16 bit words to be read from the I/O port.

DESCRIPTION

The **repinsw** function provides a C language interface to the machine instructions that read a string of 16 bit short words from a 16 bit I/O port using the I/O address space, instead of the memory address space. The data from *cnt* reads of the I/O port is stored in the data buffer pointed to by *addr*.

Return Values

None

USAGE

The data buffer should be at least *cnt* 16 bit words in length.

This function may not be meaningful on all implementations because some implementations may not support I/O-mapped I/O (direct I/O instructions). On Intel860 systems, I/O is mapped to memory (memory-mapped I/O). Therefore, on Intel860 systems, a *port* is not really an I/O port, but rather a memory pointer that points to the memory-mapped I/O location. The *port* argument is similar to a token that can represent a 16-bit address for the I/O port for Intel386 systems or a 32-bit memory address for Intel860 systems.

Level

Initialization, Base or Interrupt.

Synchronization Constraints

Does not sleep.

Driver-defined basic locks, read/write locks, and sleep locks may be held across calls to this function.

REFERENCES

inb(D3), **inl**(D3), **inw**(D3), **outb**(D3), **outl**(D3), **outw**(D3), **repinsb**(D3), **repinsd**(D3), **repoutsb**(D3), **repoutsd**(D3), **repoutsw**(D3)

NOTICES

Availability

SVR4.0, SVR4.1ES, SVR4MP, SVR4.2

Portability

Intel386, Intel486, Intel860

repinsw (D3)

Interface
Driver-Hardware

Commitment
Level 1

NAME

repoutsb – write bytes from buffer to an I/O port

SYNOPSIS

```
#include <sys/types.h>
#include <sys/ddi.h>

void repoutsb(int port, uchar_t *addr, int cnt);
```

Arguments

port A valid 8 bit I/O port.

addr The address of the buffer from which *cnt* bytes are written to the I/O port.

cnt The number of bytes to be written to the I/O port.

DESCRIPTION

The **repoutsb** function provides a C language interface to the machine instructions that write a string of bytes to an 8 bit I/O port using the I/O address space, instead of the memory address space. *cnt* bytes starting at the address pointed to by *addr* are written to the I/O port in *cnt* write operations.

Return Values

None

USAGE

The buffer should be at least *cnt* bytes in length.

This function may not be meaningful on all implementations because some implementations may not support I/O-mapped I/O (direct I/O instructions). On Intel860 systems, I/O is mapped to memory (memory-mapped I/O). Therefore, on Intel860 systems, a *port* is not really an I/O port, but rather a memory pointer that points to the memory-mapped I/O location. The *port* argument is similar to a token that can represent a 16-bit address for the I/O port for Intel386 systems or a 32-bit memory address for Intel860 systems.

Level

Initialization, Base or Interrupt.

Synchronization Constraints

Does not sleep.

Driver-defined basic locks, read/write locks, and sleep locks may be held across calls to this function.

REFERENCES

inb(D3), **inl**(D3), **inw**(D3), **outb**(D3), **outl**(D3), **outw**(D3), **repinsb**(D3), **repinsd**(D3), **repinsw**(D3), **repoutsd**(D3), **repoutsw**(D3)

NOTICES

Availability

SVR4.0, SVR4.1ES, SVR4MP, SVR4.2

Portability

Intel386, Intel486, Intel860

repoutsb (D3)

Interface
Driver-Hardware

Commitment
Level 1

NAME

repoutsd – write 32 bit words from buffer to an I/O port

SYNOPSIS

```
#include <sys/types.h>
#include <sys/ddi.h>

void repoutsd(int port, ulong_t *addr, int cnt);
```

Arguments

port A valid 32 bit I/O port.

addr The address of the buffer from which *cnt* 32 bit words are written to the I/O port.

cnt The number of 32 bit words to be written to the I/O port.

DESCRIPTION

The **repoutsd** function provides a C language interface to the machine instructions that write a string of 32 bit long words to a 32 bit I/O port using the I/O address space, instead of the memory address space. *cnt* 32 bit words starting at the address pointed to by *addr* are written to the I/O port in *cnt* write operations.

Return Values

None

USAGE

The buffer should be at least *cnt* 32 bit words in length.

This function may not be meaningful on all implementations because some implementations may not support I/O-mapped I/O (direct I/O instructions). On Intel860 systems, I/O is mapped to memory (memory-mapped I/O). Therefore, on Intel860 systems, a *port* is not really an I/O port, but rather a memory pointer that points to the memory-mapped I/O location. The *port* argument is similar to a token that can represent a 16-bit address for the I/O port for Intel386 systems or a 32-bit memory address for Intel860 systems.

Level

Initialization, Base or Interrupt.

Synchronization Constraints

Does not sleep.

Driver-defined basic locks, read/write locks, and sleep locks may be held across calls to this function.

REFERENCES

inb(D3), **inl**(D3), **inw**(D3), **outb**(D3), **outl**(D3), **outw**(D3), **repinsb**(D3), **repinsd**(D3), **repinsw**(D3), **repoutsb**(D3), **repoutsw**(D3)

NOTICES

Availability

SVR4.0, SVR4.1ES, SVR4MP, SVR4.2

Portability

Intel386, Intel486, Intel860

repoutsd (D3)

Interface

Driver-Hardware

Commitment

Level 1

NAME

repoutsw – write 16 bit words from buffer to an I/O port

SYNOPSIS

```
#include <sys/types.h>
#include <sys/ddi.h>

void repoutsw(int port, ushort_t *addr, int cnt);
```

Arguments

port A valid 16 bit I/O port.

addr The address of the buffer from which *cnt* 16 bit words are written to the I/O port.

cnt The number of 16 bit words to be written to the I/O port.

DESCRIPTION

The **repoutsw** function provides a C language interface to the machine instructions that write a string of 16 bit short words to a 16 bit I/O port using the I/O address space, instead of the memory address space. *cnt* 16 bit words starting at the address pointed to by *addr* are written to the I/O port in *cnt* write operations.

Return Values

None

USAGE

The buffer should be at least *cnt* 16 bit words in length.

This function may not be meaningful on all implementations because some implementations may not support I/O-mapped I/O (direct I/O instructions). On Intel860 systems, I/O is mapped to memory (memory-mapped I/O). Therefore, on Intel860 systems, a *port* is not really an I/O port, but rather a memory pointer that points to the memory-mapped I/O location. The *port* argument is similar to a token that can represent a 16-bit address for the I/O port for Intel386 systems or a 32-bit memory address for Intel860 systems.

Level

Initialization, Base or Interrupt.

Synchronization Constraints

Does not sleep.

Driver-defined basic locks, read/write locks, and sleep locks may be held across calls to this function.

REFERENCES

inb(D3), **inl**(D3), **inw**(D3), **outb**(D3), **outl**(D3), **outw**(D3), **repinsb**(D3), **repinsd**(D3), **repinsw**(D3), **repoutsb**(D3), **repoutsd**(D3)

NOTICES

Availability

SVR4.0, SVR4.1ES, SVR4MP, SVR4.2

Portability

Intel386, Intel486, Intel860

repoutsw (D3)

Interface
Driver-Hardware

Commitment
Level 1

NAME

`rmalloc` – allocate space from a private space management map

SYNOPSIS

```
#include <sys/types.h>
#include <sys/map.h>
#include <sys/ddi.h>

ulong_t rmalloc(struct map *mp, size_t size);
```

Arguments

mp Pointer to the map from which space is to be allocated.

size Number of units of space to allocate.

DESCRIPTION

rmalloc allocates space from the private space management map pointed to by *mp*.

Return Values

Upon successful completion, **rmalloc** returns the base of the allocated space. If *size* units cannot be allocated, 0 is returned.

USAGE

Drivers can use **rmalloc** to allocate space from a previously allocated and initialized private space management map.

On systems where the **rmallocmap** function is available, the map must have been allocated by a call to **rmallocmap**(D3) and the space managed by the map must have been added using **rmfree**(D3) prior to the first call to **rmalloc** for the map.

On systems where the **rmallocmap** function is not available, the map must be initially allocated either as a data array, or by the **kmem_alloc**(D3) function. The map must have been initialized by a call to **rminit**(D3) and the space managed by the map must have been added using **rmfree**(D3) prior to the first call to **rmalloc** for the map.

size specifies the amount of space to allocate and is in arbitrary units. The driver using the map places whatever semantics on the units are appropriate for the type of space being managed. For example, units may be byte addresses, pages of memory, or blocks on a device.

The system allocates space from the memory map on a first-fit basis and coalesces adjacent space fragments when space is returned to the map by **rmfree**.

Level

Initialization, Base or Interrupt.

Synchronization Constraints

Does not sleep.

Driver-defined basic locks, read/write locks, and sleep locks may be held across calls to this function.

Examples

The following example is a simple memory map, but it illustrates the principles of map management. A driver declares a map table (line 4) and initializes the map table by calling both the **rminit** and **rmfree** functions. There are 35 entries in the map table, 32 of which can be used to represent space allocated. In the driver's

start(D2) routine, we allocate 16 Kbytes of memory using **kmem_alloc**(D3) (line 8). This is the space to be managed. Then we call **rminit** to establish the number of slots or entries in the map (line 10), and **rmfree** to populate the map with the space it is to manage (line 11).

In the driver's **read**(D2) and **write**(D2) routines, we use **rmalloc** to allocate buffers for data transfer. This example illustrates the **write** routine. Assuming the device can only transfer **XX_MAXBUFSZ** bytes at a time, we calculate the amount of data to copy (line 22) and use **rmalloc** to allocate some space from the map. The call to **rmalloc** is protected against interrupts (line 23) from the device that may result in freeing map space. This way, if space is freed, we won't miss the corresponding **wakeup**(D3).

If the appropriate space cannot be allocated, we use **rmsetwant**(D3) to indicate that we want space (line 25) and then we sleep until a buffer is available. When a buffer becomes available, **rmfree** is called to return the space to the map and to wake the sleeping process. Then the call to **rmalloc** will succeed and the driver can then transfer data.

```
 1  #define XX_MAPSIZE       35
 2  #define XX_MEMSIZE       (16*1024)
 3  #define XX_MAXBUFSZ      1024
 4  struct map xx_map[XX_MAPSIZE];
    ...
 5  xx_start()
 6  {
 7     caddr_t bp;
 8     if ((bp = kmem_alloc(XX_MEMSIZE, KM_NOSLEEP)) == 0)
 9             cmn_err(CE_PANIC, "xx_start: could not allocate %d bytes", XX_MEMSIZE);
10     rminit(xx_map, XX_MAPSIZE);
11     rmfree(xx_map, XX_MEMSIZE, bp);
12  }
    ...
13  xx_write(dev, uiop, crp)
14     dev_t dev;
15     uio_t *uiop;
16     cred_t *crp;
17  {
18     caddr_t addr;
19     size_t size;
20     int s;
       ...
21     while (uiop->uio_resid > 0) {
22             size = min(uiop->uio_resid, XX_MAXBUFSZ);
23             s = spl4();
24             while ((addr = (caddr_t)rmalloc(xx_map, size)) == NULL) {
25                     rmsetwant(xx_map);
26                     sleep((caddr_t)xx_map, PZERO);
27             }
28             splx(s);
               ...
29     }
       ...
```

On systems where the **rmallocmap** function is available, line 4 could become:

```
struct map *xx_map;
```

and line 10 could become:

```
if ((mp=rmallocmap(xx_MAPSIZE) == 0
    cmn_err (CE_PANIC, "xx_start: could not allocate map");
```

REFERENCES

`rmalloc_wait`(D3), **rmallocmap**(D3), **rmfree**(D3), **rmfreemap**(D3), `rminit`(D3), `rmsetwant`(D3)

NOTICES

Availability

SVR4.0, SVR4.1ES, SVR4MP, SVR4.2

Portability

All processors

Interface

Driver-Kernel

Commitment

Level 1

rmallocmap (D3)

NAME

`rmallocmap` – allocate and initialize a private space management map

SYNOPSIS

```
#include <sys/types.h>
#include <sys/map.h>
#include <sys/ddi.h>

struct map *rmallocmap(ulong_t mapsize);
```

Arguments

mapsize Number of entries for the map.

DESCRIPTION

`rmallocmap` allocates and initializes a private map array that can be used for the allocation of space.

Return Values

On success, `rmallocmap` returns a pointer to the newly allocated map. On failure, a `NULL` pointer is returned.

USAGE

Although `rmallocmap` allocates and initializes the map array itself, it does not allocate the space that the map will manage. This space must be allocated separately and must be added to the map using `rmfree`(D3) prior to attempting to allocate space from the map using `rmalloc`(D3) or `rmalloc_wait`(D3).

The system maintains the map list structure by size and index. The caller places whatever semantics on the units of size are appropriate for the type of space being managed. For example, units may be byte addresses, pages of memory, or blocks.

On systems where the the `rmallocmap` function is available, DDI/DKI conforming drivers may only use `map` structures which have been allocated and initialized using `rmallocmap`. Use of `map` structures which have been obtained by any other means is prohibited on such systems.

Level

Initialization, Base or Interrupt.

Synchronization Constraints

Does not sleep.

Driver-defined basic locks, read/write locks, and sleep locks may be held across calls to this function.

REFERENCES

`rmalloc`(D3), `rmalloc_wait`(D3), `rmfree`(D3), `rmfreemap`(D3)

NOTICES

Availability

SVR4MP

Portability

All processors

Interface

Driver-Kernel

Commitment

Level 1

rmalloc_wait (D3)

NAME

`rmalloc_wait` – allocate space from a private space management map

SYNOPSIS

```
#include <sys/types.h>
#include <sys/map.h>
#include <sys/ddi.h>

ulong_t rmalloc_wait(struct map *mp, size_t size);
```

Arguments

mp Pointer to map to resource map.

size Number of units to allocate.

DESCRIPTION

`rmalloc_wait` allocates space from a private map previously allocated using `rmallocmap`(D3).

Return Values

`rmalloc_wait` returns the base of the allocated space.

USAGE

`rmalloc_wait` is identical to `rmalloc`(D3), except that a call to `rmalloc_wait` will sleep (uninterruptible by signals), if necessary, until space becomes available.

Space allocated using `rmalloc_wait` may be returned to the map using `rmfree`(D3).

Level

Base only.

Synchronization Constraints

May sleep.

Driver-defined basic locks and read/write locks may not be held across calls to this function.

Driver-defined sleep locks may be held across calls to this function, but the driver writer must be cautious to avoid deadlock between the process holding the lock and trying to acquire the resource and another process holding the resource and trying to acquire the lock.

REFERENCES

`rmalloc`(D3), `rmallocmap`(D3), `rmfree`(D3), `rmfreemap`(D3)

NOTICES

Availability

SVR4MP

Portability

All processors

Interface

Driver-Kernel

Commitment

Level 1

rmfree (D3)

NAME

`rmfree` – free space into a private space management map

SYNOPSIS

```
#include <sys/types.h>
#include <sys/map.h>
#include <sys/ddi.h>

void rmfree(struct map *mp, size_t size, ulong_t index);
```

Arguments

mp Pointer to the map.

size Number of units to free into the map.

index Index of the first unit of the space being freed.

DESCRIPTION

rmfree releases space into the private space management map pointed to by *mp* and wakes up any processes that are waiting for space.

Return Values

None

USAGE

rmfree should be called to return space that had been allocated by a previous call to **rmalloc**(D3), in which case *index* is the value returned from the corresponding call to **rmalloc**. **rmfree** should also be called to add space to a newly allocated map prior to the first call to **rmalloc**, in which case *index* specifies the base of the space being added.

Both *size* and *index* are in arbitrary units. The driver using the map places whatever semantics on the units are appropriate for the type of space being managed. For example, units may be byte addresses, pages of memory, or blocks on a device.

If the space being returned is adjacent to other space in the map, **rmfree** will coalesce the adjacent fragments.

If the **rmfree** call causes the number of fragments in the map to exceed the number of map entries specified by **rminit**(D3) (for singlethreaded drivers) or **rmallocmap**(D3) (for multithreaded drivers) the following warning message is displayed on the console:

WARNING: rmfree map overflow *mp* **lost** *size* **items at** *index*

This implies that the driver should specify a larger number of map entries when initializing the map.

Level

Base or Interrupt.

Synchronization Constraints

Does not sleep.

Driver-defined basic locks, read/write locks, and sleep locks may be held across calls to this function.

Examples

See `rmalloc`(D3) for an example of `rmfree`.

REFERENCES

`rmalloc`(D3), `rmalloc_wait`(D3), `rmallocmap`(D3), `rmfreemap`(D3), `rminit`(D3), `rmsetwant`(D3)

NOTICES

Availability

SVR4.0, SVR4.1ES, SVR4MP, SVR4.2

Portability

All processors

Interface

Driver-Kernel

Commitment

Level 1

rmfreemap (D3)

NAME

rmfreemap – free a private space management map

SYNOPSIS

```
#include <sys/map.h>
#include <sys/ddi.h>

void rmfreemap(struct map *mp);
```

Arguments

mp Pointer to the map to be freed.

DESCRIPTION

rmfreemap frees the map pointed to by *mp*.

Return Values

None

USAGE

The **map** structure array pointed to by *mp* must have been previously allocated by a call to **rmallocmap**(D3).

Before freeing the map, the caller must ensure that nobody is using space managed by the map, and that nobody is waiting for space in the map.

Level

Initialization, Base or Interrupt.

Synchronization Constraints

Does not sleep.

Driver-defined basic locks, read/write locks, and sleep locks may be held across calls to this function.

REFERENCES

rmalloc(D3), **rmalloc_wait**(D3), **rmallocmap**(D3), **rmfree**(D3)

NOTICES

Availability

SVR4MP

Portability

All processors

Interface

Driver-Kernel

Commitment

Level 1

NAME

`rminit` – initialize a private space management map

SYNOPSIS

```
#include <sys/map.h>
#include <sys/ddi.h>

void rminit(struct map *mp, unsigned long mapsize);
```

Arguments

mp Pointer to the map describing the private space.

mapsize Number of entries in the map table.

DESCRIPTION

The **rminit** function initializes a private space management map structure that can be used for the allocation of space.

Return Values

None

USAGE

Although **rminit** initializes the map structure itself, it does not allocate the space that the map will manage. This space must be allocated separately and must be added to the map using **rmfree**(D3) prior to attempting to allocate space from the map using **rmalloc**(D3).

The system maintains the map list structure by size and index. The caller places whatever semantics on the units of size are appropriate for the type of space being managed. For example, units may be byte addresses, pages of memory, or blocks. The elements of the map are sorted by index.

The map array must be initialized to zero before calling **rminit**.

Three map entries are reserved for use by the system and are not available for general map use. Therefore, *mapsize* must be greater than three.

Level

Initialization, Base or Interrupt.

Synchronization Constraints

Does not sleep.

Examples

See **rmalloc**(D3) for an example of **rminit**.

REFERENCES

rmalloc(D3), **rmfree**(D3), **rmsetwant**(D3)

NOTICES

Availability

SVR4.0, SVR4.1ES, SVR4.2

Portability

All processors

rminit (D3)

Interface
Driver-Kernel

Commitment
Level 2 effective October 8, 1991

Future Directions
In SVR4MP, `rminit` is replaced by `rmallocmap`(D3).

NAME

rmsetwant – set the map's wait flag for a wakeup

SYNOPSIS

```
#include <sys/map.h>
#include <sys/ddi.h>

void rmsetwant(struct map *mp);
```

Arguments

mp Pointer to the map from which the driver is waiting for space.

DESCRIPTION

The **rmsetwant** function increments the counter on the wait flag of the map pointed to by *mp*.

Return Values

None

USAGE

rmsetwant is typically called from the driver after an unsuccessful attempt to allocate space from the map using **rmalloc**(D3).

The driver should sleep on *mp* after calling **rmsetwant**. When the **rmfree**(D3) function returns space to the map, it wakes up any processes waiting for space.

Level

Base only.

Synchronization Constraints

Does not sleep.

Examples

See **rmalloc**(D3) for an example of **rmsetwant**.

REFERENCES

rmalloc(D3), **rmalloc_wait**(D3), **rmfree**(D3), **rminit**(D3)

NOTICES

Availability

SVR4.0, SVR4.1ES, SVR4.2

Portability

All processors

Interface

Driver-Kernel

Commitment

Level 2 effective October 8, 1991

Future Directions

In SVR4MP, **rmsetwant** is replaced by **rmalloc_wait**(D3).

rmvb (D3)

NAME

`rmvb` – remove a message block from a message

SYNOPSIS

```
#include <sys/stream.h>
#include <sys/ddi.h>

mblk_t *rmvb(mblk_t *mp, mblk_t *bp);
```

Arguments

mp	Pointer to the message from which a message block is to be removed.
bp	Pointer to the message block to be removed.

DESCRIPTION

`rmvb` removes the message block specified by *bp* from the message specified *mp* and returns a pointer to the altered message.

Return Values

On success, a pointer to the message (minus the removed block) is returned. If *bp* was the only block in the message before **`rmvb`** was called, **`NULL`** is returned. If the designated message block (*bp*) was not in the message, –1 is returned.

USAGE

The message block is not freed, merely removed from the message. It is the caller's responsibility to free the message block.

Level

Base or Interrupt.

Synchronization Constraints

Does not sleep.

Driver-defined basic locks, read/write locks, and sleep locks may be held across calls to this function.

Examples

This routine removes all zero-length **`M_DATA`** message blocks from the given message. For each message block in the message, we save the next message block (line 9). If the current message block is of type **`M_DATA`** and has no data in its buffer (lines 10–11), then we remove the message block from the message (line 12) and free it (line 13). In either case, we continue with the next message block (line 15), until we have checked every message block in the message.

```
 1  void
 2  xxclean(mp)
 3      mblk_t *mp;
 4  {
 5      mblk_t *tmp;
 6      mblk_t *nmp;

 7      tmp = mp;
 8      while (tmp) {
 9              nmp = tmp->b_next;
10              if ((tmp->b_datap->db_type == M_DATA) &&
11                  (tmp->b_rptr == tmp->b_wptr)) {
12                      mp = rmvb(mp, tmp);
13                      freeb(tmp);
```

```
                }
                tmp = nmp;
        }
}
```

NOTICES

Availability

SVR4.0, SVR4.1ES, SVR4MP, SVR4.2

Portability

All processors

Interface

Driver-Kernel (STREAMS)

Commitment

Level 1

rmvq (D3)

NAME

rmvq – remove a message from a queue

SYNOPSIS

```
#include <sys/stream.h>
#include <sys/ddi.h>

void rmvq(queue_t *q, mblk_t *mp);
```

Arguments

q Pointer to the queue containing the message to be removed.

mp Pointer to the message to remove.

DESCRIPTION

rmvq removes the message specified by *mp* from the queue specified by *q*.

Return Values

None

USAGE

A message can be removed from anywhere in a queue. To prevent modules and drivers from having to deal with the internals of message linkage on a queue, either **rmvq** or **getq**(D3) should be used to remove a message from a queue.

Level

Base or Interrupt.

Synchronization Constraints

Does not sleep.

Driver-defined basic locks, read/write locks, and sleep locks may be held across calls to this function.

The caller cannot have the stream frozen [see **freezestr**(D3)] when calling this function.

Warnings

mp must point to an existing message in the queue pointed to by *q*, or a system panic will occur.

Examples

See **insq**(D3) for an example of **rmvq**.

REFERENCES

freezestr(D3), **getq**(D3), **insq**(D3), **unfreezestr**(D3)

NOTICES

Availability

SVR4.0, SVR4.1ES, SVR4MP, SVR4.2

Portability

All processors

Interface

Driver-Kernel (STREAMS)

Commitment
Level 1

RW_ALLOC(D3)

NAME

RW_ALLOC – allocate and initialize a read/write lock

SYNOPSIS

```
#include <sys/types.h>
#include <sys/kmem.h>
#include <sys/ksynch.h>
#include <sys/ddi.h>

rwlock_t *RW_ALLOC(uchar_t hierarchy, pl_t min_pl, lkinfo_t *lkinfop,
        int flag);
```

Arguments

hierarchy Hierarchy value which asserts the order in which this lock will be acquired relative to other basic and read/write locks.

min_pl Minimum priority level argument which asserts the minimum priority level that will be passed in with any attempt to acquire this lock [see **RW_RDLOCK**(D3) and **RW_WRLOCK**(D3)].

lkinfop Pointer to a **lkinfo**(D4) structure.

flag Specifies whether the caller is willing to sleep waiting for memory.

DESCRIPTION

RW_ALLOC dynamically allocates and initializes an instance of a read/write lock. The lock is initialized to the unlocked state.

If *flag* is set to **KM_SLEEP**, the caller will sleep if necessary until sufficient memory is available. If *flag* is set to **KM_NOSLEEP**, the caller will not sleep, but **RW_ALLOC** will return **NULL** if sufficient memory is not immediately available.

Return Values

Upon successful completion, **RW_ALLOC** returns a pointer to the newly allocated lock. If **KM_NOSLEEP** is specified and sufficient memory is not immediately available, **RW_ALLOC** returns a **NULL** pointer.

USAGE

hierarchy Argument

This assertion is enforced by the system when the driver is compiled with the **DEBUG** and **_LOCKTEST** compilation options defined. *hierarchy* must be within the range 1 through 32 inclusive and must be chosen such that locks are normally acquired in order of increasing *hierarchy* number. In other words, when acquiring a read/write lock using any function other than **RW_TRYRDLOCK**(D3) or **RW_TRYWRLOCK**(D3), the lock being acquired must have a *hierarchy* value that is strictly greater than the *hierarchy* values associated with all locks currently held by the calling context.

Implementations of lock testing may differ in whether they assume a separate range of *hierarchy* values for each interrupt priority level or a single range that spans all interrupt priority levels. In order to be portable across different implementations, drivers which may acquire locks at more than one interrupt priority level should define the *hierarchy* among those locks such that the *hierarchy* is strictly increasing with increasing priority level. For example, if M is the maximum *hierarchy* value defined for any lock that may be acquired at priority level N, then M + 1 should be the minimum hierarchy value defined for any lock that may be acquired at any priority level greater than N.

min_pl Argument

This assertion may be enforced by the system when the driver is compiled with the **DEBUG** and **_LOCKTEST** compilation options defined. Implementations which do not require that the interrupt priority level be raised during lock acquisition may choose not to enforce the *min_pl* assertion, even when the appropriate compilation options have been defined. The valid values for this argument are as follows:

plbase	Block no interrupts
pltimeout	Block functions scheduled by itimeout and dtimeout
pldisk	Block disk device interrupts
plstr	Block STREAMS interrupts
plhi	Block all interrupts

The notion of a *min_pl* assumes a defined order of priority levels. The following partial order is defined:

```
plbase < pltimeout <= pldisk,plstr <= plhi
```

The ordering of **pldisk** and **plstr** relative to each other is not defined.

Setting a given priority level will block interrupts associated with that level as well as any levels that are defined to be less than or equal to the specified level. In order to be portable a driver should not acquire locks at different priority levels where the relative order of those priority levels is not defined above.

The *min_pl* argument should specify a priority level that would be sufficient to block out any interrupt handler that might attempt to acquire this lock. In addition, potential deadlock problems involving multiple locks should be considered when defining the *min_pl* value. For example, if the normal order of acquisition of locks A and B (as defined by the lock hierarchy) is to acquire A first and then B, lock B should never be acquired at a priority level less than the *min_pl* for lock A. Therefore, the *min_pl* for lock B should be greater than or equal to the *min_pl* for lock A.

Note that the specification of *min_pl* with a **RW_ALLOC** call does not actually cause any interrupts to be blocked upon lock acquisition, it simply asserts that subsequent **RW_RDLOCK/RW_WRLOCK** calls to acquire this lock will pass in a priority level at least as great as *min_pl*.

lkinfop Argument

The **lk_name** member of the **lkinfo** structure points to a character string defining a name that will be associated with the lock for the purpose of statistics gathering. The name should begin with the driver prefix and should be unique to the lock or group of locks for which the driver wishes to collect a uniquely identifiable set of statistics (that is, if a given name is shared by a group of locks, the statistics of individual locks within the group will not be uniquely identifiable). There are no flags defined within the **lk_flags** member of the **lkinfo** structure for use with **RW_ALLOC**.

The *lkinfop* pointer is recorded in a statistics buffer along with the lock statistics when the driver is compiled with the **DEBUG** and **_MPSTATS** compilation options defined. A given **lkinfo** structure may be shared among multiple read/write locks and basic locks but a **lkinfo** structure may not be shared between a read/write lock and a sleep lock. The caller must ensure that the **lk_flags** and **lk_pad** members of the **lkinfo** structure are zeroed out before passing it to **RW_ALLOC**.

flag Argument

Under the _MPSTATS compilation option, if KM_NOSLEEP is specified and sufficient memory can be immediately allocated for the lock itself but not for an accompanying statistics buffer, RW_ALLOC will return a pointer to the allocated lock but individual statistics will not be collected for the lock.

Level

Base only if *flag* is set to KM_SLEEP.

Initialization, Base or Interrupt if *flag* is set to KM_NOSLEEP.

Synchronization Constraints

May sleep if flag is set to KM_SLEEP.

Driver-defined basic locks and read/write locks may be held across calls to this function if *flag* is KM_NOSLEEP but may not be held if *flag* is KM_SLEEP.

Driver-defined sleep locks may be held across calls to this function regardless of the value of *flag*.

REFERENCES

RW_DEALLOC(D3), RW_RDLOCK(D3), RW_TRYRDLOCK(D3), RW_TRYWRLOCK(D3), RW_UNLOCK(D3), RW_WRLOCK(D3), lkinfo(D4)

NOTICES

Availability

SVR4MP

Portability

All processors

Interface

Driver-Kernel

Commitment

Level 1

NAME

RW_DEALLOC – deallocate an instance of a read/write lock

SYNOPSIS

```
#include <sys/types.h>
#include <sys/ksynch.h>
#include <sys/ddi.h>

void RW_DEALLOC(rwlock_t *lockp);
```

Arguments

lockp Pointer to the read/write lock to be deallocated.

DESCRIPTION

RW_DEALLOC deallocates the read/write lock specified by *lockp*.

Return Values

None

USAGE

Attempting to deallocate a lock that is currently locked or is being waited for is an error and will result in undefined behavior.

Level

Base or Interrupt.

Synchronization Constraints

Does not sleep.

Driver-defined locks, read/write locks (other than the one being deallocated), and sleep locks may be held across calls to this function.

REFERENCES

RW_ALLOC(D3), RW_RDLOCK(D3), RW_TRYRDLOCK(D3), RW_TRYWRLOCK(D3), RW_UNLOCK(D3), RW_WRLOCK(D3)

NOTICES

Availability

SVR4MP

Portability

All processors

Interface

Driver-Kernel

Commitment

Level 1

RW_RDLOCK(D3)

NAME

RW_RDLOCK – acquire a read/write lock in read mode

SYNOPSIS

```
#include <sys/types.h>
#include <sys/ksynch.h>
#include <sys/ddi.h>

pl_t RW_RDLOCK(rwlock_t *lockp, pl_t pl);
```

Arguments

lockp Pointer to the read/write lock to be acquired.

pl The interrupt priority level to be set while the lock is held by the caller.

DESCRIPTION

RW_RDLOCK sets the interrupt priority level in accordance with the value specified by *pl* (if required by the implementation) and acquires the lock specified by *lockp* in read mode. If the lock cannot be acquired immediately in read mode, the caller will wait until the lock is available in read mode. (A read/write lock is available in read mode when the lock is not held by any context or when the lock is held by one or more readers and there are no waiting writers). It is implementation defined whether the caller will block during the wait. Some implementations may cause the caller to spin for the duration of the wait, while on others the caller may block at some point.

Return Values

Upon acquiring the lock, RW_RDLOCK returns the previous interrupt priority level (plbase – plhi).

USAGE

Because some implementations require that interrupts that might attempt to acquire the lock be blocked on the processor on which the lock is held, portable drivers must specify a *pl* value that is sufficient to block out any interrupt handler that might attempt to acquire this lock. See the description of the *min_pl* argument to RW_ALLOC(D3) for additional discussion and a list of the valid values for *pl*. Implementations which do not require that the interrupt priority level be raised during lock acquisition may choose to ignore this argument.

When called from interrupt level, the *pl* argument must not specify a priority level below the level at which the interrupt handler is running.

Level

Base or Interrupt.

Synchronization Constraints

Driver-defined sleep locks may be held across calls to this function.

Driver-defined basic locks and read/write locks may be held across calls to this function subject to the hierarchy and recursion restrictions described below.

Warnings

Read/write locks are not recursive. A call to LOCK attempting to acquire a lock that is currently held by the calling context may result in deadlock.

Calls to **RW_RDLOCK** should honor the ordering defined by the lock hierarchy [see **RW_ALLOC**(D3)] in order to avoid deadlock.

REFERENCES

RW_ALLOC(D3), **RW_DEALLOC**(D3), **RW_TRYRDLOCK**(D3), **RW_TRYWRLOCK**(D3), **RW_UNLOCK**(D3), **RW_WRLOCK**(D3)

NOTICES

Availability

SVR4MP

Portability

All processors

Interface

Driver-Kernel

Commitment

Level 1

RW_TRYRDLOCK(D3)

NAME

RW_TRYRDLOCK – try to acquire a read/write lock in read mode

SYNOPSIS

```
#include <sys/types.h>
#include <sys/ksynch.h>
#include <sys/ddi.h>

pl_t RW_TRYRDLOCK(rwlock_t *lockp, pl_t pl);
```

Arguments

lockp Pointer to the read/write lock to be acquired.

pl The interrupt priority level to be set while the lock is held by the caller.

DESCRIPTION

If the lock specified by *lockp* is immediately available in read mode (there is not a writer holding the lock and there are no waiting writers), the **RW_TRYRDLOCK** function sets the interrupt priority level in accordance with the value specified by *pl* (if required by the implementation) and acquires the lock in read mode. If the lock is not immediately available in read mode, **RW_TRYLOCK** returns without acquiring the lock.

Return Values

If the lock is acquired, **RW_TRYRDLOCK** returns the previous interrupt priority level (**plbase** – **plhi**). If the lock is not acquired the value **invpl** is returned.

USAGE

Because some implementations require that interrupts that might attempt to acquire the lock be blocked on the processor on which the lock is held, portable drivers must specify a *pl* value that is sufficient to block out any interrupt handler that might attempt to acquire this lock. See the description of the *min_pl* argument to RW_ALLOC(D3) for additional discussion and a list of the valid values for *pl*. Implementations which do not require that the interrupt priority level be raised during lock acquisition may choose to ignore this argument.

When called from interrupt level, the *pl* argument must not specify a priority level below the level at which the interrupt handler is running.

RW_TRYRDLOCK may be used to acquire a lock in a different order from the order defined by the lock hierarchy.

Level

Base or Interrupt.

Synchronization Constraints

Does not sleep.

Driver-defined basic locks, read/write locks, and sleep locks may be held across calls to this function.

REFERENCES

RW_ALLOC(D3), RW_DEALLOC(D3), RW_RDLOCK(D3), RW_TRYWRLOCK(D3), RW_UNLOCK(D3), RW_WRLOCK(D3)

NOTICES

Availability
SVR4MP

Portability
All processors

Interface
Driver-Kernel

Commitment
Level 1

RW_TRYWRLOCK(D3)

NAME

RW_TRYWRLOCK – try to acquire a read/write lock in write mode

SYNOPSIS

```
#include <sys/types.h>
#include <sys/ksynch.h>
#include <sys/ddi.h>

pl_t RW_TRYWRLOCK(rwlock_t *lockp, pl_t pl);
```

Arguments

lockp Pointer to the read/write lock to be acquired.

pl The interrupt priority level to be set while the lock is held by the caller.

DESCRIPTION

If the lock specified by *lockp* is immediately available in write mode (no context is holding the lock in read mode or write mode), the **RW_TRYWRLOCK** function sets the interrupt priority level in accordance with the value specified by *pl* (if required by the implementation) and acquires the lock in write mode. If the lock is not immediately available in write mode, **RW_TRYWRLOCK** returns without acquiring the lock.

Return Values

If the lock is acquired, **RW_TRYWRLOCK** returns the previous interrupt priority level (**plbase** – **plhi**). If the lock is not acquired the value **invpl** is returned.

USAGE

Because some implementations require that interrupts that might attempt to acquire the lock be blocked on the processor on which the lock is held, portable drivers must specify a *pl* value that is sufficient to block out any interrupt handler that might attempt to acquire this lock. See the description of the *min_pl* argument to **RW_ALLOC**(D3) for additional discussion and a list of the valid values for *pl*. Implementations which do not require that the interrupt priority level be raised during lock acquisition may choose to ignore this argument.

When called from interrupt level, the *pl* argument must not specify a priority level below the level at which the interrupt handler is running. **RW_TRYWRLOCK** may be used to acquire a lock in a different order from the order defined by the lock hierarchy.

Level

Base or Interrupt.

Synchronization Constraints

Does not sleep.

Driver-defined basic locks, read/write locks, and sleep locks may be held across calls to this function.

REFERENCES

RW_ALLOC(D3), **RW_DEALLOC**(D3), **RW_RDLOCK**(D3), **RW_TRYRDLOCK**(D3), **RW_UNLOCK**(D3), **RW_WRLOCK**(D3)

NOTICES

Availability

SVR4MP

Portability

All processors

Interface

Driver-Kernel

Commitment

Level 1

RW_UNLOCK(D3)

NAME

RW_UNLOCK – release a read/write lock

SYNOPSIS

```
#include <sys/types.h>
#include <sys/ksynch.h>
#include <sys/ddi.h>

void RW_UNLOCK(rwlock_t *lockp, pl_t pl);
```

Arguments

lockp Pointer to the read/write lock to be released.

pl The interrupt priority level to be set after releasing the lock.

DESCRIPTION

The RW_UNLOCK function releases the read/write lock specified by *lockp* and then sets the interrupt priority level in accordance with the value specified by *pl* (if required by the implementation). If the lock is held in read mode by multiple contexts, RW_UNLOCK releases the lock in the calling context but does not cause the lock to be released in any other context.

Return Values

None

USAGE

See the description of the *min_pl* argument to RW_ALLOC(D3) for a list of the valid values for *pl*.

If lock calls are not being nested or if the caller is unlocking in the reverse order that locks were acquired, the *pl* argument will typically be the value that was returned from the corresponding call to acquire the lock. The caller may need to specify a different value for *pl* if nested locks are released in some order other than the reverse order of acquisition, so as to ensure that the interrupt priority level is kept sufficiently high to block interrupt code that might attempt to acquire locks which are still held. Although portable drivers must always specify an appropriate *pl* argument, implementations which do not require that the interrupt priority level be raised during lock acquisition may choose to ignore this argument.

Level

Base or Interrupt.

Synchronization Constraints

Does not sleep.

Driver-defined basic locks, read/write locks, and sleep locks may be held across calls to this function.

REFERENCES

RW_ALLOC(D3), RW_DEALLOC(D3), RW_RDLOCK(D3), RW_TRYRDLOCK(D3), RW_TRYWRLOCK(D3), RW_WRLOCK(D3)

NOTICES

Availability

SVR4MP

Portability
All processors

Interface
Driver-Kernel

Commitment
Level 1

RW_WRLOCK(D3)

NAME

`RW_WRLOCK` – acquire a read/write lock in write mode

SYNOPSIS

```
#include <sys/types.h>
#include <sys/ksynch.h>
#include <sys/ddi.h>

pl_t RW_WRLOCK(rwlock_t *lockp, pl_t pl);
```

Arguments

lockp Pointer to the read/write lock to be acquired.

pl The interrupt priority level to be set while the lock is held by the caller.

DESCRIPTION

The `RW_WRLOCK` function sets the interrupt priority level in accordance with the value specified by *pl* (if required by the implementation) and acquires the lock specified by *lockp* in write mode. If the lock cannot be acquired immediately in write mode, the caller will wait until the lock is available in write mode. (A read/write lock is available in write mode when the lock is not held by any context). It is implementation defined whether the caller will block during the wait. Some implementations may cause the caller to spin for the duration of the wait, while on other implementations the caller may block at some point.

Return Values

Upon acquiring the lock, `RW_WRLOCK` returns the previous interrupt priority level (`plbase` - `plhi`).

USAGE

Because some implementations require that interrupts that might attempt to acquire the lock be blocked on the processor on which the lock is held, portable drivers must specify a *pl* value that is sufficient to block out any interrupt handler that might attempt to acquire this lock. See the description of the *min_pl* argument to `RW_ALLOC`(D3) for additional discussion and a list of the valid values for *pl*. Implementations which do not require that the interrupt priority level be raised during lock acquisition may choose to ignore this argument.

When called from interrupt level, the *pl* argument must not specify a priority level below the level at which the interrupt handler is running.

Level

Base or Interrupt.

Synchronization Constraints

Driver-defined sleep locks may be held across calls to this function.

Driver-defined basic locks and read/write locks may be held across calls to this function subject to the hierarchy and recursion restrictions described below.

Warnings

Read/write locks are not recursive. A call to `LOCK` attempting to acquire a lock that is currently held by the calling context may result in deadlock.

Calls to **RW_WRLOCK** should honor the ordering defined by the lock hierarchy [see **RW_ALLOC**(D3)] in order to avoid deadlock.

REFERENCES

RW_ALLOC(D3), **RW_DEALLOC**(D3), **RW_RDLOCK**(D3), **RW_TRYRDLOCK**(D3), **RW_TRYWRLOCK**(D3), **RW_UNLOCK**(D3)

NOTICES

Availability

SVR4MP

Portability

All processors

Interface

Driver-Kernel

Commitment

Level 1

SAMESTR (D3)

NAME

`SAMESTR` – test if next queue is of the same type

SYNOPSIS

```
#include <sys/stream.h>
#include <sys/ddi.h>

int SAMESTR(queue_t *q);
```

Arguments

q Pointer to the queue.

DESCRIPTION

The **SAMESTR** function checks whether the next queue in a stream (if it exists) is of the same type as the current queue (that is, both are read queues or both are write queues).

Return Values

SAMESTR returns 1 if the next queue is of the same type as the current queue. It returns 0 if the next queue does not exist or if it is not of the same type.

USAGE

This function can be used to determine the point in a STREAMS-based pipe where a read queue is linked to a write queue.

In multithreaded drivers, the *q* argument may not reference **q_next** (for example, an argument of **q->q_next** is erroneous in a multithreaded driver and is disallowed by the DDI/DKI).

Level

Base or Interrupt.

Synchronization Constraints

Does not sleep.

Driver-defined basic locks, read/write locks, and sleep locks may be held across calls to this function.

The caller cannot have the stream frozen [see **freezestr**(D3)] when calling this function.

Examples

See the **put**(D2) manual page for an example of **SAMESTR**.

REFERENCES

`OTHERQ`(D3)

NOTICES

Availability

SVR4.0, SVR4.1ES, SVR4MP, SVR4.2

Portability

All processors

Interface

Driver-Kernel (STREAMS)

Commitment
Level 1

sleep (D3)

NAME

`sleep` – suspend process execution pending occurrence of an event

SYNOPSIS

```
#include <sys/types.h>
#include <sys/param.h>
#include <sys/ddi.h>

int sleep(caddr_t event, int priority);
```

Arguments

event Kernel address signifying an event for which the caller wishes to wait.

priority A hint to the scheduling policy as to the relative priority the caller wishes to be assigned while running in the kernel after waking up.

DESCRIPTION

sleep suspends execution of a process to await certain events such as reaching a known system state in hardware or software. For instance, when a process wants to read a device and no data are available, the driver may need to call **sleep** to wait for data to become available before returning. This causes the kernel to suspend execution of the process that called **sleep** and schedule another process. The process that called **sleep** can be resumed by a call to the **wakeup** function with the same *event* specified as that used to call **sleep**.

Return Values

sleep returns `0` if the caller woke up because of a call to **wakeup**, or if the caller was stopped by a job control signal and subsequently continued. If the sleep is interrupted by a signal that does not cause the process to be stopped and the *priority* argument includes the **PCATCH** flag, the **sleep** call returns a value of `1`. If the sleep is interrupted by a signal and the **PCATCH** flag is not set, the process will **longjmp** out of the driver and the **sleep** call will never return to the calling code.

USAGE

event Argument

The address has no significance except that the same address must be passed to **wakeup**(D3) to resume the sleeping process. The address used should be the address of a kernel data structure associated with the driver, or one of the driver's own data structures. Use of arbitrary addresses not associated with a private data structure can result in conflict with other, unrelated **sleep** and **wakeup** operations in the kernel.

priority Argument

Valid values for *priority* are `0` through `39` inclusive. In general, a lower value will result in more favorable scheduling although the exact semantic of the priority argument is specific to the scheduling class of the caller, and some scheduling classes may choose to ignore the argument for the purposes of assigning a scheduling priority.

In addition to the scheduling semantics, the value of the *priority* argument determines whether the sleep may be interrupted by signals. If the value of *priority* is less than or equal to the value of the constant **PZERO** (defined in **sys/param.h**), the sleeping process will not be awakened by a signal. If the value of *priority* is greater than **PZERO** and the **PCATCH** bit flag is **OR**ed into the *priority* argument, the process will wake up prematurely (without a call to **wakeup**) upon receipt of a non-ignored, non-held signal and will normally return **1** to the calling code. If *priority* is greater than **PZERO** and **PCATCH** is not set, the **sleep** function will **longjmp** out of the driver upon receipt of a signal and will never return to the caller.

General Considerations

If a process were to sleep while it is manipulating global data inside a critical section of driver code, it would be possible for another process to execute base level driver code which manipulates the same data while the first process was sleeping, resulting in data corruption. A driver should not sleep inside such a critical section unless it takes explicit steps to prevent concurrent access to the data (for example, the driver could implement its own locking protocol to protect the data).

The value for *priority* should be selected based on whether or not a **wakeup** is certain to occur as well as the importance of the driver and of any resources that the driver will hold after waking up. If the driver is holding or waiting for a critical kernel resource or is otherwise crucial to the performance of the system, and the corresponding call to **wakeup** is guaranteed to happen, the driver should specify a *priority* argument less than or equal to **PZERO**. If the driver is less performance critical or it is possible that the **wakeup** may not occur, the driver should specify a *priority* argument greater than **PZERO**.

If there is any driver state that needs to be cleaned up in the event of a signal, the driver should **OR** the **PCATCH** flag in with the priority argument. Typical items that need cleaning up are locked data structures that should be unlocked or dynamically allocated resources that need to be freed. When **PCATCH** is specified **sleep** will normally return a **1** in the event of a signal, indicating that the calling routine should perform any necessary cleanup and then return.

If **sleep** is called from the driver **strategy**(D2) routine, the caller should **OR** the *priority* argument with **PCATCH** or select a *priority* of **PZERO** or less.

Level

Base only.

Synchronization Constraints

Can sleep.

REFERENCES

wakeup(D3)

NOTICES

Availability

SVR4.0, SVR4.1ES, SVR4.2

Portability

All processors

Interface

Driver-Kernel

Commitment

Level 2 effective October 8, 1991

Future Directions

In SVR4MP, **sleep** is replaced by **SV_WAIT_SIG**(D3).

NAME

SLEEP_ALLOC – allocate and initialize a sleep lock

SYNOPSIS

```
#include <sys/types.h>
#include <sys/kmem.h>
#include <sys/ksynch.h>
#include <sys/ddi.h>

sleep_t *SLEEP_ALLOC(int arg, lkinfo_t *lkinfop, int flag);
```

Arguments

arg Reserved for future use (must be equal to zero).

lkinfop Pointer to a **lkinfo**(D4) structure. The **lk_name** member of the **lkinfo** structure points to a character string defining a name that will be associated with the lock for the purpose of statistics gathering.

flag Specifies whether the caller is willing to sleep waiting for memory.

DESCRIPTION

SLEEP_ALLOC dynamically allocates and initializes an instance of a sleep lock. The lock is initialized to the unlocked state.

If *flag* is set to **KM_SLEEP**, the caller will sleep if necessary until sufficient memory is available. If *flag* is set to **KM_NOSLEEP**, the caller will not sleep, but **SLEEP_ALLOC** will return **NULL** if sufficient memory is not immediately available.

Return Values

Upon successful completion, **SLEEP_ALLOC** returns a pointer to the newly allocated lock. If **KM_NOSLEEP** is specified and sufficient memory is not immediately available, **SLEEP_ALLOC** returns a **NULL** pointer.

USAGE

lkinfop Argument

The name should begin with the driver prefix and should be unique to the lock or group of locks for which the driver wishes to collect a uniquely identifiable set of statistics (that is, if a given name is shared by a group of locks, the statistics of individual locks within the group will not be uniquely identifiable). The only bit flag currently specified within the **lk_flags** member of the **lkinfo** structure is the **LK_NOSTATS** flag, which specifies that statistics are not to be collected for this particular lock under the **_MPSTATS** compilation option. If the **LK_NOSTATS** flag is not specified, statistics will be collected for this lock under the **_MPSTATS** compilation option, and the *lkinfop* pointer will be recorded in the statistics buffer along with the lock statistics.

A given **lkinfo** structure may be shared among multiple sleep locks but a **lkinfo** structure may not be shared between a sleep lock and a basic or read/write lock. The caller must ensure that the **lk_pad** member of the **lkinfo** structure is zeroed out before passing it to **SLEEP_ALLOC**.

flag Argument

Under the **_MPSTATS** compilation option, if **KM_NOSLEEP** is specified and sufficient memory can be immediately allocated for the lock itself but not for an accompanying statistics buffer, **SLEEP_ALLOC** will return a pointer to the allocated lock but individual statistics will not be collected for the lock.

SLEEP_ALLOC (D3)

Level

Base only if *flag* is set to **KM_SLEEP**.

Initialization, Base or Interrupt if *flag* is set to **KM_NOSLEEP**.

Synchronization Constraints

May sleep if flag is set to **KM_SLEEP**.

Driver-defined basic locks and read/write locks may be held across calls to this function if *flag* is **KM_NOSLEEP** but may not be held if *flag* is **KM_SLEEP**.

Driver-defined sleep locks may be held across calls to this function regardless of the value of *flag*.

REFERENCES

SLEEP_DEALLOC(D3), **SLEEP_LOCK**(D3), **SLEEP_LOCK_SIG**(D3), **SLEEP_LOCKAVAIL**(D3), **SLEEP_LOCKOWNED**(D3), **SLEEP_TRYLOCK**(D3), **SLEEP_UNLOCK**(D3), **lkinfo**(D4)

NOTICES

Availability

SVR4MP

Portability

All processors

Interface

Driver-Kernel

Commitment

Level 1

NAME

`SLEEP_DEALLOC` – deallocate an instance of a sleep lock

SYNOPSIS

```
#include <sys/ksynch.h>
#include <sys/ddi.h>

void SLEEP_DEALLOC(sleep_t *lockp);
```

Arguments

lockp Pointer to the sleep lock to be deallocated.

DESCRIPTION

`SLEEP_DEALLOC` deallocates the lock specified by *lockp*.

Return Values

None

USAGE

Attempting to deallocate a lock that is currently locked or is being waited for is an error and results in undefined behavior.

Level

Base or Interrupt.

Synchronization Constraints

Does not sleep.

Driver-defined basic locks, read/write locks, and sleep locks (other than the one being deallocated), may be held across calls to this function.

REFERENCES

`SLEEP_ALLOC`(D3), `SLEEP_LOCK`(D3), `SLEEP_LOCK_SIG`(D3), `SLEEP_LOCKAVAIL`(D3), `SLEEP_LOCKOWNED`(D3) `SLEEP_TRYLOCK`(D3), `SLEEP_UNLOCK`(D3)

NOTICES

Availability

SVR4MP

Portability

All processors

Interface

Driver-Kernel

Commitment

Level 1

SLEEP_LOCK(D3)

NAME

`SLEEP_LOCK` – acquire a sleep lock

SYNOPSIS

```
#include <sys/ksynch.h>
#include <sys/ddi.h>

void SLEEP_LOCK(sleep_t *lockp, int priority);
```

Arguments

lockp Pointer to the sleep lock to be acquired.

priority A hint to the the scheduling policy as to the relative priority the caller wishes to be assigned while running in the kernel after waking up.

DESCRIPTION

`SLEEP_LOCK` acquires the sleep lock specified by *lockp*. If the lock is not immediately available, the caller is put to sleep (the caller's execution is suspended and other processes may be scheduled) until the lock becomes available to the caller, at which point the caller wakes up and returns with the lock held.

The caller will not be interrupted by signals while sleeping inside `SLEEP_LOCK`.

Return Values

None

USAGE

priority Argument

Valid values for *priority* are:

`pridisk`	Priority appropriate for disk driver.
`prinet`	Priority appropriate for network driver.
`pritty`	Priority appropriate for terminal driver.
`pritape`	Priority appropriate for tape driver.
`prihi`	High priority.
`primed`	Medium priority.
`prilo`	Low priority.

Drivers may use these values to request a priority appropriate to a given type of device or to request a priority that is high, medium or low relative to other activities within the kernel.

It is also permissible to specify positive or negative offsets from the values defined above. Positive offsets result in more favorable priority. The maximum allowable offset in all cases is 3 (for example, `pridisk+3` and `pridisk-3` are valid values but `pridisk+4` and `pridisk-4` are not valid). Offsets can be useful in defining the relative importance of different locks or resources that may be held by a given driver. In general, a higher relative priority should be used when the caller is attempting to acquire a highly contended lock or resource, or when the caller is already holding one or more locks or kernel resources upon entry to `SLEEP_LOCK`.

The exact semantic of the *priority* argument is specific to the scheduling class of the caller, and some scheduling classes may choose to ignore the argument for the purposes of assigning a scheduling priority.

Level

Base only.

Synchronization Constraints

Can sleep.

Driver-defined basic locks and read/write locks may not be held across calls to this function.

Driver-defined sleep locks may be held across calls to this function subject to the recursion restrictions described below.

Warnings

Sleep locks are not recursive. A call to **SLEEP_LOCK** attempting to acquire a lock that is currently held by the calling context will result in deadlock.

REFERENCES

SLEEP_ALLOC(D3), **SLEEP_DEALLOC**(D3), **SLEEP_LOCK_SIG**(D3), **SLEEP_LOCKAVAIL**(D3), **SLEEP_LOCKOWNED**(D3), **SLEEP_TRYLOCK**(D3), **SLEEP_UNLOCK**(D3)

NOTICES

Availability

SVR4MP

Portability

All processors

Interface

Driver-Kernel

Commitment

Level 1

SLEEP_LOCKAVAIL(D3)

NAME

`SLEEP_LOCKAVAIL` – query whether a sleep lock is available

SYNOPSIS

```
#include <sys/types.h>
#include <sys/ksynch.h>
#include <sys/ddi.h>

bool_t SLEEP_LOCKAVAIL(sleep_t *lockp);
```

Arguments

lockp Pointer to the sleep lock to be queried.

DESCRIPTION

`SLEEP_LOCKAVAIL` returns an indication of whether the sleep lock specified by *lockp* is currently available.

Return Values

`SLEEP_LOCKAVAIL` returns `TRUE` (a non-zero value) if the lock was available or `FALSE` (zero) if the lock was not available.

USAGE

The state of the lock may change and the value returned may no longer be valid by the time the caller sees it. The caller is expected to understand that this is ''stale data'' and is either using it as a heuristic or has arranged for the return value to be meaningful by other means.

Level

Base or Interrupt.

Synchronization Constraints

Does not sleep.

Driver-defined basic locks, read/write locks, and sleep locks may be held across calls to this function.

REFERENCES

`SLEEP_ALLOC`(D3), `SLEEP_DEALLOC`(D3), `SLEEP_LOCK`(D3), `SLEEP_LOCK_SIG`(D3), `SLEEP_LOCKOWNED`(D3), `SLEEP_TRYLOCK`(D3), `SLEEP_UNLOCK`(D3)

NOTICES

Availability

SVR4MP

Portability

All processors

Interface

Driver-Kernel

Commitment

Level 1

NAME

SLEEP_LOCKOWNED – query whether a sleep lock is held by the caller

SYNOPSIS

```
#include <sys/types.h>
#include <sys/ksynch.h>
#include <sys/ddi.h>

bool_t SLEEP_LOCKOWNED(sleep_t *lockp);
```

Arguments

lockp Pointer to the sleep lock to be queried.

DESCRIPTION

SLEEP_LOCKOWNED returns an indication of whether the sleep lock specified by *lockp* is currently held by the calling context.

Return Values

SLEEP_LOCKOWNED returns **TRUE** (a non-zero value) if the lock is currently held by the calling context or **FALSE** (zero) if the lock is not currently held by the calling context.

USAGE

SLEEP_LOCKOWNED is intended for use only within **ASSERT** expressions [see **ASSERT**(D3)] and other code that is conditionally compiled under the **DEBUG** compilation option. The **SLEEP_LOCKOWNED** function is only defined under the **DEBUG** compilation option, and therefore calls to **SLEEP_LOCKOWNED** will not compile when **DEBUG** is not defined.

Level

Base only.

Synchronization Constraints

Does not sleep.

Driver-defined basic locks, read/write locks, and sleep locks may be held across calls to this function.

REFERENCES

SLEEP_ALLOC(D3), **SLEEP_DEALLOC**(D3), **SLEEP_LOCK**(D3), **SLEEP_LOCK_SIG**(D3), **SLEEP_LOCKAVAIL**(D3), **SLEEP_TRYLOCK**(D3), **SLEEP_UNLOCK**(D3)

NOTICES

Availability

SVR4MP

Portability

All processors

Interface

Driver-Kernel

Commitment

Level 1

SLEEP_LOCK_SIG (D3)

NAME

SLEEP_LOCK_SIG – acquire a sleep lock

SYNOPSIS

```
#include <sys/types.h>
#include <sys/ksynch.h>
#include <sys/ddi.h>

bool_t SLEEP_LOCK_SIG(sleep_t *lockp, int priority);
```

Arguments

lockp Pointer to the sleep lock to be acquired.

priority A hint to the the scheduling policy as to the relative priority the caller wishes to be assigned while running in the kernel after waking up.

DESCRIPTION

SLEEP_LOCK_SIG acquires the sleep lock specified by *lockp*. If the lock is not immediately available, the caller is put to sleep (the caller's execution is suspended and other processes may be scheduled) until the lock becomes available to the caller, at which point the caller wakes up and returns with the lock held.

SLEEP_LOCK_SIG may be interrupted by a signal, in which case it may return early without acquiring the lock.

If the function is interrupted by a job control stop signal (e.g. **SIGSTOP**, **SIGTSTP**, **SIGTTIN**, **SIGTTOU**) which results in the caller entering a stopped state, the **SLEEP_LOCK_SIG** function will transparently retry the lock operation upon continuing (the call will not return without the lock).

If the function is interrupted by a signal other than a job control stop signal, or by a job control stop signal that does not result in the caller stopping (because the signal has a non-default disposition), the **SLEEP_LOCK_SIG** call will return early without acquiring the lock.

Return Values

SLEEP_LOCK_SIG returns **TRUE** (a non-zero value) if the lock is successfully acquired or **FALSE** (zero) if the function returned early because of a signal.

USAGE

priority Argument

Valid values for *priority* are:

`pridisk`	Priority appropriate for disk driver.
`prinet`	Priority appropriate for network driver.
`pritty`	Priority appropriate for terminal driver.
`pritape`	Priority appropriate for tape driver.
`prihi`	High priority.
`primed`	Medium priority.
`prilo`	Low priority.

Drivers may use these values to request a priority appropriate to a given type of device or to request a priority that is high, medium or low relative to other activities within the kernel.

It is also permissible to specify positive or negative offsets from the values defined above. Positive offsets result in more favorable priority. The maximum allowable offset in all cases is 3 (that is, **pridisk+3** and **pridisk-3** are valid values but **pridisk+4** and **pridisk-4** are not valid). Offsets can be useful in defining the relative importance of different locks or resources that may be held by a given driver. In general, a higher relative priority should be used when the caller is attempting to acquire a highly contended lock or resource, or when the caller is already holding one or more locks or kernel resources upon entry to **SLEEP_LOCK_SIG**.

The exact semantic of the *priority* argument is specific to the scheduling class of the caller, and some scheduling classes may choose to ignore the argument for the purposes of assigning a scheduling priority.

Level

Base only.

Synchronization Constraints

Can sleep.

Driver-defined basic locks and read/write locks may not be held across calls to this function.

Driver-defined sleep locks may be held across calls to this function subject to the recursion restrictions described below.

Warnings

Sleep locks are not recursive. A call to **SLEEP_LOCK_SIG** attempting to acquire a lock that is currently held by the calling context will result in deadlock.

REFERENCES

SLEEP_ALLOC(D3), **SLEEP_DEALLOC**(D3), **SLEEP_LOCK**(D3), **SLEEP_LOCKAVAIL**(D3), **SLEEP_LOCKOWNED**(D3), **SLEEP_TRYLOCK**(D3), **SLEEP_UNLOCK**(D3), **signals**(D5)

NOTICES

Availability

SVR4MP

Portability

All processors

Interface

Driver-Kernel

Commitment

Level 1

SLEEP_TRYLOCK(D3)

NAME

SLEEP_TRYLOCK – try to acquire a sleep lock

SYNOPSIS

```
#include <sys/types.h>
#include <sys/ksynch.h>
#include <sys/ddi.h>

bool_t SLEEP_TRYLOCK(sleep_t *lockp);
```

Arguments

lockp Pointer to the sleep lock to be acquired.

DESCRIPTION

If the lock specified by *lockp* is immediately available (can be acquired without sleeping) the **SLEEP_TRYLOCK** function acquires the lock. If the lock is not immediately available, **SLEEP_TRYLOCK** returns without acquiring the lock.

Return Values

SLEEP_TRYLOCK returns **TRUE** (a non-zero value) if the lock is successfully acquired or **FALSE** (zero) if the lock is not acquired.

USAGE

Level

Base only.

Synchronization Constraints

Does not sleep.

Driver-defined basic locks, read/write locks, and sleep locks may be held across calls to this function.

REFERENCES

SLEEP_ALLOC(D3), **SLEEP_DEALLOC**(D3), **SLEEP_LOCK**(D3), **SLEEP_LOCK_SIG**(D3), **SLEEP_LOCKAVAIL**(D3), **SLEEP_LOCKOWNED**(D3), **SLEEP_UNLOCK**(D3)

NOTICES

Availability

SVR4MP

Portability

All processors

Interface

Driver-Kernel

Commitment

Level 1

NAME

`SLEEP_UNLOCK` – release a sleep lock

SYNOPSIS

```
#include <sys/ksynch.h>
#include <sys/ddi.h>

void SLEEP_UNLOCK(sleep_t *lockp);
```

Arguments

lockp Pointer to the sleep lock to be released.

DESCRIPTION

`SLEEP_UNLOCK` releases the sleep lock specified by *lockp*. If there are processes waiting for the lock, one of the waiting processes is awakened.

Return Values

None

USAGE

Level

Base or Interrupt.

Synchronization Constraints

Does not sleep.

Driver-defined basic locks, read/write locks, and sleep locks may be held across calls to this function.

REFERENCES

`SLEEP_ALLOC`(D3), `SLEEP_DEALLOC`(D3), `SLEEP_LOCK`(D3), `SLEEP_LOCK_SIG`(D3), `SLEEP_LOCKAVAIL`(D3), `SLEEP_LOCKOWNED`(D3), `SLEEP_TRYLOCK`(D3)

NOTICES

Availability

SVR4MP

Portability

All processors

Interface

Driver-Kernel

Commitment

Level 1

spl (D3)

NAME

`spl` – block/allow interrupts on a processor

SYNOPSIS

```
#include &lt;sys/ddi.h&gt;

pl_t splbase();
pl_t spltimeout();
pl_t spldisk();
pl_t splstr();
pl_t spltty();
pl_t splhi();
pl_t spl0();
pl_t spl7();

pl_t splx(pl_t oldlevel);
```

Arguments

oldlevel	Last set priority value (only **splx** has an input argument).

DESCRIPTION

The **spl** functions block or allow servicing of interrupts on the processor on which the function is called.

Return Values

All **spl** functions return the previous priority level.

USAGE

Hardware devices are assigned to interrupt priority levels depending on the type of device. Each **spl** function which blocks interrupts is associated with some machine dependent interrupt priority level and will prevent interrupts occurring at or below this priority level from being serviced on the processor on which the **spl** function is called.

On a multiprocessor system, interrupts may be serviced by more than one processor and, therefore, use of a **spl** function alone is not sufficient to prevent interrupt code from executing and manipulating driver data structures during a critical section. Drivers that must prevent execution of interrupt-level code in order to protect the integrity of their data should use basic locks or read/write locks for this purpose [see **LOCK_ALLOC**(D3) or **RW_ALLOC**(D3)].

The **spl** functions include the following:

`splbase`	Block no interrupts. Should only be used by base-level code that knows it is not nested within any section of protected critical code.
`spltimeout`	Block functions scheduled by `itimeout` and `dtimeout`.
`spldisk`	Block disk device interrupts.
`splstr`	Block STREAMS interrupts.
`spltty`	Used by a TTY driver to protect critical code. `spltty` is mapped to `splstr`.

`splhi` Block all interrupts. Can be used in any type of driver to mask out all interrupts including the clock, and should be used very sparingly.

`slp0` Equivalent to **splbase**.

`slp7` On Intel processors, equivalent to **splhi**.

To ensure driver portability, the named **spl** functions (such as **splbase** or **spltimeout**) should be used whenever possible. The numbered **spl** functions (**spl0** and **spl7**) should be used only when an interrupt priority level must be set to a specific value.

Calling a given **spl** function will block interrupts specified for that function as well as interrupts at equal and lower levels. The notion of low vs. high levels assumes a defined order of priority levels. The following partial order is defined:

```
splbase <= spltimeout <= spldisk,splstr <= splhi
```

The ordering of **spldisk** and **splstr** relative to each other is not defined.

When setting a given priority level, the previous level returned should be saved and **splx**, **UNLOCK**(D3), or **RW_UNLOCK**(D3) should be used as appropriate to restore this level.

Interrupt-level code must never lower the interrupt priority level below the level at which the interrupt handler was entered. For example, if an interrupt handler is entered at the priority level associated with **spldisk**, the handler must not call **spltimeout**.

Level

Base or Interrupt.

Synchronization Considerations

All **spl** functions do not sleep.

Driver-defined basic locks and read/write locks may be held across calls to these functions, but the **spl** call must not cause the priority level to be lowered below the level associated with the lock.

Driver-defined sleep locks may be held across calls to these functions.

REFERENCES

LOCK(D3), **LOCK_ALLOC**(D3), **RW_RDLOCK**(D3), **RW_UNLOCK**(D3), **RW_WRLOCK**(D3), **RW_ALLOC**(D3)

Availability

SVR4.0, SVR4.1ES, SVR4MP, SVR4.2

Portability

The named **spl** functions are supported on all processors. Implementation of the numbered **spl** functions may vary across processors.

Interface

Driver-Kernel (STREAMS)

Commitment

Level 1

strcat (D3)

NAME

`strcat` – concatenate strings

SYNOPSIS

```
#include <sys/types.h>
#include <sys/ddi.h>

char *strcat(char *sptr1, const char *sptr2)
```

Arguments

The arguments *sptr1* and *sptr2* each point to strings, and each string is an array of characters terminated by a null-character.

DESCRIPTION

The function **strcat** appends a copy of the string pointed to by *sptr2* including the terminating null-character to the end of the string pointed to by *sptr1*. The initial character in the string pointed to by *sptr2* replaces the null-character at the end of the string pointed to by *sptr1*.

The function **strcat** alters *sptr1* without checking for overflow of the array pointed to by *sptr1*. If copying takes place between strings that overlap, the behavior is undefined.

Return Values

The function **strcat** returns the value of *sptr1*, which points to the null-terminated result.

USAGE

Character movement is performed differently in different implementations; thus, overlapping moves may yield surprises.

The **<sys/ddi.h>** header file declares this function.

Level

Base or Interrupt.

Synchronization Constraints

Does not sleep.

Driver-defined basic locks, read/write locks, and sleep locks may be held across calls to this function.

REFERENCES

bcmp(D3), **bcopy**(D3), **strncat**(D3)

NOTICES

Availability

SVR4.2

Portability

All processors

Interface

General-purpose utility

Commitment

Level 1

NAME

strcpy – copy a string

SYNOPSIS

```
#include <sys/types.h>
#include <sys/ddi.h>

char *strcpy (char *sptr1, const char *sptr2)
```

Arguments

The arguments *sptr1* and *sptr2* each point to strings, and each string is an array of characters terminated by a null-character.

DESCRIPTION

The function **strcpy** copies the string pointed to by *sptr2* (including the terminating null-character) into the string pointed to by *sptr1*, stopping after the null-character has been copied, and returns the string pointed to by *sptr1*.

The function **strcpy** alters *sptr1* without checking for overflow of the string pointed to by *sptr1*. If copying takes place between strings that overlap, the behavior is undefined.

Return Values

The function **strcpy** returns the value of *sptr1*, which points to the null-terminated result.

USAGE

Character movement is performed differently in different implementations; thus, overlapping moves may yield surprises.

The **<sys/ddi.h>** header file declares this function.

Level

Base or Interrupt.

Synchronization Constraints

Does not sleep.

Driver-defined basic locks, read/write locks, and sleep locks may be held across calls to this function.

REFERENCES

bcmp(D3), **bcopy**(D3), **strncpy**(D3)

NOTICES

Availability

SVR4.2

Portability

All processors

Interface

General-purpose utility

Commitment

Level 1

strlen (D3)

NAME

strlen – determine the length of a string

SYNOPSIS

```
#include <sys/types.h>
#include <sys/ddi.h>

size_t strlen (const char *sptr)
```

Arguments

The argument *sptr* points to a string, which is an array of characters terminated by a null-character.

DESCRIPTION

The function **strlen** determines the length of characters in the string pointed to by *sptr*.

Return Values

The function **strlen** returns the number of characters, not including the terminating null-character, in the string pointed to by *sptr*.

USAGE

Character movement is performed differently in different implementations; thus, overlapping moves may yield surprises.

The **<sys/ddi.h>** header file declares this function.

Level

Base or Interrupt.

Synchronization Constraints

Does not sleep.

Driver-defined basic locks, read/write locks, and sleep locks may be held across calls to this function.

REFERENCES

bcmp(D3), **bcopy**(D3), **strncat**(D3), **strncmp**(D3), **strncpy**(D3)

NOTICES

Availability

SVR4.2

Portability

All processors

Interface

General-purpose utility

Commitment

Level 1

NAME

strlog – submit messages to the **log** driver

SYNOPSIS

```
#include <sys/types.h>
#include <sys/stream.h>
#include <sys/strlog.h>
#include <sys/log.h>
#include <sys/ddi.h>

int strlog(short mid, short sid, char level, ushort_t flags,
      char *fmt, ... /* args */);
```

Arguments

mid	Identification number of the module or driver submitting the message.
sid	Identification number for a particular minor device.
level	Tracing level for selective screening of low priority messages.
flags	Bitmask of flags indicating message purpose.
fmt	**printf**(3S) style format string.
args	Zero or more arguments to **printf**.

DESCRIPTION

strlog submits formatted messages to the **log**(7) driver. The messages can be retrieved with the **getmsg**(2) system call. The *flags* argument specifies the type of the message and where it is to be sent. **strace**(1M) receives messages from the **log** driver and sends them to the standard output. **strerr**(1M) receives error messages from the **log** driver and appends them to a file called **/var/adm/streams/error.***mm-dd*, where *mm-dd* identifies the date of the error message.

Return Values

strlog returns **0** if the message is not seen by all the readers, **1** otherwise.

USAGE

flags Argument

Valid values for *flags* are:

SL_ERROR	Message is for error logger.
SL_TRACE	Message is for tracing.
SL_CONSOLE	Message is for console logger.
SL_NOTIFY	If **SL_ERROR** is also set, mail copy of message to system administrator.
SL_FATAL	Modifier indicating error is fatal.
SL_WARN	Modifier indicating error is a warning.
SL_NOTE	Modifier indicating error is a notice.

fmt Argument

The **%s**, **%e**, **%g**, and **%G** formats are not allowed.

printf args

`args` can specify a maximum of `NLOGARGS`, currently three.

Level

Base or Interrupt.

Synchronization Constraints

Does not sleep.

Driver-defined basic locks, read/write locks, and sleep locks may be held across calls to this function.

REFERENCES

`log`(7), `strace`(1M), `strerr`(1M)

NOTICES

Availability

SVR4.0, SVR4.1ES, SVR4MP, SVR4.2

Portability

All processors

Interface

Driver-Kernel (STREAMS)

Commitment

Level 1

NAME

`strncat` – concatenate strings appending a specified number of characters

SYNOPSIS

```
#include <sys/types.h>
#include <sys/ddi.h>
```

`char *strncat (char *`*sptr1*`, const char *`*sptr2*`, size_t` *nchr*`)`

Arguments

The arguments *sptr1* and *sptr2* each point to strings, and each string is an array of characters terminated by a null-character.

DESCRIPTION

The function **strncat** appends to the end of the string pointed to by *sptr1* at most *nchr* characters from the string pointed to by *sptr2* (a null-character and characters that follow it are not appended). The initial character of *sptr2* replaces the null-character at the end of *sptr1*. Thus, the maximum number of characters that can end up in the string pointed to by *sptr1* equals **strlen(sptr1)+nchr+1** [see **strlen**(D3)].

The function **strncat** alters *sptr1* without checking for overflow of the string pointed to by *sptr1*. If copying takes place between strings that overlap, the behavior is undefined.

Return Values

The function **strncat** returns the value of *sptr1*, which points to the null-terminated result.

USAGE

Character movement is performed differently in different implementations; thus, overlapping moves may yield surprises.

The **<sys/ddi.h>** header file declares this function.

Level

Base or Interrupt.

Synchronization Constraints

Does not sleep.

Driver-defined basic locks, read/write locks, and sleep locks may be held across calls to this function.

REFERENCES

bcmp(D3), **bcopy**(D3), **strcat**(D3), **strlen**(D3)

NOTICES

Availability

SVR4.2

Portability

All processors

Interface

General-purpose utility

Commitment

Level 1

NAME

strncmp – compare strings using a specified number of characters

SYNOPSIS

```
#include <sys/types.h>
#include <sys/ddi.h>

int strncmp (char *sptr1, const char *sptr2, size_t nchr)
```

Arguments

The arguments *sptr1* and *sptr2* each point to strings, and each string is an array of characters terminated by a null-character.

DESCRIPTION

The function **strncmp** compares at most *nchr* characters (characters that follow a null-character are not compared) of the string pointed to by *sptr1* to the string pointed to by *sptr2*.

Return Values

The function **strncmp** returns an integer value less than, equal to or greater than zero to indicate whether at most *nchr* characters of the possibly null-terminated string pointed to by *sptr1* is lexicographically less than, equal to or greater than the possibly null-terminated string pointed to by *sptr2*.

USAGE

The function **strncmp** uses native character comparison. The sign of the value returned when one of the characters has its high-order bit set is implementation-dependent.

The **<sys/ddi.h>** header file declares this function.

Level

Base or Interrupt.

Synchronization Constraints

Does not sleep.

Driver-defined basic locks, read/write locks, and sleep locks may be held across calls to this function.

REFERENCES

bcmp(D3), **bcopy**(D3), **strcmp**(D3), **strlen**(D3)

NOTICES

Availability

SVR4.2

Portability

All processors

Interface

General-purpose utility

Commitment

Level 1

strncpy (D3)

NAME

`strncpy` – copy a string using a specified number of characters

SYNOPSIS

```
#include <sys/types.h>
#include <sys/ddi.h>

char *strncpy (char *sptr1, const char *sptr2, size_t nchr)
```

Arguments

The arguments *sptr1* and *sptr2* each point to strings, and each string is an array of characters terminated by a null-character unless the length of *sptr2* is *nchr* or more.

DESCRIPTION

The function **strncpy** copies exactly *nchr* characters from the string pointed to by *sptr2* into the string pointed to by *sptr1*. The function **strncpy** refrains from copying any characters following a null-character; **strncpy** truncates *sptr2* or adds null-characters to *sptr1* if necessary until *nchr* characters in all are copied from *sptr2* into *sptr1*. The result is not null-terminated if the length of *sptr2* is *nchr* or more.

A terminating null-character is always appended to the result; thus, if there is no null-character in the initial *nchr* characters of the string pointed to by *sptr2*, the result is not terminated by a null-character.

The function **strncpy** alters *sptr1* without checking for overflow of the array pointed to by *sptr1*. If copying takes place between strings that overlap, the behavior is undefined.

Return Values

The function **strcmp** returns the value of *sptr1*, which points to an string of *nchr* characters in length.

USAGE

Character movement is performed differently in different implementations; thus, overlapping moves may yield surprises.

The **<sys/ddi.h>** header file declares this function.

Level

Base or Interrupt.

Synchronization Constraints

Does not sleep.

Driver-defined basic locks, read/write locks, and sleep locks may be held across calls to this function.

REFERENCES

bcmp(D3), **bcopy**(D3), **strcpy**(D3), **strlen**(D3)

NOTICES

Availability

SVR4.2

Portability

All processors

Interface

General-purpose utility

Commitment

Level 1

strqget (D3)

NAME

strqget – get information about a queue or band of the queue

SYNOPSIS

```
#include <sys/types.h>
#include <sys/stream.h>
#include <sys/ddi.h>

int strqget(queue_t *q, qfields_t what, uchar_t pri, long *valp);
```

Arguments

q	Pointer to the queue.
what	The field of the queue about which to return information.
pri	Priority band of the queue about which to obtain information.
valp	Pointer to the memory location where the value is to be stored.

DESCRIPTION

strqget gives drivers and modules a way to get information about a queue or a particular priority band of a queue without directly accessing STREAMS data structures.

Return Values

On success, 0 is returned. An error number is returned on failure. The actual value of the requested field is returned through the reference parameter, *valp*.

USAGE

Valid *what* values are:

QHIWAT	High water mark of the specified priority band.
QLOWAT	Low water mark of the specified priority band.
QMAXPSZ	Maximum packet size of the specified priority band.
QMINPSZ	Minimum packet size of the specified priority band.
QCOUNT	Number of bytes of data in messages in the specified priority band.
QFIRST	Pointer to the first message in the specified priority band.
QLAST	Pointer to the last message in the specified priority band.
QFLAG	Flags for the specified priority band [see **queue**(D4)].

Level

Base or Interrupt.

Synchronization Constraints

Does not sleep.

Driver-defined basic locks, read/write locks, and sleep locks may be held across calls to this function.

The caller must have the stream frozen [see **freezestr**(D3)] when calling this function.

REFERENCES

`freezestr`(D3), `queue`(D4), `strqset`(D3), `unfreezestr`(D3)

NOTICES

Availability

SVR4.0, SVR4.1ES, SVR4MP, SVR4.2

Portability

All processors

Interface

Driver-Kernel (STREAMS)

Commitment

Level 1

strqset (D3)

NAME

`strqset` – change information about a queue or band of the queue

SYNOPSIS

```
#include <sys/types.h>
#include <sys/stream.h>
#include <sys/ddi.h>

int strqset(queue_t *q, qfields_t what, uchar_t pri, long val);
```

Arguments

q	Pointer to the queue.
what	The field of the queue to change.
pri	Priority band of the queue to be changed.
val	New value for the field to be changed.

DESCRIPTION

`strqset` gives drivers and modules a way to change information about a queue or a particular priority band of a queue without directly accessing STREAMS data structures.

Return Values

On success, `0` is returned. An error number is returned on failure.

USAGE

Valid values for *what* are:

`QHIWAT`	High water mark of the specified priority band.
`QLOWAT`	Low water mark of the specified priority band.
`QMAXPSZ`	Maximum packet size of the specified priority band.
`QMINPSZ`	Minimum packet size of the specified priority band.

Level

Base or Interrupt.

Synchronization Constraints

Does not sleep.

Driver-defined basic locks, read/write locks, and sleep locks may be held across calls to this function.

The caller must have the stream frozen [see `freezestr`(D3)] when calling this function.

REFERENCES

`freezestr`(D3), `queue`(D4), `strqget`(D3) `unfreezestr`(D3),

NOTICES

Availability

SVR4.0, SVR4.1ES, SVR4MP, SVR4.2

Portability

All processors

Interface

Driver-Kernel (STREAMS)

Commitment

Level 1

SV_ALLOC(D3)

NAME

SV_ALLOC – allocate and initialize a synchronization variable

SYNOPSIS

```
#include <sys/kmem.h>
#include <sys/ksynch.h>
#include <sys/ddi.h>

sv_t *SV_ALLOC(int flag);
```

Arguments

flag Specifies whether the caller is willing to sleep waiting for memory.

DESCRIPTION

SV_ALLOC dynamically allocates and initializes an instance of a synchronization variable. If *flag* is set to **KM_SLEEP**, the caller will sleep if necessary until sufficient memory is available. If *flag* is set to **KM_NOSLEEP**, the caller will not sleep, but **SV_ALLOC** will return **NULL** if sufficient memory is not immediately available.

Return Values

Upon successful completion, **SV_ALLOC** returns a pointer to the newly allocated synchronization variable. If **KM_NOSLEEP** is specified and sufficient memory is not immediately available, **SV_ALLOC** returns a **NULL** pointer.

USAGE

Level

Base only if *flag* is set to **KM_SLEEP**.

Initialization, Base or Interrupt if *flag* is set to **KM_NOSLEEP**.

Synchronization Constraints

May sleep if flag is set to **KM_SLEEP**.

Driver-defined basic locks and read/write locks may be held across calls to this function if *flag* is **KM_NOSLEEP** but may not be held if *flag* is **KM_SLEEP**.

Driver-defined sleep locks may be held across calls to this function regardless of the value of *flag*.

REFERENCES

SV_BROADCAST(D3), **SV_DEALLOC**(D3), **SV_SIGNAL**(D3), **SV_WAIT**(D3), **SV_WAIT_SIG**(D3)

NOTICES

Availability

SVR4MP

Portability

All processors

Interface

Driver-Kernel

Commitment

Level 1

NAME

`SV_BROADCAST` – wake up all processes sleeping on a synchronization variable

SYNOPSIS

```
#include <sys/ksynch.h>
#include <sys/ddi.h>

void SV_BROADCAST(sv_t *svp, int flags);
```

Arguments

svp Pointer to the synchronization variable to be broadcast signaled.

flags Bit field for flags. No flags are currently defined for use in drivers and the *flags* argument must be set to zero.

DESCRIPTION

If one or more processes are blocked on the synchronization variable specified by *svp*, `SV_BROADCAST` wakes up all of the blocked processes.

Return Values

None

USAGE

Note that synchronization variables are stateless, and therefore calls to `SV_BROADCAST` only affect processes currently blocked on the synchronization variable and have no effect on processes that block on the synchronization variable at a later time.

Level

Base or Interrupt.

Synchronization Constraints

Does not sleep.

Driver-defined basic locks, read/write locks, and sleep locks may be held across calls to this function.

REFERENCES

`SV_ALLOC`(D3), `SV_DEALLOC`(D3), `SV_SIGNAL`(D3), `SV_WAIT`(D3), `SV_WAIT_SIG`(D3)

NOTICES

Availability

SVR4MP

Portability

All processors

Interface

Driver-Kernel

Commitment

Level 1

SV_DEALLOC(D3)

NAME

SV_DEALLOC – deallocate an instance of a synchronization variable

SYNOPSIS

```
#include <sys/ksynch.h>
#include <sys/ddi.h>

void SV_DEALLOC(sv_t *svp);
```

Arguments

lockp Pointer to the synchronization variable to be deallocated.

DESCRIPTION

SV_DEALLOC deallocates the synchronization variable specified by *svp*.

Return Values

None

USAGE

Level

Base or Interrupt.

Synchronization Constraints

Does not sleep.

Driver-defined basic locks, read/write locks, and sleep locks may be held across calls to this function.

REFERENCES

SV_ALLOC(D3), SV_BROADCAST(D3), SV_SIGNAL(D3), SV_WAIT(D3), SV_WAIT_SIG(D3)

NOTICES

Availability

SVR4MP

Portability

All processors

Interface

Driver-Kernel

Commitment

Level 1

NAME

SV_SIGNAL – wake up one process sleeping on a synchronization variable

SYNOPSIS

```
#include <sys/ksynch.h>
#include <sys/ddi.h>

void SV_SIGNAL(sv_t *svp, int flags);
```

Arguments

svp Pointer to the synchronization variable to be signaled.

flags Bit field for flags. No flags are currently defined for use in drivers and the *flags* argument must be set to zero.

DESCRIPTION

If one or more processes are blocked on the synchronization variable specified by *svp*, **SV_SIGNAL** wakes up a single blocked process.

Return Values

None

USAGE

Note that synchronization variables are stateless, and therefore calls to **SV_SIGNAL** only affect processes currently blocked on the synchronization variable and have no effect on processes that block on the synchronization variable at a later time.

Level

Base or Interrupt.

Synchronization Constraints

Does not sleep.

Driver-defined basic locks, read/write locks, and sleep locks may be held across calls to this function.

REFERENCES

SV_ALLOC(D3), **SV_BROADCAST**(D3), **SV_DEALLOC**(D3), **SV_WAIT**(D3), **SV_WAIT_SIG**(D3)

NOTICES

Availability

SVR4MP

Portability

All processors

Interface

Driver-Kernel

Commitment

Level 1

SV_WAIT(D3)

NAME

`SV_WAIT` – sleep on a synchronization variable

SYNOPSIS

```
#include <sys/types.h>
#include <sys/ksynch.h>
#include <sys/ddi.h>
```

```
void SV_WAIT(sv_t *svp, int priority, lock_t *lkp);
```

Arguments

svp — Pointer to the synchronization variable on which to sleep.

priority — A hint to the the scheduling policy as to the relative priority the caller wishes to be assigned while running in the kernel after waking up.

lkp — Pointer to a basic lock which must be locked when **`SV_WAIT`** is called. The basic lock is released when the calling process goes to sleep, as described below.

DESCRIPTION

`SV_WAIT` causes the calling process to go to sleep (the caller's execution is suspended and other processes may be scheduled) waiting for a call to **`SV_SIGNAL`**(D3) or **`SV_BROADCAST`**(D3) for the synchronization variable specified by *svp*.

Return Values

None

USAGE

priority Argument

Valid values for *priority* are:

`pridisk`	Priority appropriate for disk driver.
`prinet`	Priority appropriate for network driver.
`pritty`	Priority appropriate for terminal driver.
`pritape`	Priority appropriate for tape driver.
`prihi`	High priority.
`primed`	Medium priority.
`prilo`	Low priority.

Drivers may use these values to request a priority appropriate to a given type of device or to request a priority that is high, medium or low relative to other activities within the kernel.

It is also permissible to specify positive or negative offsets from the values defined above. Positive offsets result in more favorable priority. The maximum allowable offset in all cases is 3 (that is, **`pridisk+3`** and **`pridisk-3`** are valid values but **`pridisk+4`** and **`pridisk-4`** are not valid). Offsets can be useful in defining the relative importance of different locks or resources that may be held by a given driver. In general, a higher relative priority should be used when the caller is sleeping waiting for a highly contended kernel resource, or when the caller is already holding one or more locks or kernel resources upon entry to **`SV_WAIT`**.

The exact semantic of the *priority* argument is specific to the scheduling class of the caller, and some scheduling classes may choose to ignore the argument for the purposes of assigning a scheduling priority.

lkp Argument

The basic lock specified by *lkp* must be held by the caller upon entry. The lock is released and the interrupt priority level is set to **pl0** after the process is queued on the synchronization variable but prior to context switching to another process. When the caller returns from **SV_WAIT** the basic lock is not held and the interrupt priority level is equal to **pl0**.

General Considerations

The caller will not be interrupted by signals while sleeping inside **SV_WAIT**.

Level

Base only.

Synchronization Constraints

Can sleep.

Driver-defined basic locks (with the exception of the lock specified by *lkp*) and read/write locks may not be held across calls to this function.

Driver-defined sleep locks may be held across calls to this function.

REFERENCES

SV_ALLOC(D3), **SV_BROADCAST**(D3), **SV_DEALLOC**(D3), **SV_SIGNAL**(D3), **SV_WAIT_SIG**(D3)

NOTICES

Availability

SVR4MP

Portability

All processors

Interface

Driver-Kernel

Commitment

Level 1

SV_WAIT_SIG (D3)

NAME

SV_WAIT_SIG – sleep on a synchronization variable

SYNOPSIS

```
#include <sys/types.h>
#include <sys/ksynch.h>
#include <sys/ddi.h>

bool_t SV_WAIT_SIG(sv_t *svp, int priority, lock_t *lkp);
```

Arguments

svp Pointer to the synchronization variable on which to sleep.

priority A hint to the the scheduling policy as to the relative priority the caller wishes to be assigned while running in the kernel after waking up.

lkp Pointer to a basic lock which must be locked when `SV_WAIT_SIG` is called. The basic lock is released when the calling process goes to sleep, as described below.

DESCRIPTION

`SV_WAIT_SIG` causes the calling process to go to sleep (the caller's execution is suspended and other processes may be scheduled) waiting for a call to `SV_SIGNAL`(D3) or `SV_BROADCAST`(D3) for the synchronization variable specified by *svp*.

Return Values

`SV_WAIT_SIG` returns `TRUE` (a non-zero value) if the caller woke up because of a call to `SV_SIGNAL` or `SV_BROADCAST`, or if the caller was stopped and subsequently continued. `SV_WAIT_SIG` returns `FALSE` (zero) if the caller woke up and returned early because of a signal other than a job control stop signal, or by a job control stop signal that did not result in the caller stopping because the signal had a non-default disposition.

USAGE

priority Argument

Valid values for *priority* are:

`pridisk`	Priority appropriate for disk driver.
`prinet`	Priority appropriate for network driver.
`pritty`	Priority appropriate for terminal driver.
`pritape`	Priority appropriate for tape driver.
`prihi`	High priority.
`primed`	Medium priority.
`prilo`	Low priority.

Drivers may use these values to request a priority appropriate to a given type of device or to request a priority that is high, medium or low relative to other activities within the kernel.

It is also permissible to specify positive or negative offsets from the values defined above. Positive offsets result in more favorable priority. The maximum allowable offset in all cases is 3 (that is, `pridisk+3` and `pridisk-3` are valid values but

Interface
Driver-Kernel (STREAMS)

Commitment
Level 1

UNLOCK(D3)

NAME

UNLOCK – release a basic lock

SYNOPSIS

```
#include <sys/types.h>
#include <sys/ksynch.h>
#include <sys/ddi.h>

void UNLOCK(lock_t *lockp, pl_t pl);
```

Arguments

lockp Pointer to the basic lock to be released.

pl The interrupt priority level to be set after releasing the lock.

DESCRIPTION

UNLOCK releases the basic lock specified by *lockp* and then sets the interrupt priority level in accordance with the value specified by *pl* (if required by the implementation).

Return Values

None

USAGE

See the description of the *min_pl* argument to **LOCK_ALLOC**(D3) for a list of the valid values for *pl*. If lock calls are not being nested or if the caller is unlocking in the reverse order that locks were acquired, the *pl* argument will typically be the value that was returned from the corresponding call to acquire the lock. The caller may need to specify a different value for *pl* if nested locks are released in some order other than the reverse order of acquisition, so as to ensure that the interrupt priority level is kept sufficiently high to block interrupt code that might attempt to acquire locks which are still held.

Although portable drivers must always specify an appropriate *pl* argument, implementations which do not require that the interrupt priority level be raised during lock acquisition may choose to ignore this argument.

Level

Base or Interrupt.

Synchronization Constraints

Does not sleep.

Driver-defined basic locks, read/write locks, and sleep locks may be held across calls to this function.

REFERENCES

LOCK(D3), **LOCK_ALLOC**(D3), **LOCK_DEALLOC**(D3), **TRYLOCK**(D3)

NOTICES

Availability

SVR4MP

Portability

All processors

Interface

Driver-Kernel

Commitment

Level 1

untimeout(D3)

NAME

`untimeout` – cancel previous timeout request

SYNOPSIS

```
#include <sys/types.h>
#include <sys/ddi.h>

void untimeout(toid_t id);
```

Arguments

id Non-zero identifier returned from a prior call to **`timeout`**(D3) (singlethreaded drivers) or from a prior call to **`dtimeout`**(D3) or **`itimeout`**(D3) (multithreaded drivers).

DESCRIPTION

`untimeout` cancels the pending timeout request specified by *id*.

Return Values

None

USAGE

On uniprocssor systems, if **`untimeout`** is called while any function called by the pending timeout request is running, then there is no effect.

On multiprocssor systems, if **`untimeout`** is called while any function called by the pending timeout request is running, **`untimeout`** will not return until the function completes.

Note that any function that runs as a result of a call to **`timeout`** (or to **`dtimeout`** or **`itimeout`**) cannot use **`untimeout`** to cancel itself.

Level

Base or Interrupt, with the following exception on multiprocessor systems: For **`itimeout`**(D3) and **`dtimeout`**(D3), the **`untimeout`** can only be performed from interrupt levels less than, or equal to, the level specified when the function was scheduled.

Synchronization Constraints

Does not sleep.

Driver-defined basic locks, read/write locks, and sleep locks may not be held across calls to this function if these locks are contended by the function being canceled.

Examples

See **`unbufcall`**(D3) for an example of **`untimeout`**.

REFERENCES

`delay`(D3), **`dtimeout`**(D3), **`itimeout`**(D3), **`timeout`**(D3), **`unbufcall`**(D3)

NOTICES

Availability

SVR4.0, SVR4.1ES, SVR4MP, SVR4.2

Portability

All processors

Interface
Driver-Kernel

Commitment
Level 1

ureadc (D3)

NAME

ureadc – copy a character to space described by **uio**(D4) structure

SYNOPSIS

```
#include <sys/uio.h>
#include <sys/ddi.h>

int ureadc(int c, uio_t *uiop);
```

Arguments

c The character to be copied.

uiop Pointer to the **uio** structure.

DESCRIPTION

ureadc copies the character *c* into the space described by the **uio** structure pointed to by *uiop*.

The **uio_segflg** member of the **uio** structure specifies the type of space to which the copy is made. If **uio_segflg** is set to **UIO_SYSSPACE** the character is copied to a kernel address. If **uio_segflg** is set to **UIO_USERSPACE** the character is copied to a user address.

If the character is successfully copied, **ureadc** updates the appropriate members of the **uio** and **iovec**(D4) structures to reflect the copy (**uio_offset** and **iov_base** are incremented and **uio_resid** and **iov_len** are decremented).

Return Values

ureadc returns 0 on success or an error number on failure.

USAGE

Level

Base only if **uio_segflg** is set to **UIO_USERSPACE**.

Base or Interrupt if **uio_segflg** is set to **UIO_SYSSPACE**.

Synchronization Constraints

May sleep if **uio_segflg** is set to **UIO_USERSPACE**.

Driver-defined basic locks and read/write locks may be held across calls to this function if **uio_segflg** is **UIO_SYSSPACE** but may not be held if **uio_segflg** is **UIO_USERSPACE**.

Driver-defined sleep locks may be held across calls to this function regardless of the value of **uio_segflg**.

Warnings

When holding locks across calls to this function, multithreaded drivers must be careful to avoid creating a deadlock. During the data transfer, page fault resolution might result in another I/O to the same device. For example, this could occur if the driver controls the disk drive used as the swap device.

REFERENCES

iovec(D4), **uio**(D4), **uiomove**(D3), **uwritec**(D3)

NOTICES

Availability
SVR4.0, SVR4.1ES, SVR4MP, SVR4.2

Portability
All processors

Interface
Driver-Kernel

Commitment
Level 1

uwritec (D3)

NAME

uwritec – return a character from space described by **uio**(D4) structure

SYNOPSIS

```
#include <sys/uio.h>
#include <sys/ddi.h>

int uwritec(uio_t *uiop);
```

Arguments

uiop Pointer to the **uio** structure.

DESCRIPTION

uwritec copies a character from the space described by the **uio** structure pointed to by *uiop* and returns the character to the caller.

The **uio_segflg** member of the **uio** structure specifies the type of space from which the copy is made. If **uio_segflg** is set to **UIO_SYSSPACE** the character is copied from a kernel address. If **uio_segflg** is set to **UIO_USERSPACE** the character is copied from a user address.

If the character is successfully copied, **uwritec** updates the appropriate members of the **uio** and **iovec**(D4) structures to reflect the copy (**uio_offset** and **iov_base** are incremented and **uio_resid** and **iov_len** are decremented) and returns the character to the caller.

Return Values

If successful, **uwritec** returns the character. **-1** is returned if the space described by the **uio** structure is empty or there is an error.

USAGE

Level

Base only if **uio_segflg** is set to **UIO_USERSPACE**.

Base or Interrupt if **uio_segflg** is set to **UIO_SYSSPACE**.

Synchronization Constraints

May sleep if **uio_segflg** is set to **UIO_USERSPACE**.

Driver-defined basic locks and read/write locks may be held across calls to this function if **uio_segflg** is **UIO_SYSSPACE** but may not be held if **uio_segflg** is **UIO_USERSPACE**.

Driver-defined sleep locks may be held across calls to this function regardless of the value of **uio_segflg**.

Warnings

When holding locks across calls to this function, multithreaded drivers must be careful to avoid creating a deadlock. During the data transfer, page fault resolution might result in another I/O to the same device. For example, this could occur if the driver controls the disk drive used as the swap device.

REFERENCES

iovec(D4), **uio**(D4), **uiomove**(D3), **ureadc**(D3)

NOTICES

Availability

SVR4.0, SVR4.1ES, SVR4MP, SVR4.2

Portability

All processors

Interface

Driver-Kernel

Commitment

Level 1

vtop (D3)

NAME

vtop – convert virtual address to physical address

SYNOPSIS

```
#include <sys/types.h>
#include <sys/ddi.h>

paddr_t vtop(caddr_t vaddr, proc_t *p);
```

Arguments

vaddr Virtual address to convert.

p Pointer to the process structure used by **vtop** to locate the information tables used for memory management.

DESCRIPTION

vtop converts a virtual address to a physical address.

Return Values

On success, the physical address is returned. Otherwise, if there is no physical memory mapped to the virtual address, 0 is returned.

USAGE

When a driver receives a memory address from the kernel, that address is virtual. Generally, memory management is performed by the MMU. However, devices that access memory directly using physical DMA deal only with physical memory addresses. In such cases, the driver must provide the device with physical memory addresses.

p Argument

To indicate that the address is in kernel virtual space, *p* must be set to **NULL**. Block drivers that can transfer data directly in and out of user memory space must set *p* to the **b_proc** member of the **buf**(D4) structure. A pointer to the currently running process can be obtained by calling **drv_getparm**(D3) with the **UPROCP** parameter.

vaddr Argument

The only addresses that are safe to pass to **vtop** are those provided to drivers from the kernel through driver entry points, DDI/DKI kernel routines, DDI/DKI kernel data structures, or statically-allocated global driver variables.

Level

Initialization, Base or Interrupt.

Synchronization Constraints

Does not sleep.

Driver-defined basic locks, read/write locks, and sleep locks may be held across calls to this function.

Warnings

If *vaddr* specifies an invalid kernel address, a system panic will occur.

REFERENCES

btop(D3), **btopr**(D3), **buf**(D4), **drv_getparm**(D3), **ptob**(D3)

NOTICES

Availability

SVR4.0, SVR4.1ES, SVR4MP, SVR4.2

Portability

All processors

Interface

Driver-Kernel

Commitment

Level 1

wakeup (D3)

NAME

wakeup – resume suspended process execution

SYNOPSIS

```
#include <sys/types.h>
#include <sys/ddi.h>

void wakeup(caddr_t event);
```

Arguments

event Address that was passed to the corresponding call to **sleep**(D3) which caused the process to be suspended.

DESCRIPTION

wakeup awakens all processes sleeping on the address specified by *event* and makes them eligible for scheduling.

Return Values

None

USAGE

The same *event* argument must be used for corresponding calls to **sleep** and **wakeup**. It is recommended for code readability and for efficiency to have a one-to-one correspondence between events and **sleep** addresses.

Whenever a driver returns from a call to **sleep**, it should test to ensure that the event for which the driver slept actually occurred. There is an interval between the time the process that called **sleep** is awakened and the time it resumes execution where the state forcing the **sleep** may have been reentered. This can occur because all processes waiting for an event are awakened at the same time. The first process selected for execution by the scheduler usually gains control of the event. All other processes awakened should recognize that they cannot continue and should reissue the **sleep** call.

Level

Base or Interrupt.

Synchronization Constraints

Does not sleep.

REFERENCES

sleep(D3)

NOTICES

Availability

SVR4.0, SVR4.1ES, SVR4.2

Portability

All processors

Interface

Driver-Kernel

Commitment

Level 2 effective October 8, 1991

Future Directions

In SVR4MP, **wakeup** is replaced by **SV_BROADCAST**(D3).

WR(D3)

NAME

WR – get a pointer to the write queue

SYNOPSIS

```
#include <sys/stream.h>
#include <sys/ddi.h>

queue_t *WR(queue_t *q);
```

Arguments

q Pointer to the queue whose write queue is to be returned.

DESCRIPTION

The WR function accepts a queue pointer as an argument and returns a pointer to the write queue of the same module.

Return Values

The pointer to the write queue.

USAGE

Note that when WR is passed a write queue pointer as an argument, it returns a pointer to this write queue.

Level

Base or Interrupt.

Synchronization Constraints

Does not sleep.

Driver-defined basic locks, read/write locks, and sleep locks may be held across calls to this function.

Examples

In a STREAMS **open**(D2) routine, the driver or module is passed a pointer to the read queue. The driver or module can store a pointer to a private data structure in the **q_ptr** field of both the read and write queues if it needs to identify the data structures from its **put**(D2) or **srv**(D2) routines.

```
extern struct xxx_dev[];
...
xxxopen(queue_t *q, dev_t *devp, int flag, int sflag, cred_t *crp)
{
   ...
   q->q_ptr = (caddr_t)&xxx_dev[getminor(*devp)];
   WR(q)->q_ptr = (caddr_t)&xxx_dev[getminor(*devp)];
   ...
}
```

REFERENCES

OTHERQ(D3), RD(D3)

NOTICES

Availability

SVR4.0, SVR4.1ES, SVR4MP, SVR4.2

Portability

All processors

Interface

Driver-Kernel (STREAMS)

Commitment

Level 1

NAME

`intro` – introduction to kernel data structures

SYNOPSIS

```
#include <sys/types.h>
#include <sys/ddi.h>
```

DESCRIPTION

This section describes the kernel data structures a developer might need to use in a device driver.

USAGE

Driver developers should not declare arrays of these structures, as the size of any structure might change between releases. Two exceptions to this are the **iovec**(D4) and **uio**(D4) structures.

Drivers can only reference those structure members described on the manual page. The actual data structures may have additional structure members beyond those described, but drivers must not reference them.

Some structure members are flags fields that consist of a bitmask of flags. Drivers must never directly assign values to these structure members. Drivers should only set and clear flags they are interested in, since the actual implementation may contain unlisted flags.

Data structures that are "black boxes" to drivers are not described in this section. These structures are referenced on the manual pages where they are used. Drivers should not be written to use any of their structure members. Their only valid use is passing pointers to the structures to the particular kernel routines.

buf (D4)

NAME

buf – block I/O data transfer structure

SYNOPSIS

```
#include <sys/types.h>
#include <sys/proc.h>
#include <sys/buf.h>
#include <sys/ddi.h>
```

DESCRIPTION

The **buf** structure is the basic data structure for block I/O transfers.

USAGE

Each block I/O transfer has an associated buffer header. The header contains all the buffer control and status information. For drivers, the buffer header pointer is the sole argument to a block driver **strategy**(D2) routine. Do not depend on the size of the **buf** structure when writing a driver.

It is important to note that a buffer header may be linked in multiple lists simultaneously. Because of this, most of the members in the buffer header cannot be changed by the driver, even when the buffer header is in one of the drivers' work lists.

Buffer headers may be used by the system to describe a portion of the kernel data space for I/O for block drivers. Buffer headers are also used by the system for physical I/O for block drivers. In this case, the buffer describes a portion of user data space that is locked into memory [see **physiock**(D3)].

Block drivers often chain block requests so that overall throughput for the device is maximized. The **av_forw** and the **av_back** members of the **buf** structure can serve as link pointers for chaining block requests.

Structure Definitions

The **buf** structure contains the following members:

```
int             b_flags;          /* Buffer status */
struct buf      *b_forw;          /* Kernel/driver list link */
struct buf      *b_back;          /* Kernel/driver list link */
struct buf      *av_forw;         /* Driver work list link */
struct buf      *av_back;         /* Driver work list link */
unsigned int    b_bcount;         /* # of bytes to transfer */
union {
        caddr_t b_addr;           /* Buffer's virtual address */
} b_un;
daddr_t         b_blkno;          /* Block number on device */
unsigned int    b_resid;          /* # of bytes not transferred */
clock_t         b_start;          /* Request start time */
struct proc     *b_proc;          /* Process structure pointer */
long            b_bufsize;        /* Size of allocated buffer */
void            (*b_iodone)();    /* Function called by biodone */
int             b_error;          /* Expanded error field */
dev_t           b_edev;           /* Expanded dev field */
```

```
void            (*b_writestrat)();  /* Function called by bwrite */
void            *b_private;         /* For driver's use in SVR4MP only*/
```

The members of the buffer header available to test or set by a driver are described below:

b_flags is a bitmask that stores the buffer status and tells the driver whether to read from or write to the device. To avoid an error condition, the driver must never clear the **b_flags** member or modify its value, except by setting or clearing individual flag bits as described below.

Valid flags are as follows:

B_BUSY The buffer is in use. The driver may change this flag only if it acquired the buffer with **getrbuf**(D3), and if no I/O operation is in progress.

B_DONE The data transfer has completed. The driver should not change this flag [see **bioreset(D3)].**

B_ERROR The driver sets **B_ERROR** to indicate an error occurred during an I/O transfer. On systems where the **bioerror**(D3) function is available, drivers should not access this flag directly.

B_PAGEIO The buffer is being used in a paged I/O request. If **B_PAGEIO** is set, the **b_pages** field of the buffer header points to a list of page structures sorted by block location on the device. Also, the **b_un.b_addr** field of the buffer header is the offset into the first page of the page list. If **B_PAGEIO** is not set, the **b_pages** field of the buffer header is not used and the **b_un.b_addr** field of the buffer header contains the starting virtual address of the I/O request (in user address space if **B_PHYS** is set or kernel address space otherwise). The driver must not set or clear the **B_PAGEIO** flag.

B_PHYS The buffer header is being used for physical (direct) I/O to a user data area. The **b_un.b_addr** member contains the starting virtual address of the user data area. Note that **B_PHYS** and **B_PAGEIO** are never set simultaneously and must not be changed by the driver.

B_READ Data are to be read from the peripheral device into main memory. The driver may change this flag only if it acquired the buffer with **getrbuf**(D3), **geteblk**(D3), or **ngeteblk**(D3), and if no I/O operation is in progress.

B_WRITE Data are to be transferred from main memory to the peripheral device. **B_WRITE** is a pseudo-flag that occupies the same bit location as **B_READ**. **B_WRITE** cannot be directly tested; it is only detected as the absence of **B_READ** (**!(bp->b_flags&B_READ)**.)

b_forw and b_back may only be used by the driver if the buffer was acquired by the driver with the getrbuf routine. In that case, these members can be used to link the buffer into driver work lists.

av_forw and av_back can be used by the driver to link the buffer into driver work lists.

b_bcount specifies the number of bytes to be transferred for both paged and non-paged I/O requests. The driver may change this member.

b_un.b_addr is either the virtual address of the I/O request, or an offset into the first page of a page list depending on whether B_PAGEIO is set. If it is set, the b_pages field of the buffer header points to a sorted list of page structures and b_un.b_addr is the offset into the first page. If B_PAGEIO is not set, b_un.b_addr is the virtual address from which data are read or to which data are written. It represents a user virtual address if B_PHYS is set, or a kernel virtual address otherwise. The driver may change this member.

b_blkno identifies which logical block on the device is to be accessed. The driver may have to convert this logical block number to a physical location such as a cylinder, track, and sector of a disk. The driver may change this member only if it allocated the buffer via geteblk, ngeteblk, or getrbuf, and if no I/O operation is in progress.

b_resid indicates the number of bytes not transferred. The driver must set this member prior to calling biodone(D3).

b_start holds the time the I/O request was started. It is provided for the driver's use in calculating response time and is set by the driver. Its type, clock_t, is an integral type upon which direct integer calculations can be performed. It represents clock ticks.

b_proc contains the process structure address for the process requesting an unbuffered (direct) data transfer to or from a user data area (this member is set to NULL when the transfer is buffered). The process table entry is used to perform proper virtual to physical address translation of the b_un.b_addr member [see vtop(D3)]. The driver should not change this member.

b_bufsize contains the size in bytes of the allocated buffer. The driver may change this member only if it acquired the buffer with getrbuf, and if no I/O operation is in progress.

(*b_iodone) identifies a specific driver routine to be called by the system when the I/O is complete. If a routine is specified, the biodone(D3) routine does not return the buffer to the system. The driver may change this member if no I/O operation is in progress.

b_error holds an error code that can be passed as a return code from the driver routine. b_error is set in conjunction with the B_ERROR flag. The error codes are described in errnos(D5). On systems where the bioerror(D3) function is available, drivers should not access this member directly.

b_edev contains the external device number of the device. The driver may change this member only if it allocated the buffer via geteblk, ngeteblk, or getrbuf, and if no I/O operation is in progress.

(*b_writestrat) is valid on SVR4.2 systems only. It identifies the routine to be called from **bwrite()** when the system writes buffers. If a routine is specified, the routine assumes responsibility for calling the device's **strategy**(D2) routine. Only the creator of the buffer may change this member.

b_private is a private field for use by the driver on SVR4MP systems only. Note that on SVR4.0, SVR4.1ES and SVR4.2 systems, the **b_private** field is reserved for use by the kernel, and therefore should not be used by the driver. When used by an SVR4MP driver, the system does not interpret this field. The SVR4MP driver is free to use it in whatever manner it chooses. For example, the SVR4MP driver could use the field as part of a disk block sorting algorithm.

Warnings

Buffers are a shared resource within the kernel. Drivers should only read or write the members listed in this section in accordance with the rules given above. Drivers that attempt to use undocumented members of the **buf** structure risk corrupting data in the kernel and on the device.

DDI/DKI-conforming drivers may only use buffer headers that have been allocated using **geteblk**, **ngeteblk**, or **getrbuf**, or have been passed to the driver **strategy** routine.

REFERENCES

biodone(D3), **bioreset**(D3), **biowait**(D3), **brelse**(D3), **clrbuf**(D3), **freerbuf**(D3), **geteblk**(D3), **geterror**(D3), **getrbuf**(D3), **iovec**(D4), **ngeteblk**(D3), **physiock**(D3), **strategy**(D2), **uio**(D4)

NOTICES

Availability

SVR4.0, SVR4.1ES, SVR4MP, SVR4.2

Portability

All processors

Interface

Driver-Kernel

Commitment

Level 1

copyreq (D4)

NAME

copyreq – STREAMS transparent ioctl copy request structure

SYNOPSIS

```
#include <sys/stream.h>
#include <sys/ddi.h>
```

DESCRIPTION

The copyreq structure contains the information necessary to process transparent ioctls.

USAGE

The copyreq structure is used in M_COPYIN and M_COPYOUT messages. The module or driver usually converts an M_IOCTL or M_IOCDATA message into an M_COPYIN or M_COPYOUT message. The copyreq structure is thus overlaid on top of the iocblk(D4) or copyresp(D4) structure. The stream head guarantees that the message is large enough to contain the different structures.

Structure Definitions

The copyreq structure contains the following members:

```
int       cq_cmd;        /* ioctl command */
cred_t    *cq_cr;        /* user credentials */
uint_t    cq_id;         /* ioctl ID */
caddr_t   cq_addr;       /* copy buffer address */
uint_t    cq_size;       /* number of bytes to copy */
int       cq_flag;       /* for future use */
mblk_t    *cq_private;   /* module private data */
```

The cq_cmd field is the ioctl command, copied from the ioc_cmd field of the iocblk structure. If the same message is used, then the cq_cmd field directly overlays the ioc_cmd field (that is, it need not be copied.)

The cq_cr field contains a pointer to the user credentials. It is copied from the ioc_cr field of the iocblk structure. If the same message is used, then the cq_cr field directly overlays the ioc_cr field (that is, it need not be copied.)

The cq_id field is the ioctl ID, copied from the ioc_id field of the iocblk structure. It is used to uniquely identify the ioctl request in the stream. If the same message is used, then the cq_id field directly overlays the ioc_id field (that is, it need not be copied.)

For an M_COPYIN message, the cq_addr field contains the user address from which the data are to be copied. For an M_COPYOUT message, the cq_addr field contains the user address to which the data are to be copied. In both cases, the cq_size field contains the number of bytes to copy.

The cq_flag field is reserved for future use and should be set to 0 by the module or driver.

The cq_private field is a field set aside for use by the driver. It can be used to hold whatever state information is necessary to process the ioctl. It is copied to the cp_private field in the resultant M_IOCDATA message. When the M_COPYIN or M_COPYOUT message is freed, any message that cq_private refers to is not freed by the STREAMS subsystem. It is the responsibility of the module or driver to free it.

REFERENCES

`copyresp`(D4), `datab`(D4), `iocblk`(D4), `messages`(D5), `msgb`(D4)

NOTICES

Availability

SVR4.0, SVR4.1ES, SVR4MP, SVR4.2

Portability

All processors

Interface

Driver-Kernel (STREAMS)

Commitment

Level 1

copyresp (D4)

NAME

copyresp – STREAMS transparent **ioctl** copy response structure

SYNOPSIS

```
#include <sys/stream.h>
#include <sys/ddi.h>
```

DESCRIPTION

The **copyresp** structure contains information in response to a prior copy request necessary to continue processing transparent **ioctl**s.

USAGE

M_IOCDATA messages, generated by the stream head, contain the **copyresp** structure.

If an **M_IOCDATA** message is reused, any unused fields in the new message should be cleared.

Structure Definitions

The **copyresp** structure contains the following members:

```
int       cp_cmd;        /* ioctl command */
cred_t    *cp_cr;        /* user credentials */
uint_t    cp_id;         /* ioctl ID */
caddr_t   cp_rval;       /* status of request */
mblk_t    *cp_private;   /* module private data */
```

The **cp_cmd** field is the **ioctl** command, copied from the **cq_cmd** field of the **copyreq** structure.

The **cp_cr** field contains a pointer to the user credentials. It is copied from the **cq_cr** field of the **copyreq** structure.

The **cp_id** field is the **ioctl** ID, copied from the **cq_id** field of the **copyreq** structure. It is used to uniquely identify the **ioctl** request in the stream.

The **cq_rval** field contains the return value from the last copy request. If the request succeeded, it is set to 0. Otherwise, if it is non-zero, the request failed. On success, the module or driver should continue processing the **ioctl**. On failure, the module or driver should abort **ioctl** processing and free the message. No **M_IOCNAK** message need be generated.

The **cp_private** field is copied from the **cq_private** field of the **copyreq** structure. It is available so that the module or driver can regain enough state information to continue processing the **ioctl** request. When the **M_IOCDATA** message is freed, any message that **cp_private** refers to is not freed by the STREAMS subsystem. It is the responsibility of the module or driver to free it.

REFERENCES

copyreq(D4), **datab**(D4), **iocblk**(D4), **messages**(D5), **msgb**(D4)

NOTICES

Availability

SVR4.0, SVR4.1ES, SVR4MP, SVR4.2

Portability
All processors

Interface
Driver-Kernel (STREAMS)

Commitment
Level 1

datab (D4)

NAME

datab – STREAMS data block structure

SYNOPSIS

```
#include <sys/types.h>
#include <sys/stream.h>
#include <sys/ddi.h>
```

DESCRIPTION

The **datab** structure describes the data of a STREAMS message.

USAGE

The actual data contained in a STREAMS message is stored in a data buffer pointed to by this structure. A message block structure [**msgb**(D4)] includes a field that points to a **datab** structure.

A data block can have more than one message block pointing to it at one time, so the **db_ref** member keeps track of a data block's references, preventing it from being deallocated until all message blocks are finished with it.

Structure Definitions

The **datab** structure is defined as type **dblk_t** and contains the following members:

```
uchar_t     *db_base;    /* first byte of buffer */
uchar_t     *db_lim;     /* last byte (+1) of buffer */
uchar_t     db_ref;      /* # of message pointers to this data */
uchar_t     db_type;     /* message type */
```

The **db_base** field points to the beginning of the data buffer. Drivers and modules should not change this field.

The **db_lim** field points to one byte past the end of the data buffer. Drivers and modules should not change this field.

The **db_ref** field contains a count of the number of message blocks sharing the data buffer. If it is greater than 1, drivers and modules should not change the contents of the data buffer. Drivers and modules should not change this field.

The **db_type** field contains the message type associated with the data buffer. This field can be changed by the driver. However, if the **db_ref** field is greater than 1, this field should not be changed.

REFERENCES

free_rtn(D4), **messages**(D5), **msgb**(D4)

NOTICES

Availability

SVR4.0, SVR4.1ES, SVR4MP, SVR4.2

Portability

All processors

Interface

Driver-Kernel (STREAMS)

Commitment

Level 1

NAME

dma_buf – DMA buffer descriptor structure

SYNOPSIS

```
#include <sys/types.h>
#include <sys/dma.h>
#include <sys/ddi.h>
```

DESCRIPTION

The DMA buffer descriptor structure is used to specify the data to be transferred by a DMA operation.

USAGE

Each DMA operation is controlled by a DMA command block [see dma_cb(D4)] structure that includes pointers to two dma_buf structures.

Each dma_buf structure provides the physical address and size of a data block involved in a DMA transfer. Scatter/gather operations involving multiple data blocks may be implemented by linking together multiple dma_bufs in a singly-linked list. Each dma_buf includes both the virtual and physical address of the next DMA buffer descriptor in the list.

DMA buffer descriptor structures should only be allocated via dma_get_buf(D3). Although drivers may access the members listed below, they should not make any assumptions about the size of the structure or the contents of other fields in the structure.

Structure Definitions

The dma_buf structure contains the following members:

```
ushort_t        count;      /* size of block*/
paddr_t         address;    /* physical address of data block */
paddr_t         physical;   /* physical address of next dma_buf */
struct dma_buf  *next_buf;  /* next buffer descriptor */
ushort_t        count_hi;   /* for big blocks */
```

The members of the dma_buf structure are:

count specifies the low-order 16 bits of the size of the data block in bytes.

address specifies the physical address of the data block.

physical specifies the physical address of the next dma_buf in a linked list of DMA buffers descriptors. It should be NULL if the buffer descriptor is the last one in the list. Note that a DMA buffer descriptor allocated by dma_get_buf will be zeroed out initially, thus no explicit initialization is required for this field if a value of NULL is desired.

next_buf specifies the virtual address of the next dma_buf in a linked list of DMA buffer descriptors. It should be NULL if the buffer descriptor is the last one in the list. Note that a DMA buffer descriptor allocated by dma_get_buf will be zeroed out initially, thus no explicit initialization is required for this field if a value of NULL is desired.

count_hi specifies the high-order 16 bits of the size of the data block in bytes. Since a dma_buf allocated by dma_get_buf is initially zeroed out, no explicit initialization is required for this field if the size of the data block may be specified by a ushort_t.

REFERENCES

dma_cb(D4), dma_free_buf(D3), dma_get_buf(D3)

NOTICES

Availability
SVR4.0, SVR4.1ES, SVR4MP, SVR4.2

Portability
AT-compatible architectures

Interface
Driver-Kernel

Commitment
Level 2

NAME

dma_cb – DMA command block structure

SYNOPSIS

```
#include <sys/types.h>
#include <sys/dma.h>
#include <sys/ddi.h>
```

DESCRIPTION

The DMA command block structure is used to control a DMA operation.

USAGE

Each DMA operation requested by a driver is controlled by a command block structure whose fields specify the operation to occur.

A number of fields of the DMA control block come in pairs: one for the requestor and one for the target. The requestor is the hardware device that is requesting the DMA operation, while the target is the target of the operation. The typical case is one in which the requestor is an I/O device and the target is memory.

DMA command block structures should only be allocated via **dma_get_cb**(D3). Although drivers may access the structure members listed below, they should not make any assumptions about the size of the structure or the contents of other fields in the structure.

Structure Definitions

The **dma_cb** structure contains the following members:

```
struct dma_buf  *targbufs;    /* list of target data buffers */
struct dma_buf  *reqrbufs;    /* list of requestor data buffers */
uchar_t         command;      /* Read/Write/Translate/Verify */
uchar_t         targ_type;    /* Memory/IO */
uchar_t         reqr_type;    /* Memory/IO  */
uchar_t         targ_step;    /* Inc/Dec/Hold  */
uchar_t         reqr_step;    /* Inc/Dec/Hold  */
uchar_t         trans_type;   /* Single/Demand/Block/Cascade */
uchar_t         targ_path;    /* 8/16/32 */
uchar_t         reqr_path;    /* 8/16/32 */
uchar_t         cycles;       /* 1 or 2 */
uchar_t         bufprocess;   /* Single/Chain/Auto-Init */
char            *procparam;   /* parameter buffer for appl call */
int             (*proc)();    /* address of application call routines */
```

The members of the **dma_cb** structure are:

targbufs is a pointer to a list of DMA buffer structures [see **dma_buf**(D4)] that describes the target of the DMA operation.

reqrbufs is a pointer to a list of DMA buffer structures [see **dma_buf**(D4)] that describes the requestor of the DMA operation.

command specifies the command for the DMA operation. It may be one of the following values:

DMA_CMD_READ Specifies a DMA read from the target to the requestor.

DMA_CMD_WRITE	Specifies a DMA write from the requestor to the target.

targ_type and reqr_type specify the type of the target and requestor, respectively. They each may have one of the following values:

DMA_TYPE_MEM	Specifies that the target (or requestor) is memory.
DMA_TYPE_IO	Specifies that the target (or requestor) is an I/O device.

targ_step and reqr_step specify how the target and requestor addresses are to be modified after each transfer. They each may have one of the following values:

DMA_STEP_INC	Specifies that the target (or requestor) address is to be incremented following each data transfer.
DMA_STEP_DEC	Specifies that the target (or requestor) address is to be decremented following each data transfer
DMA_STEP_HOLD	Specifies that the target (or requestor) address is to remain the same following each data transfer.

trans_type specifies the transfer type of the operation. It can have one of the following values:

DMA_TRANS_SNGL	Specifies that a single transfer is to occur.
DMA_TRANS_BLCK	Specifies that a block transfer is to occur. This is the only acceptable value for software-initiated transfers.
DMA_TRANS_DMND	Specifies demand transfer mode, which is a variation on block transfer in which the requestor may provide additional control flow on the transfer.

targ_path and reqr_path specify the size of the data path for the target and requestor, respectively. They each may have one of the following values:

DMA_PATH_8	Specifies that the target (or requestor) uses an eight-bit data path.
DMA_PATH_16	Specifies that the target (or requestor) uses a 16-bit data path.
DMA_PATH_32	Specifies that the target (or requestor) uses a 32-bit data path.
DMA_PATH_64	Specifies that the target (or requestor) uses a 64-bit data path.

cycles is an integer that specifies the number of cycles required for each transfer. Its value should be taken from the result of dma_get_best_mode(D3).

bufprocess specifies how the DMA target buffer structures are to be processed. It may have the following values:

DMA_BUF_SNGL	Specifies that the target consists of a single DMA Buffer.
DMA_BUF_CHAIN	Specifies that the target consists of a chain of DMA Buffers.

procparam is the parameter to be passed to the subroutine specified by the **proc** field.

proc specifies the address of a routine to be called when a DMA operation is successfully set up by **dma_swsetup**(D3). The value in the **procparam** field is passed as an argument to this routine. This field may be set to **NULL** if no procedure is to be called.

REFERENCES

dma_buf(D4), **dma_free_cb**(D3), **dma_get_cb**(D3), **dma_get_best_mode**(D3), **dma_prog**(D3), **dma_swsetup**(D3), **dma_swstart**(D3)

NOTICES

Availability

SVR4.0, SVR4.1ES, SVR4MP, SVR4.2

Portability

AT-compatible architectures

Interface

Driver-Kernel

Commitment

Level 2

free_rtn (D4)

NAME

`free_rtn` – STREAMS driver's message free routine structure

SYNOPSIS

```
#include <sys/stream.h>
#include <sys/ddi.h>
```

DESCRIPTION

A **free_rtn** structure is needed for messages allocated via **esballoc**(D3).

USAGE

Since the driver is providing the memory for the data buffer, a way is needed to notify the driver when the buffer is no longer in use. **esballoc** associates the free routine structure with the message when it is allocated. When **freeb**(D3) is called to free the message and the reference count goes to zero, the driver's message free routine is called, with the argument specified, to free the data buffer.

Structure Definitions

The **free_rtn** structure is defined as type **frtn_t** and contains the following members:

```
void  (*free_func)()   /* driver's free routine */
char  *free_arg        /* argument to free_func() */
```

The **free_func** field specifies the driver's function to be called when the message has been freed. It is called with interrupts from STREAMS devices blocked on the processor on which the function is running.

The **free_arg** field is the only argument to the driver's free routine.

REFERENCES

esballoc(D3), **freeb**(D3)

NOTICES

Availability

SVR4.0, SVR4.1ES, SVR4MP, SVR4.2

Portability

All processors

Interface

Driver-Kernel (STREAMS)

Commitment

Level 1

NAME

iocblk – STREAMS ioctl structure

SYNOPSIS

```
#include <sys/stream.h>
#include <sys/ddi.h>
```

DESCRIPTION

The **iocblk** structure describes a user's **ioctl**(2) request.

USAGE

The **iocblk** structure is used in **M_IOCTL**, **M_IOCACK**, and **M_IOCNAK** messages. Modules and drivers usually convert **M_IOCTL** messages into **M_IOCACK** or **M_IOCNAK** messages by changing the type and updating the relevant fields in the **iocblk** structure.

Data cannot be copied to the user's buffer with an **M_IOCACK** message if the **ioctl** is transparent.

No data can be copied to the user's buffer with an **M_IOCNAK** message.

When processing a transparent **ioctl**, the **iocblk** structure is usually overlaid with a **copyreq**(D4) structure. The stream head guarantees that the message is large enough to contain either structure.

Structure Definitions

The **iocblk** structure contains the following members:

```
int      ioc_cmd;     /* ioctl command */
cred_t   *ioc_cr;     /* user credentials */
uint_t   ioc_id;      /* ioctl ID */
uint_t   ioc_count;   /* number of bytes of data */
int      ioc_error;   /* error code for M_IOCACK or M_IOCNAK */
int      ioc_rval;    /* return value for M_IOCACK */
```

The **ioc_cmd** field is the **ioctl** command request specified by the user.

The **ioc_cr** field contains a pointer to the user credentials.

The **ioc_id** field is the **ioctl** ID, used to uniquely identify the **ioctl** request in the stream.

The **ioc_count** field specifies the amount of user data contained in the **M_IOCTL** message. User data will appear in **M_DATA** message blocks linked to the **M_IOCTL** message block. If **ioc_count** is set to the special value **TRANSPARENT**, then the **ioctl** request is "transparent." This means that the user did not use the **I_STR** format of STREAMS **ioctl**s and the module or driver will have to obtain any user data with **M_COPYIN** messages, and change any user data with **M_COPYOUT** messages. In this case, the **M_DATA** message block linked to the **M_IOCTL** message block contains the value of the *arg* parameter in the **ioctl** system call. For an **M_IOCACK** message, the **ioc_count** field specifies the amount of data to copy back to the user's buffer.

The **ioc_error** field can be used to set an error for either an **M_IOCACK** or an **M_IOCNAK** message.

The **ioc_rval** field can be used to set the return value in an **M_IOCACK** message. This will be returned to the user as the return value for the **ioctl** system call that generated the request.

REFERENCES

copyreq(D4), **copyresp**(D4), **datab**(D4), **messages**(D5), **msgb**(D4)

NOTICES

Availability

SVR4.0, SVR4.1ES, SVR4MP, SVR4.2

Portability

All processors

Interface

Driver-Kernel (STREAMS)

Commitment

Level 1

NAME

iovec – data storage structure for I/O using **uio**(D4)

SYNOPSIS

```
#include <sys/types.h>
#include <sys/uio.h>
#include <sys/ddi.h>
```

DESCRIPTION

The **iovec** structure describes a data storage area for transfer in a **uio** structure. Conceptually, it may be thought of as a base address and length specification.

USAGE

A separate interface does not currently exist for allocating **iovec**(D4) structures when the driver needs to create them itself. Therefore, the driver may either use **kmem_zalloc**(D3) to allocate them, or allocate them statically.

Structure Definitions

The **iovec** structure contains the following members:

```
caddr_t  iov_base;  /* base address of the data storage area */
int      iov_len;   /* size of the data storage area in bytes */
```

The driver may only set **iovec** structure members to initialize them for a data transfer for which the driver created the **iovec** structure. The driver must not otherwise change **iovec** structure members. However, drivers may read them. The **iovec** structure members available to the driver are:

iov_base contains the address for a range of memory to or from which data are transferred.

iov_len contains the number of bytes of data to be transferred to or from the range of memory starting at **iov_base**.

REFERENCES

physiock(D3), **uiomove**(D3), **ureadc**(D3), **uwritec**(D3), **uio**(D4)

NOTICES

Availability

SVR4.0, SVR4.1ES, SVR4MP, SVR4.2

Portability

All processors

Interface

Driver-Kernel

Commitment

Level 1

linkblk (D4)

NAME

`linkblk` – STREAMS multiplexor link structure

SYNOPSIS

```
#include <sys/stream.h>
#include <sys/ddi.h>
```

DESCRIPTION

The **linkblk** structure contains the information needed by a multiplexing driver to set up or take down a multiplexor link.

USAGE

The **linkblk** structure is embedded in the **M_DATA** portion of the **M_IOCTL** messages generated from the following **ioctl**(2) calls: **I_LINK**, **I_UNLINK**, **I_PLINK**, and **I_PUNLINK** [see **streamio**(7)].

Structure Definitions

The **linkblk** structure contains the following members:

```
queue_t   *l_qtop;   /* lower queue of top stream */
queue_t   *l_qbot;   /* upper queue of bottom stream */
int       l_index;   /* unique ID */
```

The `l_qtop` field is a pointer to the lowest write queue in the upper stream. In other words, it is the write queue of the multiplexing driver. If the link is persistent across closes of the driver, then this field is set to **NULL**.

The `l_qbot` field is a pointer to the upper write queue in the lower stream. The lower stream is the stream being linked under the multiplexor. The topmost read and write queues in the lower stream are given to the multiplexing driver to use for the lower half of its multiplexor processing. The **qinit**(D4) structures associated with these queues are those specified for the lower processing in the multiplexing driver's **streamtab**(D4) structure.

The `l_index` field is a unique ID that identifies the multiplexing link in the system. The driver can use this as a key on which it can multiplex or de-multiplex.

REFERENCES

datab(D4), **iocblk**(D4), **ioctl**(2), **messages**(D5), **msgb**(D4), **qinit**(D4), **streamio**(7), **streamtab**(D4)

NOTICES

Availability

SVR4.0, SVR4.1ES, SVR4MP, SVR4.2

Portability

All processors

Interface

Driver-Kernel (STREAMS)

Commitment

Level 1

NAME

module_info – STREAMS driver and module information structure

SYNOPSIS

```
#include <sys/types.h>
#include <sys/conf.h>
#include <sys/stream.h>
#include <sys/ddi.h>
```

DESCRIPTION

When a module or driver is declared, several identification and limit values can be set. These values are stored in the **module_info** structure. These values are used to initialize the module's or driver's queues when they are created.

USAGE

After the initial declaration, the **module_info** structure is intended to be read-only. However, the flow control limits (**mi_hiwat** and **mi_lowat**) and the packet size limits (**mi_minpsz** and **mi_maxpsz**) are copied to the **queue**(D4) structure, where they may be modified.

There may be one **module_info** structure per read and write queue, or the driver or module may use the same **module_info** structure for both the read and write queues.

Structure Definitions

The module_info structure contains the following members:

```
ushort_t  mi_idnum;     /* module ID number */
char      *mi_idname;   /* module name */
long      mi_minpsz;    /* minimum packet size */
long      mi_maxpsz;    /* maximum packet size */
ulong_t   mi_hiwat;     /* high water mark */
ulong_t   mi_lowat;     /* low water mark */
```

The mi_idnum field is a unique identifier for the driver or module that distinguishes the driver or module from the other drivers and modules in the system.

The **mi_idname** field points to the driver or module name. The constant **FMNAMESZ** limits the length of the name, not including the terminating **NULL**. It is currently set to eight characters.

The **mi_minpsz** field is the default minimum packet size for the driver or module queues. This is an advisory limit specifying the smallest message that can be accepted by the driver or module.

The **mi_maxpsz** field is the default maximum packet size for the driver or module queues. This is an advisory limit specifying the largest message that can be accepted by the driver or module.

The **mi_hiwat** field is the default high water mark for the driver or module queues. This specifies the number of bytes of data contained in messages on the queue such that the queue is considered full and hence flow-controlled.

The **mi_lowat** field is the default low water mark for the driver or module queues. This specifies the number of bytes of data contained in messages on the queue such that the queue is no longer flow-controlled.

REFERENCES

queue(D4)

NOTICES

Availability

SVR4.0, SVR4.1ES, SVR4MP, SVR4.2

Portability

All processors

Interface

Driver-Kernel (STREAMS)

Commitment

Level 1

NAME

msgb – STREAMS message block structure

SYNOPSIS

```
#include <sys/types.h>
#include <sys/stream.h>
#include <sys/ddi.h>
```

DESCRIPTION

A STREAMS message is made up of one or more message blocks, referenced by a pointer to a **msgb** structure. When a message is on a queue, all fields are read-only to drivers and modules.

USAGE

Structure Definitions

The **msgb** structure is defined as type **mblk_t** and contains the following members:

```
struct msgb    *b_next;   /* next message on queue */
struct msgb    *b_prev;   /* previous message on queue */
struct msgb    *b_cont;   /* next block in message */
uchar_t        *b_rptr;   /* 1st unread data byte of buffer */
uchar_t        *b_wptr;   /* 1st unwritten data byte of buffer */
struct datab   *b_datap;  /* pointer to data block */
uchar_t        b_band;    /* message priority  */
ushort_t       b_flag;    /* used by stream head  */
```

The **b_next** and **b_prev** pointers are used to link messages together on a **queue**(D4). These fields can be used by drivers and modules to create linked lists of messages.

The **b_cont** pointer links message blocks together when a message is composed of more than one block. Drivers and modules can use this field to create complex messages from single message blocks.

The **b_rptr** and **b_wptr** pointers describe the valid data region in the associated data buffer. The **b_rptr** field points to the first unread byte in the buffer and the **b_wptr** field points to the next byte to be written in the buffer.

The **b_datap** field points to the data block [see **datab**(D4)] associated with the message block. This field should never be changed by modules or drivers.

The **b_band** field contains the priority band associated with the message. Normal priority messages and high priority messages have **b_band** set to zero. High priority messages are high priority by virtue of their message type. This field can be used to alter the queuing priority of the message. The higher the priority band, the closer to the head of the queue the message is placed.

The **b_flag** field contains a bitmask of flags that can be set to alter the way the stream head will process the message. Valid flags are:

MSGMARK The last byte in the message is "marked." This condition is testable from user level via the **I_ATMARK ioctl**(2).

REFERENCES

`allocb`(D3), `datab`(D4), `esballoc`(D3), `freeb`(D3), `free_rtn`(D4), `messages`(D5)

NOTICES

Availability

SVR4.0, SVR4.1ES, SVR4MP, SVR4.2

Portability

All processors

Interface

Driver-Kernel (STREAMS)

Commitment

Level 1

NAME

qinit – STREAMS queue initialization structure

SYNOPSIS

```
#include <sys/stream.h>
#include <sys/ddi.h>
```

DESCRIPTION

The **qinit** structure contains pointers to processing procedures and default values for a **queue**(D4). Drivers and modules declare **qinit** structure for their read and write queues, and place the addresses of the structures in their **streamtab**(D4) structure. After the initial declaration, all fields are intended to be read-only.

USAGE

There is usually one **qinit** structure for the read side of a module or driver, and one **qinit** structure for the write side.

Structure Definitions

The **quinit** structure contains the following members:

```
int                  (*qi_putp)();      /* put procedure */
int                  (*qi_srvp)();      /* service procedure */
int                  (*qi_qopen)();     /* open procedure */
int                  (*qi_qclose)();    /* close procedure */
int                  (*qi_qadmin)();    /* for future use */
struct module_info   *qi_minfo;         /* module parameters */
struct module_stat   *qi_mstat;         /* module statistics */
```

The **qi_putp** field contains the address of the **put**(D2) routine for the **queue**.

The **qi_srvp** field contains the address of the service [**srv**(D2)] routine for the **queue**. If there is no service routine, this field should be set to **NULL**.

The **qi_qopen** field contains the address of the **open**(D2) routine for the driver or module. Only the read-side **qinit** structure need define contain the routine address. The write-side value should be set to **NULL**.

The **qi_qclose** field contains the address of the **close**(D2) routine for the driver or module. Only the read-side **qinit** structure need define contain the routine address. The write-side value should be set to **NULL**.

The **qi_qadmin** field is intended for future use and should be set to **NULL**.

The **qi_minfo** field contains the address of the **module_info**(D4) structure for the driver or module.

The **qi_mstat** field contains the address of the **module_stat** structure for the driver or module. The **module_stat** structure is defined in **/usr/include/sys/strstat.h**. This field should be set to **NULL** if the driver or module does not keep statistics.

REFERENCES

module_info(D4), **queue**(D4), **streamtab**(D4)

NOTICES

Availability

SVR4.0, SVR4.1ES, SVR4MP, SVR4.2

Portability

All processors

Interface

Driver-Kernel (STREAMS)

Commitment

Level 1

NAME

queue – STREAMS queue structure

SYNOPSIS

```
#include <sys/types.h>
#include <sys/stream.h>
#include <sys/ddi.h>
```

DESCRIPTION

A instance of a STREAMS driver or module consists of two **queue** structures, one for upstream (read-side) processing and one for downstream (write-side) processing.

USAGE

This structure is the major building block of a stream. It contains pointers to the processing procedures, pointers to the next queue in the stream, flow control parameters, and a list of messages to be processed.

Structure Definitions

The **queue** structure is defined as type **queue_t** and contains the following members:

```
struct qinit  *q_qinfo;  /* module or driver entry points */
struct msgb   *q_first;  /* first message in queue */
struct msgb   *q_last;   /* last message in queue */
struct queue  *q_next;   /* next queue in stream */
void          *q_ptr;    /* pointer to private data structure */
ulong_t       q_count;   /* approximate size of message queue */
ulong_t       q_flag;    /* status of queue */
long          q_minpsz;  /* smallest packet accepted by QUEUE */
long          q_maxpsz;  /* largest packet accepted by QUEUE */
ulong_t       q_hiwat;   /* high water mark */
ulong_t       q_lowat;   /* low water mark */
```

The **q_qinfo** field contains a pointer to the **qinit**(D4) structure specifying the processing routines and default values for the queue. This field should not be changed by drivers or modules.

The **q_first** field points to the first message on the queue, or is **NULL** if the queue is empty. This field should not be changed by drivers or modules.

The **q_last** field points to the last message on the queue, or is **NULL** if the queue is empty. This field should not be changed by drivers or modules.

The **q_next** field points to the next queue in the stream. This field should not be changed by drivers or modules.

The **q_ptr** field is a private field for use by drivers and modules. It provides a way to associate the driver's per-minor data structure with the queue.

The **q_count** field contains the number of bytes in messages on the queue in priority band 0. This includes normal messages and high priority messages.

The `q_flag` field contains a bitmask of flags that indicate different queue characteristics. No flags may be set or cleared by drivers or modules. However, the following flags may be tested:

`QREADR` The queue is the read queue. Absence of this flag implies a write queue.

The `q_minpsz` field is the minimum packet size for the queue. This is an advisory limit specifying the smallest message that can be accepted by the queue. It is initially set to the value specified by the `mi_minpsz` field in the `module_info`(D4) structure. This field can be changed by drivers or modules.

The `q_maxpsz` field is the maximum packet size for the queue. This is an advisory limit specifying the largest message that can be accepted by the queue. It is initially set to the value specified by the `mi_maxpsz` field in the `module_info` structure. This field can be changed by drivers or modules.

The `q_hiwat` field is the high water mark for the queue. This specifies the number of bytes of data contained in messages on the queue such that the queue is considered full, and hence flow-controlled. It is initially set to the value specified by the `mi_hiwat` field in the `module_info` structure. This field can be changed by drivers or modules.

The `q_lowat` field is the low water mark for the queue. This specifies the number of bytes of data contained in messages on the queue such that the queue is no longer flow-controlled. It is initially set to the value specified by the `mi_lowat` field in the `module_info` structure. This field can be changed by drivers or modules.

REFERENCES

`getq`(D3), `module_info`(D4), `msgb`(D4), `putq`(D3), `qinit`(D4), `strqget`(D3), `strqset`(D3)

NOTICES

Availability

SVR4.0, SVR4.1ES, SVR4MP, SVR4.2

Portability

All processors

Interface

Driver-Kernel (STREAMS)

Commitment

Level 1

NAME

streamtab – STREAMS driver and module declaration structure

SYNOPSIS

```
#include <sys/stream.h>
#include <sys/ddi.h>
```

DESCRIPTION

The **streamtab** structure is made up of pointers to **qinit** structures for both the read and write queue portions of each module or driver. (Multiplexing drivers require both upper and lower **qinit** structures.) The **qinit** structure contains the entry points through which the module or driver routines are called.

USAGE

Each STREAMS driver or module must have a **streamtab** structure. The **streamtab** structure must be named *prefix***info**, where *prefix* is the driver prefix.

Structure Definitions

The **streamtab** structure contains the following members:

```
struct qinit  *st_rdinit;     /* read queue */
struct qinit  *st_wrinit;     /* write queue */
struct qinit  *st_muxrinit;   /* lower read queue*/
struct qinit  *st_muxwinit;   /* lower write queue*/
```

The **st_rdinit** field contains a pointer to the read-side **qinit** structure. For a multiplexing driver, this is the **qinit** structure for the upper read side.

The **st_wrinit** field contains a pointer to the write-side **qinit** structure. For a multiplexing driver, this is the **qinit** structure for the upper write side.

The **st_muxrinit** field contains a pointer to the lower read-side **qinit** structure for multiplexing drivers. For modules and non-multiplexing drivers, this field should be set to **NULL**.

The **st_muxwinit** field contains a pointer to the lower write-side **qinit** structure for multiplexing drivers. For modules and non-multiplexing drivers, this field should be set to **NULL**.

REFERENCES

qinit(D4)

NOTICES

Availability

SVR4.0, SVR4.1ES, SVR4MP, SVR4.2

Portability

All processors

Interface

Driver-Kernel (STREAMS)

Commitment

Level 1

stroptions (D4)

NAME

stroptions – stream head option structure

SYNOPSIS

```
#include <sys/stream.h>
#include <sys/stropts.h>
#include <sys/ddi.h>
```

DESCRIPTION

The **stroptions** structure, used in an **M_SETOPTS** message, contains options for the stream head.

USAGE

The **M_SETOPTS** message is sent upstream by drivers and modules when they want to change stream head options for their stream.

Structure Definitions

The **stroptions** structure contains the following members:

```
ulong_t   so_flags;    /* options to set */
short     so_readopt;  /* read option */
ushort_t  so_wroff;    /* write offset */
long      so_minpsz;   /* minimum read packet size */
long      so_maxpsz;   /* maximum read packet size */
ulong_t   so_hiwat;    /* read queue high water mark */
ulong_t   so_lowat;    /* read queue low water mark */
uchar_t   so_band;     /* band for water marks */
```

The **so_flags** field determines which options are to be set, and which of the other fields in the structure are used. This field is a bitmask and is comprised of the bitwise OR of the following flags:

SO_READOPT	Set the read option to that specified by the **so_readopt** field.
SO_WROFF	Set the write offset to that specified by the **so_wroff** field.
SO_MINPSZ	Set the minimum packet size on the stream head read queue to that specified by the **so_minpsz** field.
SO_MAXPSZ	Set the maximum packet size on the stream head read queue to that specified by the **so_maxpsz** field.
SO_HIWAT	Set the high water mark on the stream head read queue to that specified by the **so_hiwat** field.
SO_LOWAT	Set the low water mark on the stream head read queue to that specified by the **so_lowat** field.
SO_ALL	Set all of the above options (**SO_READOPT | SO_WROFF | SO_MINPSZ | SO_MAXPSZ | SO_HIWAT | SO_LOWAT**).
SO_MREADON	Turn on generation of **M_READ** messages by the stream head.

SO_MREADOFF	Turn off generation of **M_READ** messages by the stream head.
SO_NDELON	Use old TTY semantics for no-delay reads and writes.
SO_NDELOFF	Use STREAMS semantics for no-delay reads and writes.
SO_ISTTY	The stream is acting as a terminal.
SO_ISNTTY	The stream is no longer acting as a terminal.
SO_TOSTOP	Stop processes on background writes to this stream.
SO_TONSTOP	Don't stop processes on background writes to this stream.
SO_BAND	The water marks changes affect the priority band specified by the **so_band** field.

The **so_readopt** field specifies options for the stream head that alter the way it handles **read**(2) calls. This field is a bitmask whose flags are grouped in sets. Within a set, the flags are mutually exclusive. The first set of flags determines how data messages are treated when they are read:

RNORM	Normal (byte stream) mode. **read** returns the lesser of the number of bytes asked for and the number of bytes available. Messages with partially read data are placed back on the head of the stream head read queue. This is the default behavior.
RMSGD	Message discard mode. **read** returns the lesser of the number of bytes asked for and the number of bytes in the first message on the stream head read queue. Messages with partially read data are freed.
RMSGN	Message non-discard mode. **read** returns the lesser of the number of bytes asked for and the number of bytes in the first message on the stream head read queue. Messages with partially read data are placed back on the head of the stream head read queue.

The second set of flags determines how protocol messages (**M_PROTO** and **M_PCPROTO**) are treated during a **read**:

RPROTNORM	Normal mode. **read** fails with the error code **EBADMSG** if there is a protocol message at the front of the stream head read queue. This is the default behavior.
RPROTDIS	Protocol discard mode. **read** discards the **M_PROTO** or **M_PCPROTO** portions of the message and return any **M_DATA** portions that may be present. **M_PASSFP** messages are also freed in this mode.
RPROTDAT	Protocol data mode. **read** treats the **M_PROTO** or **M_PCPROTO** portions of the message as if they were normal data (that is, they are delivered to the user.)

The **so_wroff** field specifies a byte offset to be included in the first message block of every **M_DATA** message created by a **write**(2) and the first **M_DATA** message block created by each call to **putmsg**(2).

The **so_minpsz** field specifies the minimum packet size for the stream head read queue.

The **so_maxpsz** field specifies the maximum packet size for the stream head read queue.

The **so_hiwat** field specifies the high water mark for the stream head read queue.

The **so_lowat** field specifies the low water mark for the stream head read queue.

The **so_band** field specifies the priority band to which the high and/or low water mark changes should be applied.

REFERENCES

datab(D4), **messages**(D5), **msgb**(D4), **read**(2), **streamio**(7)

NOTICES

Availability

SVR4.0, SVR4.1ES, SVR4MP, SVR4.2

Portability

All processors

Interface

Driver-Kernel (STREAMS)

Commitment

Level 1

NAME

uio – scatter/gather I/O request structure

SYNOPSIS

```
#include <sys/types.h>
#include <sys/file.h>
#include <sys/uio.h>
#include <sys/ddi.h>
```

DESCRIPTION

The **uio** structure describes an I/O request that can be broken up into different data storage areas (scatter/gather I/O). A request is a list of **iovec**(D4) structures (base/length pairs) indicating where in user space or kernel space the data are to be read/written.

USAGE

The contents of the **uio** structure passed to the driver through the entry points in section D2 should not be changed directly by the driver. The **uiomove**(D3), **ureadc**(D3), and **uwritec**(D3) functions take care of maintaining the the **uio** structure. A block driver may also use the **physiock**(D3) function to perform unbuffered I/O. **physiock** also takes care of maintaining the **uio** structure.

A driver that creates its own **uio** structures for a data transfer is responsible for zeroing it prior to initializing members accessible to the driver. The driver must not change the **uio** structure afterwards; the functions take care of maintaining the **uio** structure.

Note that a separate interface does not currently exist for allocating **uio**(D4) and **iovec**(D4) structures when the driver needs to create them itself. Therefore, the driver may either use **kmem_zalloc**(D3) to allocate them, or allocate them statically.

Structure Definitions

The **uio** structure contains the following members:

```
iovec_t  *uio_iov;     /* Pointer to the start of the iovec */
                       /* array for the uio structure */
int      uio_iovcnt;   /* The number of iovecs in the array */
off_t    uio_offset;   /* Offset into file where data are */
                       /* transferred from or to */
short    uio_segflg;   /* Identifies the type of I/O transfer */
short    uio_fmode;    /* File mode flags */
int      uio_resid;    /* Residual count */
```

The driver may only set **uio** structure members to initialize them for a data transfer for which the driver created the **uio** structure. The driver must not otherwise change **uio** structure members. However, drivers may read them. The **uio** structure members available for the driver to test or set are described below:

uio_iov contains a pointer to the **iovec** array for the **uio** structure. If the driver creates a **uio** structure for a data transfer, an associated **iovec** array must also be created by the driver.

uio_iovcnt contains the number of elements in the iovec array for the uio structure.

uio_offset contains the starting logical byte address on the device where the data transfer is to occur. Applicability of this field to the the driver is device-dependent. It applies to randomly accessed devices, but may not apply to all sequentially accessed devices.

uio_segflg identifies the virtual address space in which the transfer data areas reside. The value UIO_SYSSPACE indicates the data areas are within kernel space. The value UIO_USERSPACE indicates one data area is within kernel space and the other is within the user space of the current process context.

uio_fmode contains flags describing the file access mode for which the data transfer is to occur. Valid flags are:

FNDELAY
: The driver should not wait if the requested data transfer cannot occur immediately; it should terminate the request without indicating an error occurred. The driver's implementation of this flag's implied semantics are subject to device-dependent interpretation.

FNONBLOCK
: The driver should not wait if the requested data transfer cannot occur immediately; it should terminate the request, returning the EAGAIN error code as the completion status [see errnos(D5)]. The driver's implementation of the implied semantics of this flag are subject to device-dependent interpretation.

If the driver creates a uio structure for a data transfer, it may set the flags described above in uio_fmode.

uio_resid indicates the number of bytes that have not been transferred to or from the data area. If the driver creates a uio structure for a data transfer, uio_resid is initialized by the driver as the number of bytes to be transferred. Note that a separate interface does not currently exist for allocating

REFERENCES

iovec(D4), physiock(D3), read(D2), uiomove(D3), ureadc(D3), uwritec(D3), write(D2)

NOTICES

Availability

SVR4.0, SVR4.1ES, SVR4MP, SVR4.2

Portability

All processors

Interface

Driver-Kernel

Commitment

Level 1

NAME

`intro` – introduction to kernel **#define**'s

SYNOPSIS

```
#include <sys/types.h>
#include <sys/ddi.h>
```

DESCRIPTION

This section describes the kernel **#define**'s a developer may need to use in a device driver. Most **#define**'s are specified on the manual page in which they are used. However, some **#define**'s are too general or numerous to include in another manual page. Instead, they have been given a separate page in this section.

USAGE

#include <sys/ddi.h> must always be the last header file included.

errnos (D5)

NAME

errnos – error numbers

SYNOPSIS

```
#include <sys/errno.h>
#include <sys/ddi.h>
```

DESCRIPTION

The following is a list of the error codes that drivers may return from their entry points, or include in STREAMS messages (for example, **M_ERROR** messages).

EACCES	Permission denied. An attempt was made to access a file in a way forbidden by its file access permissions.
EADDRINUSE	The address requested is already in use.
EADDRNOTAVAIL	The address requested cannot be assigned.
EAFNOSUPPORT	The address family specified is not installed or supported on the host.
EAGAIN	Temporary resource allocation failure; try again later. Drivers can return this error when resource allocation fails, for example, **kmem_alloc**(D3) or **allocb**(D3).
EALREADY	The operation requested is already being performed.
EBUSY	Device is busy. This can be used for devices that require exclusive access.
ECONNABORTED	A received connect request was aborted when the peer closed its endpoint.
ECONNREFUSED	The connection was refused.
ECONNRESET	The connection was reset by the peer entity.
EDESTADDRREQ	The requested operation required a destination address but none was supplied.
EEXIST	Unable to register module for dynamic loading because the module is already statically configured.
EFAULT	Bad address. Drivers should return this error whenever a call to **copyin**(D3) or **copyout**(D3) fails.
EHOSTDOWN	Host is down.
EHOSTUNREACH	No route to host.
EINPROGRESS	The operation requested is now in progress.
EINTR	Interrupted operation. Drivers can return this error whenever an interruptible operation is interrupted by receipt of an asynchronous signal.
EINVAL	Invalid argument. Drivers can return this error for operations that have invalid parameters specified.

`EIO`	An I/O error has occurred. Drivers can return this error when an input or output request has failed.
`EISCONN`	The endpoint is already connected.
`EMSGSIZE`	Message too long. The protocol is such that there is a limit to the size of a message and that limit has been exceeded.
`ENETDOWN`	The network trying to be reached is down.
`ENETRESET`	The network dropped the connection because of a reset.
`ENETUNREACH`	The network trying to be reached is unreachable.
`ENOBUFS`	No buffer space available.
`ENODEV`	No such device. Drivers can return this error when an attempt is made to apply an inappropriate function to a device; for example, trying to read a write-only device such as a printer.
`ENOMEM`	Not enough memory. Drivers can return this error when resource allocation fails and it is either inconvenient or impossible for a retry to occur.
`ENOPROTOOPT`	The protocol option requested is not available at the level indicated.
`ENOSPC`	The device is out of free space.
`ENOTCONN`	The requested operation requires the endpoint to be connected but it is not.
`ENXIO`	No such device or address. Drivers can return this error when trying to open an invalid minor device, or when trying to perform I/O past the end of a device. This error may also occur when, for example, a tape drive is not online or a disk pack is not loaded on a drive.
`EOPNOTSUPP`	The operation requested is not supported.
`EPERM`	Permission denied. Drivers can return this error when a operation is attempted that requires more privilege than the current process has.
`EPROTO`	Protocol error. Drivers can return this error when they incur a protocol error, such as not being able to generate the proper protocol message because of resource exhaustion, and not being able to recover gracefully.
`ETIMEDOUT`	The connection timed out.

USAGE

The above examples are not exhaustive.

REFERENCES

`geterror`(D3)

NOTICES

Availability
SVR4.0, SVR4.1ES, SVR4MP, SVR4.2

Portability
All processors

Interface
Driver-Kernel

Commitment
Level 2

NAME

`messages` – STREAMS messages

SYNOPSIS

```
#include <sys/stream.h>
#include <sys/ddi.h>
```

DESCRIPTION

The following is a list of the STREAMS messages types that can be used by drivers and modules.

`M_DATA`	Data message.
`M_PROTO`	Protocol control message.
`M_BREAK`	Control message used to generate a line break.
`M_SIG`	Control message used to send a signal to processes.
`M_DELAY`	Control message used to generate a real-time delay.
`M_CTL`	Control message used between neighboring modules and drivers.
`M_IOCTL`	Control message used to indicate a user `ioctl`(2) request.
`M_SETOPTS`	Control message used to set stream head options.
`M_IOCACK`	High priority control message used to indicate success of an `ioctl` request.
`M_IOCNAK`	High priority control message used to indicate failure of an `ioctl` request.
`M_PCPROTO`	High priority protocol control message.
`M_PCSIG`	High priority control message used to send a signal to processes.
`M_READ`	High priority control message used to indicate the occurrence of a `read`(2) when there are no data on the stream head read queue.
`M_FLUSH`	High priority control message used to indicate that queues should be flushed.
`M_STOP`	High priority control message used to indicate that output should be stopped immediately.
`M_START`	High priority control message used to indicate that output can be restarted.
`M_HANGUP`	High priority control message used to indicate that the device has been disconnected.
`M_ERROR`	High priority control message used to indicate that the stream has incurred a fatal error.
`M_COPYIN`	High priority control message used during transparent `ioctl` processing to copy data from the user to a STREAMS message.
`M_COPYOUT`	High priority control message used during transparent `ioctl` processing to copy data from a STREAMS message to the user.

`M_IOCDATA`	High priority control message used during transparent **ioctl** processing to return the status and data of a previous **M_COPYIN** or **M_COPYOUT** request.
`M_PCCTL`	89IS THIS MP-ONLY??High priority control message used between neighboring modules and drivers.
`M_PCSETOPTS`	89IS THIS MP-ONLY??High priority control message used to set stream head options.
`M_STOPI`	High priority control message used to indicate that input should be stopped immediately.
`M_STARTI`	High priority control message used to indicate that input can be restarted.

REFERENCES

allocb(D3), **copyreq**(D4), **copyresp**(D4), **datab**(D4), **iocblk**(D4), **linkblk**(D4), **msgb**(D4), **put**(D2), **srv**(D2), **stroptions**(D4)

NOTICES

Availability

SVR4.0, SVR4.1ES, SVR4MP, SVR4.2

Portability

All processors

Interface

Driver-Kernel (STREAMS)

Commitment

Level 2

NAME

`signals` – signal numbers

SYNOPSIS

```
#include <sys/signal.h>
#include <sys/ddi.h>
```

DESCRIPTION

There are two ways to send a signal to a process. The first, **psignal**(D3), or, on multiprocessor systems, **proc_signal**(D3), can be used by non-STREAMS drivers. The second, by using an **M_SIG** or **M_PCSIG** message, can be used by STREAMS drivers and modules.

The following is a list of the signals that drivers may send to processes.

`SIGHUP`	The device has been disconnected.
`SIGINT`	The interrupt character has been received.
`SIGQUIT`	The quit character has been received.
`SIGWINCH`	The window size has changed.
`SIGURG`	Urgent data are available.
`SIGPOLL`	A pollable event has occurred.
`SIGTSTP`	Interactive stop of the process.

USAGE

The signal **SIGTSTP** cannot be generated with **psignal** or **proc_signal**. It is only valid when generated from a stream.

REFERENCES

psignal(D3), **proc_ref**(D3), **proc_signal**(D3), **proc_unref**(D3)

NOTICES

Availability

SVR4.0, SVR4.1ES, SVR4MP, SVR4.2

Portability

All processors

Interface

Driver-Kernel

Commitment

Level 1

Introduction to the Portable Device Interface

The Portable Device Interface (PDI) is an architecture for block-oriented devices. The PDI presents a framework for driver development that emphasizes the separation of hardware-dependent and hardware-independent pieces of drivers. The routines described here complement those of the Device Driver Interface/Driver–Kernel Interface (DDI/DKI). While the DDI/DKI defines a standard interface between drivers and the rest of the kernel, the PDI defines a set of routines for doing common tasks within drivers. See the driver programming guides for more information on the PDI. While we expect future versions of PDI routines to be highly compatible with those in this release, the PDI routines are not mature enough for us to make the same sorts of guarantees we make for the DDI/DKI.

NOTE Drivers may have to change as the PDI evolves.

NAME

`intro` – introduction to PDI Host Bus Adapter functions

DESCRIPTION

The Portable Device Interface (PDI) Host Bus Adapter (HBA) includes the following entry point routines:

HBA Function	Description	Computer Type	Base or Interrupt
`close`(*dev, flags, otype, cred_t*)	Close pass-through access	Any	Base
`freeblk`(*hbap*)	Free a HBA request block	Any	Base
`getblk`()	Get a HBA request block	Any	Base
`icmd`(*hbap*)	Perform command now	Any	Either
`intr`(*vect*)	Handle HBA interrupt	Any	Interrupt
`ioctl`(*dev, cmd, arg, cred_p*)	HBA ioctl pass-through command	Any	Base
`open`(*devt, flags, otype, cred_p*)	Initiate HBA pass-through access	Any	Base
`send`(*hbap*)	Queue HBA request	Any	Base
`start`()	Initialize/identify HBA controller	Any	Base
`xlat`(*hbap, flag, procp*)	Perform virtual to physical translation for **scb**	Any	Base

The "Computer Type" column indicates on which computers the function can be called. "Any" indicated in the "Computer Type" column refers to the type of computer the function is supported under. The "Base or Interrupt" column indicates which types of routines can call the listed function.

close (D2H)

NAME

close – close Host Bus Adapter pass-through access

SYNOPSIS

int *prefix***close(dev_t** *dev*, **int** *flags*, **int** *otype*, **cred_t** **cred_t*);

Arguments

dev Device number.

flags Flags for close.

otype Type of close.

cred_p Credential pointer of the closing process.

DESCRIPTION

close(D2H) returns target level access to a device, attached to a Host Bus Adapter (HBA), currently operating in pass-through mode.

Return Values

On success, **close** returns 0. On failure, it returns the appropriate error number corresponding to the failure.

USAGE

After completing pass-through access to a device, the user level application should issue the pass-through **close** to allow target level access to the device once more.

The arguments to this routine are the same as those for any standard **close**(D2) routine.

Level

Base only.

REFERENCES

close(D2), **ioctl**(D2H), **open**(D2H)

NAME

`freeblk` – free a Host Bus Adapter device-specific request block

SYNOPSIS

`long` *prefix*`freeblk(struct hbadata *`*hbap*`);`

Arguments

hbap A pointer to the device specific request block to be freed.

DESCRIPTION

`freeblk`(D2H) frees Host Bus Adapter (HBA) driver-specific request blocks previously allocated by the `getblk`(D2H) routine. This routine accepts, as an argument, a `struct hbadata *`, which points to the HBA-specific request block to be freed.

Return Values

On success, `freeblk` returns `SDI_RET_OK`. On failure, it returns `SDI_RET_ERR`.

USAGE

`freeblk`(D2H) is accessed only by SDI.

Level

Base only.

REFERENCES

`getblk`(D2H)

getblk (D2H)

NAME

getblk – get a Host Bus Adapter device-specific request block

SYNOPSIS

`struct hbadata *`*prefix*`getblk(void);`

Arguments

None.

DESCRIPTION

getblk(D2H) allocates Host Bus Adapter (HBA) driver-specific request blocks, which are used in passing requests from the target drivers to the HBA driver. Each HBA driver defines and allocates its own supply of request blocks, allowing for flexibility in servicing the needs of individual HBAs.

The **getblk** routine returns a **struct hbadata ***. Typically, the HBA drivers use some other structure and cast it to a **struct hbadata *** before returning. The request block consists, minimally, of **struct xsb *** and may contain additional HBA-specific data after the **struct xsb ***.

Return Values

On success, **getblk** returns a pointer to the newly allocated request block. On failure, it returns an appropriate error number corresponding to the failure.

USAGE

getblk is accessed only by SDI.

Level

Base only.

REFERENCES

freeblk(D2H)

NAME

`icmd` – perform a request immediately on a Host Bus Adapter

SYNOPSIS

long *prefix***icmd(struct hbadata** ***hbap*);**

Arguments

hbap A pointer to the device-specific request block defining the request to be performed.

DESCRIPTION

icmd(D2H) is a special case of the Host Bus Adapter (HBA) **send**(D2H) routine. It sends the request directly to the controller, bypassing the queue mechanism used by **send**(D2H).

Return Values

On success, **icmd** returns **SDI_RET_OK**. On failure, it returns **SDI_RET_ERR**.

USAGE

The main use for this routine is in instances where the HBA controller is in some bad state and flushing the jobs from the queue is required to return the controller to a normal state.

At minimum, the HBA driver's **icmd** routine needs to support the following commands:

SFB_ABORTM	Send an abort message to the specified device.
SFB_FLUSHR	Flush the HBA's job queue.
SFB_RESETM	Reset the bus (SCSI bus or controller device).
SFB_RESUME	Resume sending queued jobs to the HBA.
SFB_SUSPEND	Suspend sending queued jobs to the HBA.

In addition to these SCSI SFB commands, the HBA's **icmd** routine should accept and pass to the controller all supported SCSI SCB commands.

Level

Base or Interrupt.

REFERENCES

send(D2H)

intr (D2H)

NAME

`intr` – handle Host Bus Adapter interrupts

SYNOPSIS

`void` *prefix*`intr(unsigned int *`*vect*`);`

Arguments

vect The number used by the operating system to associate a driver's interrupt handler with an interrupting device, normally the interrupt vector number.

DESCRIPTION

`intr`(D2H) is called whenever an interrupt occurs on one of the indicated vectors for the Host Bus Adapter (HBA). The routine's argument is the vector at which the interrupt occurred.

Return Values

None.

USAGE

Since interrupts can be shared, all HBA driver interrupt routines must determine, from internal status, whether or not an interrupt is pending for a device it controls whose IRQ (interrupt) matches *vect*. After processing the interrupt, the routine should check the controller to verify that the requested operation has completed successfully. If neither case is true, the routine should return without displaying a message, and should not modify the system state affecting the interrupt being processed.

Level

Interrupt only.

REFERENCES

`intr`(D2)

NAME

`ioctl` – send Host Bus Adapter pass-through commands

SYNOPSIS

int *prefix***ioctl(dev_t** *dev***, int** *cmd***, caddr_t** *arg***, int** *mode***,**
cred_t ****cred_p*, int ****rval_p***);**

Arguments

dev	Device number.
cmd	Type of pass-through command.
arg	Data for pass-through command.
cred_p	Credential pointer of the calling process.

DESCRIPTION

`ioctl`(D2H) is used for pass-through access with Host Bus Adapters (HBAs). After pass-through access has been established with the HBA device through `open`(D2H), the HBA pass-through `ioctl`(D2H) routine is used to send commands to the device.

Return Values

On success, `ioctl` returns `0`. On failure, it returns the appropriate error number corresponding to the failure.

USAGE

At minimum, `ioctl` should understand the following command types:

`B_GETTYPE`	Get the HBA driver type information.
`HA_VER`	Get the HBA driver version number.
`SDI_BRESET`	Reset the SCSI bus or the controller.
`SDI_SEND`	Send the SCSI command, supplied in *arg*, to the requested device.

Level

Base only.

REFERENCES

`close`(D2H), `ioctl`(D2), `open`(D2H)

open (D2H)

NAME

`open` – initiate Host Bus Adapter pass-through access

SYNOPSIS

`int` *prefix*`open(dev_t *`*devp*`, int` *flags*`, int` *otype*`, cred_t *`*cred_t*`);`

Arguments

devt A pointer to device number.

flags Flags for open.

otype Type of open.

cred_p Credential pointer of the opening process.

DESCRIPTION

`open`(D2H) provides pass-through access to a device attached to a Host Bus Adapter (HBA). The pass-through mechanism allows an application to have direct access to PDI devices.

Return Values

On success, `open` returns `0`. On failure, it returnes the appropriate error number corresponding to the failure.

USAGE

This mechanism provides exclusive access to a device. For this reason, the pass-through `open` routine must verify that the device being requested is valid, and that no other requests are pending for the device.

The arguments to this routine are the same as those for any standard `open`(D2) routine.

Level

Base only.

REFERENCES

`close`(D2H), `ioctl`(D2H), `open`(D2)

NAME

send – queue a request for Host Bus Adapter

SYNOPSIS

`long` *prefix*`send(struct hbadata *`*hbap*`);`

Arguments

hbap A pointer to the device-specific request block defining the request to be queued.

DESCRIPTION

send(D2H) queues requests for Host Bus Adapters (HBAs), and generally is used for every request. After the target driver has entered the pointer to the SCSI command block in the device-specific request block (previously allocated by the **getblk**(D2H) routine), it calls **sdi_send**(D3I), which invokes the appropriate HBA-specific **send** routine. The target driver has no awareness of the HBA request block.

Return Values

On success, **send** returns `SDI_RET_OK`. On failure, it returns `SDI_RET_ERR`. For a request retry, it returns `SDI_RET_RETRY`.

USAGE

Each HBA **send** routine should be capable of handling an unlimited number of **send** requests. Rather than requiring target drivers to know how many requests an HBA driver can handle under the best of conditions to achieve the maximum throughput from the HBA hardware, target drivers should send down all possible requests. With this scheme, each HBA driver can have the optimum number of jobs active when under heavy load. The maximum number of active requests varies from 1 to 42 for the HBA drivers currently provided with PDI. Using this approach, a HBA driver should have a simple and fast queuing mechanism.

The argument passed to this routine is a **`struct hbadata *`**. If the HBA hardware supports scatter-gather or programmed-I/O, merging requests should be attempted while queuing the request. As would be expected, if no requests are currently pending, the request being sent to the HBA driver should be started immediately.

Level

Base only.

REFERENCES

getblk(D2H), **sdi_send**(D3I)

start (D2H)

NAME

`start` – initialize and register a Host Bus Adapter

SYNOPSIS

`int` *prefix*`start(void);`

Arguments

None.

DESCRIPTION

`start`(D2H) performs Host Bus Adapter (HBA)-specific initialization and allocation of data structures (command blocks, queues, and so on). It is also used to inform the PDI subsystem whether a HBA controller is present.

Return Values

On success, **`start`** returns `0`. On failure, it returns `-1`, indicating no hardware found or other error.

USAGE

`start`(D2H) has two main purposes. Its first (and primary) purpose is to perform any HBA-specific initialization and allocation of data structures (command blocks, queues, and so on). As part of this initialization, the **`start`** routine needs to determine whether that type of HBA controller is present. Each HBA **`start`** routine needs to search for the presence of controllers without causing problems for the other devices present. Therefore, it should use only the minimum number of **`inb`** and **`outb`** steps needed to detect an HBA controller. If an action is needed only after a controller is detected, this action should not be performed until the detection is complete. Examples of post-detection steps include DMA initialization or other actions which can effect the system or other controllers.

The second purpose of the **`start`** routine is to let the PDI subsystem know whether the HBA controller is present. If the controller is present, and at least one device is found, the routine must register the controller with PDI by first calling **`sdi_gethbano`**(D3I), then calling the **`sdi_register`**(D3I) routine. The **`sdi_gethbano`** call returns the *external* HBA number that is used by the system to generate the node name. The HBA driver needs this number to generate the mapping from the external number to its own internal controller number. A positive return value for **`sdi_gethbano`** represents a valid and available controller number. A negative value indicates that the requested controller number is either invalid or unavailable, or that there are no available numbers to allocate.

The **`sdi_register`** routine is called after all the controller initialization has been completed. A successful registry of the HBA enters the controller into the **`HBA_tbl`** switch table, which is PDI's interface to the driver. In addition, the controller and its devices are entered into the PDI equipped device table, EDT.

If the controller is registered with PDI, the **`start`** routine should return the value `0`. If no controller is found or no devices are attached, or any other error condition is detected such that the controller is not registered, the routine should return `-1`. However, before **`start`** returns the error condition, any memory allocated for the HBA controller should be freed.

Drivers that probe I/O ports to verify that the associated hardware is present should read and save the value from the port before modifying it. If it is determined that the hardware is not present, drivers should restore the port value. This procedure will not prevent all conflicts, but does reduce the possibility of catastrophic failure.

Level

Base only.

REFERENCES

sdi_gethbano(D3I), **sdi_register**(D3I)

xlat (D2H)

NAME

`xlat` – perform virtual to physical translation on SCSI command block

SYNOPSIS

`void` *prefix*`xlat(struct hbadata *`*hbap*`, int` *flag*`, struct proc *`*procp*`);`

Arguments

hbap A pointer to the SCSI command block requiring translation.

flag Flag indicating the type of I/O.

procp Pointer to the process structure.

DESCRIPTION

`xlat` enables Host Bus Adapter (HBA) drivers to translate SCSI command block virtual addresses to physical addresses. Because many HBA devices require the physical address of the command block, this routine allows each HBA driver to facilitate its own needs in performing this translation.

Return Values

None.

USAGE

The arguments passed to **`xlat`** are **`struct hbadata *`**, the buffer flags, and the *proc* pointer. Depending on the type of I/O (determined by the flags), the *proc* pointer is used for **`vtop`**(D3) from virtual to physical addresses.

Level

Base only.

REFERENCES

`vtop`(D3)

NAME

`intro` – introduction to SDI target driver functions

DESCRIPTION

The SCSI Device Interface (SDI) consists of the functions summarized in the following table:

SDI Function	Description	Computer Type	Base or Interrupt
sdi_access(*edtp, access, owner*)	Claim or release access to a device	Any	Base
sdi_aen(*event, hba, scsi_id, lun*)	Notify an asynchronous event occurred	Any	Interrupt
sdi_blkio(*obp, sshift, strategy*)	Block and issue request	Any	Base
sdi_callback(*sbp*)	Signal target driver request completed	Any	Either
sdi_clrconfig(*op, flags, rinit*)	Free claimed device	Any	Base
sdi_doconfig(*dev_cfg, dev_cfg_size, drvrname, drv_maj, rinit*)	Find devices in EDT	Any	Base
sdi_errmsg(*dev_id, addr, sbp, sense, type, err_code*)	Format and print error message	Any	Base
sdi_findspec(*edtp, dev_spec*)	Allocate structure	Any	Base
sdi_free(*headp, fp*)	Return allocated memory to pool	Any	Either
sdi_freeblk(*pt*)	Release an **scb**	Any	Either
sdi_get(*headp, flag*)	Allocate structure	Any	Base
sdi_getblk()	Get an **scb**	Any	Base
sdi_getdev(*addr, dev*)	Get pass-through device number	Any	Either
sdi_gethbano(*cntlnum*)	Get HBA controller number	Any	Base
sdi_icmd(*pt*)	Perform command now	Any	Either
sdi_init()	Initialize HBA driver	Any	Base
sdi_name(*addr, name*)	Get controller name	Any	Either

SDI Function	Description	Computer Type	Base or Interrupt
`sdi_poolinit`(*headp*)	Initialize dynamic structure pool	Any	Base
`sdi_redt`(*hba, scsi_id, lun*)	Search EDT for existing entry	Any	Base
`sdi_register`(*infop, idatap*)	Register HBA device	Any	Base
`sdi_send`(*pt*)	Send command to device	Any	Either
`sdi_swap16`(*arg*)	Swaps bytes in 16-bit data type	Any	Base
`sdi_swap24`(*arg*)	Swaps bytes in 24-bit data type	Any	Base
`sdi_swap32`(*arg*)	Swaps bytes in 32-bit data type	Any	Base
`sdi_translate`(*pt, bflags, procp*)	Translate **scb** virtual address	Any	Base
`sdi_wedt`(*edtp, devtype, inq*)	Modify existing EDT entry	Any	Base

The "Computer Type" column indicates on which computers the function can be called. "Any" indicated in the "Computer Type" column refers to the type of computer the function is supported under. The "Base or Interrupt" column indicates which kinds of routines can call the function. HBA stands for Host Bus Adapter.

NAME

sdi_access – claim or release ownership of a given device

SYNOPSIS

int
sdi_access(struct sdi_edt ***edtp*****, int** *access***, struct owner** ***owner*****);**

Arguments

edtp Pointer to the Equipped Device Table entry associated with the device.

access Flag indicating whether ownership is to be claimed or released.

owner Defines the owner for the device.

DESCRIPTION

If the requested device is currently claimed by a target driver, **sdi_access** refuses any requests to add the device to an owner list and any attempts to claim the device.

If the device is not currently claimed by a target driver, **sdi_access**:

1. Adds the device to the calling target driver's list for **SDI_ADD** requests
2. Makes the device the target driver's current drive for **SDI_CLAIM** requests

Return Values

On success, **sdi_access** returns **SDI_RET_OK**, indicating that the access is allowed and has been set up. On failure, it returns **SDI_RET_ERR**, indicating the requested access is not allowed.

USAGE

sdi_access is used internally by SDI to claim and release ownership of devices on target driver's behalf.

Level

Base only.

sdi_aen (D3I)

NAME

sdi_aen – asynchronous event notification routine

SYNOPSIS

```
void
sdi_aen(int event, int hba, int scsi_id, int lun)
```

Arguments

event The code value of the asynchronous event which occurred on the HBA device.

hba The HBA number of the HBA device which experienced the event.

scsi_id The target ID of a specific device, or -1 if the event affects all devices for the HBA device.

lun The logical unit number of a specific device, or -1 if the event affects all logical units for the HBA device.

DESCRIPTION

sdi_aen calls the target driver fault handling routine to signal an asynchronous event, such as bus error or device error. Use of this routine is not required since many HBA drivers handle errors without help from the target drivers. Also target drivers are not required to provide a fault handling routine.

Return Values

None.

USAGE

When some critical asynchronous event (a bus reset) occurs on a HBA device which may require target driver actions, **sdi_aen** is the provided mechanism to signal target drivers. A target driver must provide a fault handling routine which is associated with the EDT structure for the device. When an event occurs, **sdi_aen** is called with the event code, the HBA number, and the target ID and LUN. The target ID and LUN can be -1 if all target drivers for devices connected to the HBA should have their fault routines called.

Level

Interrupt only.

NOTICES

The **sdi_aen** originates in pre-PDI versions of the architecture, when the devices involved required greater interaction to keep them in a sane state. Current devices require less intervention, so the need for **sdi_aen** has greatly diminished. This routine is being considered for removal in a future release.

NAME

sdi_blkio – blocks and issues non-block-aligned or non-block-sized requests

SYNOPSIS

```
void
sdi_blkio(buf_t *obp, unsigned int sshift, void (*strategy)())
```

Arguments

obp Pointer to the original buffer request.

sshift Shift value needed to shift from blocks to sectors.

strategy
Pointer to the driver's strategy routine through which the blocked requests will be issued.

DESCRIPTION

sdi_blkio blocks requests which are not on the sector boundary, or which specify a non-sector size, into sizes which can be issued to the device. Most disks and tapes will only except 512 byte (or multiples of 512) size requests. Some optical devices require 2048 byte blocks. However, there are many valid user operations which issue requests which are less than the device block size or are not a multiple of it. **sdi_blkio** uses temporary buffers to issue the needed requests, using the target driver's strategy routine to fulfill the user request. Upon successful completion of the needed transfers, **sdi_blkio** signals completion of the user request.

Return Values

None.

USAGE

sdi_blkio is typically used in a target driver's strategy routine. The strategy routine checks the size and alignment of the request for any nonaligned requests. **sdi_blkio** is then called to break the request up into valid sector/block aligned read or write requests. If the request is a write, the entire sector/block is read, the portion requested is updated, and then the entire sector/block is written. When all the separate requests (needed to formulate the original request) are completed, a call is made to **biodone**(D3I) to signal completion of the request. If any portion of the original request fails, a error result is posted for the original request, and the remaining requests are not issued.

Level

Base only.

REFERENCES

biodone(D3I)

sdi_callback (D3I)

NAME

sdi_callback – call the target driver interrupt routine to signal completion of a request

SYNOPSIS

```
void
sdi_callback(struct sb *sbp);
```

Arguments

sbp The command block associated with the completed command.

DESCRIPTION

sdi_callback calls the the target driver's interrupt routine. It calls either the *sc_int* or *sf_int* based on whether the associated command is an SCB or an SFB type.

USAGE

This routine is used to return control back to the associated target driver upon the completion of a command request.

Level

Base or Interrupt.

REFERENCES

sb(D4I), **scb**(D4I), **sfb**(D4I)

NAME

sdi_clrconfig – free devices claimed by target controllers

SYNOPSIS

```
void
sdi_clrconfig(struct owner *op, int flags, void (*rinit)());
```

Arguments

op A pointer to the head of an owner list previously returned by **sdi_doconfig**.

flags As defined for **sdi_access**.

rinit The address of the driver's **rinit** routine, which should be the same address that was previously passed to **sdi_doconfig**.

DESCRIPTION

sdi_clrconfig essentially undoes what was done by a prior call to **sdi_doconfig**. When the value of *flags* is **SDI_DISCLAIM|SDI_REMOVE**, all devices claimed by the calling target driver are freed. The address of the driver's **rinit** routine is then removed from the system's **rinit** table.

Return Values

None.

USAGE

This function is typically called by the **_unload** routine of dynamically loadable target drivers, in preparation to unload the driver.

Level

Base only.

REFERENCES

sdi_access(D3I), **sdi_doconfig**(D3I), **_unload**(D2DK)

sdi_doconfig (D3I)

NAME

sdi_doconfig – allow a target driver to find devices in the Equipped Device Table (EDT)

SYNOPSIS

```
struct owner *
sdi_doconfig(struct dev_cfg dev_cfg[], int dev_cfg_size, char *drvrname,
      struct drv_majors *drv_maj, void (*rinit()))
```

Arguments

dev_cfg
: The target driver's device configuration table.

dev_cfg_size
: Byte size of the target driver's device configuration table.

drvrname
: Target driver's name.

drv_maj
: Driver block and character major numbers.

rinit
: Target driver's **rinit**() function.

DESCRIPTION

sdi_doconfig searches the Equipped Device Table (EDT) looking for devices of the type controlled by the calling target driver.

The *rinit* argument controls how **sdi_doconfig** manipulates the *sdi_rinits* table entry for the associated device. If the **SDI_REMOVE** flag is set in the *dev_cfg* argument, the routine sets the entry to NULL. If the **SDI_REMOVE** flag is clear, the associated *sdi_rinits* entry is set to the *rinit* argument.

Return Values

The return value for **sdi_doconfig** is a pointer to a list of initialized *owner* structures associated with the target driver's devices. If no matching devices were found in the EDT, a **NULL** pointer is returned.

USAGE

sdi_doconfig is called by the target driver's *init* and *rinit* routines to claim devices of the appropriate type found in the EDT.

Level

Base only.

NAME

sdi_errmsg – format and print an error message

SYNOPSIS

```
int
sdi_errmsg(char *dev_id, struct scsi_ad *addr, struct sb *sbp,
     struct sense *sense, int type, int err_code);
```

Arguments

dev_id Pointer to a character string giving the device name.

addr Pointer to the SCSI address structure for the device returning the error.

sbp Pointer to the SCSI block for the request that generated the error.

sense Pointer to the sense data structure for the request that generated the error.

type A code indicating the type of condition that generated the error.

err_code
A code used to uniquely identify this invocation of **sdi_errmsg**.

DESCRIPTION

sdi_errmsg formats and prints **cmn_err** warning messages. The format and content of the messages changes depending on the message type argument. When the sense data is valid, **sdi_errmsg** also expands the sense data and extended sense data into meaningful phrases. When the sense key indicates a recovered error or a not ready condition, the messages go to **putbuf** instead of the system console. An optional **err_code** can be used to uniquely identify messages. No validity checking is performed on any of the values specified.

Return Values

None.

USAGE

sdi_errmsg is used in the existing target drivers to format and print error messages. It supports the production of messages in a common format. It should be used whenever a non-fatal error condition is to be presented at the system console. This routine produces **CE_WARN** error messages.

The argument *dev_id* should point to a string which will be used to identify the target returning an error. Typically, this is a single word like "Disk" or "Tape." The argument *addr* is used along with the LUN contained in the structure pointed to by *sbp* to construct a SCSI-like name for the device returning the error. This combination results in a string like "**HA** *x* **TC** *x* **LU** *x*," where the *x*s are replaced by HBA number, target number and logical unit number.

The four supported values for *type* are **SDI_SFB_ERR**, **SDI_CKCON_ERR**, **SDI_CKSTAT_ERR**, and **SDI_DEFAULT_ERR**. When executed with **SDI_SFB_ERR**, the routine interprets the *sbp* as an SFB and extracts only the logical unit and SDI completion code from the *sbp*. The other values for type cause the routine to interpret the sbp as an SCB. This allows the routine to extract and print the relevant information from the *sbp*.

When executed with **SDI_CKCON_ERR**, **sdi_errmsg** expands the available sense information into phrases. This allows the production of meaningful error messages. When executed with **SDI_CKSTAT_ERR**, the routine prints the target status information available in the SCB as part of the text. When executed with **SDI_DEFAULT_ERR**, the routine prints the SDI completion code as part of the message text.

If *err_code* is non-zero, it is printed as a hexadecimal number on the end of the first line of the error output. This may be useful to identify exactly where in a driver the call to **sdi_errmsg** occurred, if all the invocations are uniquely numbered.

Level

Base only.

REFERENCES

sb(D4I), **scb**(D4I), **scsi_ad**(D4I), **sfb**(D4I)

NAME

`sdi_findspec` – allocate a structure from the pool of structures

SYNOPSIS

```
struct struct *
sdi_findspec(struct sdi_edt *edtp, struct dev_spec *dev_spec[])
```

Arguments

edtp Pointer to an EDT structure for the desired device.

dev_spec
An array of pointers to device specific functions relative to each of the target driver entry points.

Return Values

Pointer to a *dev_spec* entry or **NULL** if no match is found.

DESCRIPTION

sdi_findspec finds a matching device specification routine. Target drivers may need special handling of certain devices. An example is a disk which requires a power-up command on the first open. This routine looks for a match of an inquiry string of a device against those kept in the **dev_spec** structure defined in the **space.c** file of the target driver.

USAGE

During a target driver init routine, the **sdi_findspec** is called to get the **dev_spec** structure (if defined) of the various function pointers of the device specific routines. The device specific routines which can be defined are **first_open**, **last_close**, **intr**, and the command helper. Only the needed functions should be defined. Included in the **dev_spec** structure is the inquiry string of the device which has the need for the special functions. It is also possible to define standard supported commands for the device and those which should use the command helper routine.

Level

Base only.

REFERENCES

space.c(4)

NOTICES

sdi_findspec appeared to be necessary while PDI was being designed, but during implementation the function was found to be unnecessary. We are considering removing it for the next release. If you feel this function is critical for your target driver please provide us with that feedback.

sdi_free (D3I)

NAME

sdi_free – return a previously allocated piece of memory back to the pool

SYNOPSIS

```
void
sdi_free(struct head *headp, struct jpool *jp);
```

Arguments

headp Pointer to the head structure of the pool from which the memory piece was allocated.

jp Pointer to the memory piece to be returned to the pool.

DESCRIPTION

sdi_free returns the allocated area of memory back to the pool it was taken from. After the completion of the use of the memory, the target or HBA driver should return the memory to the pool, because the pool is shared between all target and HBA drivers. Since each target driver and HBA driver needs large numbers of either job structures or SCSI command blocks, **sdi_get** and **sdi_free**, facilitate sharing of kernel memory. The routines allocate from and return memory to the kernel, based on demand.

Return Values

None.

USAGE

sdi_free is typically used in a local **freeblk/freejob** routine. Rather than having a local pool of job or command structures, PDI drivers should use one of the two existing shared pools. If the size of structures in these pools is too small, a new pool can be created and used by a PDI driver.

Level

Base or Interrupt.

REFERENCES

sdi_get(D3I)

NAME

sdi_freeblk – release a previously allocated **sb**

SYNOPSIS

```
long
sdi_freeblk(struct sb *pt);
```

Arguments

pt Pointer to the **sb** (command block) structure.

DESCRIPTION

sdi_freeblk returns an **sb** (command block) to the free block pool. The **sb_type** member of the **sb** structure is checked to ensure that a valid **sb** is returned.

Return Values

The normal return is **SDI_RET_OK**. A return value of **SDI_RET_ERR** indicates an error with the pointer.

USAGE

sdi_freeblk is typically used after a job completes.

Level

Base or Interrupt.

Examples

In this example, **diskfreejob** cleans up after a disk job completes and is called with a pointer to a structure, **job**. **job** contains information about the disk job, including a pointer to the **sb** for the job. **sdi_freeblk** is called with the pointer to the **job** structure as part of the clean-up operation.

```
struct job {
        struct sb *j_sbptr;
         ...
}

diskfreejob(jp)
struct job *jp;
{
         /* Perform job clean up */
         ...

         /*  Return SB to SDI */
         if( sdi_freeblk(jp->j_sbptr) != SDI_RET_OK)
         {
          /* SB rejected - print error message */
          cmn_err(CE_WARN, "DISK: SB rejected by SDI.");
         }
         ...
}
```

REFERENCES

sb(D4I), **sdi_getblk**(D3I)

sdi_get (D3I)

NAME

sdi_get – allocate a structure from the pool of structures

SYNOPSIS

```
struct jpool *
sdi_get(struct head *headp, int flag);
```

Arguments

headp Pointer to the head structure of the pool from which the memory piece was allocated.

flag The flag which is used to decide whether **sdi_get** can sleep if no structures are currently available (this flag is not currently used).

DESCRIPTION

sdi_get allocates a structure from the available pool of *headp*. If the pool is empty, an attempt is made to allocate more kernel kernel memory to satisfy the current request. If additional memory cannot be allocated, the routine will sleep.

Return Values

Pointer to a **jpool** structure.

USAGE

sdi_get is typically used in a local **getblk/getjob** routine. Rather than having a local pool of job or command structures, PDI drivers should use one of the two existing shared pools. If the size of structures in these pools are too small, a new pool can be created and used by the PDI driver.

Before making the first call to **sdi_get**, a call to **sdi_poolinit** must be done. The call to **sdi_poolinit** for *lg_poolhead* and *sm_poolhead* will be performed in **sdi_init** and should not be done again by other PDI drivers.

sdi_get should only be used by PDI drivers. This function may sleep and should not be called at interrupt level.

There are two pools initialized and used by existing PDI drivers. They are **struct head** *sm_poolhead* (28 bytes per structure) and **struct head** *lg_poolhead* (76 bytes per structure). Currently, most of the HBA drivers use the small structures for command blocks, and the target drivers use the large structures for job structures.

There are two rules for use of the structures:

1. The third word (long/bytes 8 through 11) is reserved and must not be modified.

2. Once a structure is freed, the driver cannot keep references to the structure or reference the structure in any way.

If you need to **bcopy** another structure into the structure allocated from **sdi_get**, save the third word and restore it after the copy.

Level

Base only.

REFERENCES

sdi_get(D3I), **sdi_poolinit**(D3I)

NAME

sdi_getblk – allocate an **sb** (command block) for the target driver

SYNOPSIS

```
struct sb *
sdi_getblk();
```

DESCRIPTION

sdi_getblk allocates an **sb** from PDI.

Return Values

Pointer to an **sb** structure.

USAGE

Only **sdi_getblk** should be used to allocate an **sb**. This function may sleep and should not be called at interrupt level. *sc_comp_code* is set to **SDI_UNUSED** in the returned **sb**.

PDI may add fields to the end of the **sb** for use by PDI. This implies that target drivers may not use **sb** structures allocated themselves. Target drivers must allocate an **sb** structure with **sdi_getblk**. Some of the information added at the end of the **sb** includes physical addresses. If these addresses do not exist, the computer will panic.

Level

Base only.

Examples

In the following example, **diskopen1** is called by the **open** routine for a disk target driver. In the routine, a disk-specific structure is initialized the first time the disk is accessed. This initialization includes allocating an **sb** for sending request sense commands to the disk. The **disk_st** structure is used in the example.

```
struct disk_st {
  long disk_state;          /* State of this disk */
  struct scsi_ad disk_addr; /* Major/Minor number of device */
  struct sb *disk_fltreq;   /* SCSI block for request sense */
      ...
};

diskopen1(major, minor)
long major, minor;
{
      struct disk_st *disk;
      /* Based on the major and minor numbers of the disk,
       * index into the array of disk structures and get the
       * pointer to the one for this disk.
       */
      disk = &Disk[diskintmin(major, minor)];
      /* Check to see if this disk has been initialized */
      if ((disk->disk_state & DISK_INIT) == 0)
         {
            /* This is first access to the disk so initialize
```

```
                 * some of the data structures for the disk.
                 */
                /* Get SB for request sense jobs for this disk */
                disk->disk_fltreq = sdi_getblk();

                /* Fill in the major and minor numbers and the
                 * logical unit number in the address structure.
                 */
                disk->disk_addr.sa_major = major;
                disk->disk_addr.sa_minor = minor;
                disk->disk_addr.sa_lun = LUN(minor);
        }
        ...
```

REFERENCES

sb(D4I), scsi_ad(D4I), sdi_freeblk(D3I)

NAME

sdi_getdev – convert device number to SCSI pass-through device number

SYNOPSIS

```
void
sdi_getdev(struct scsi_ad *addr, dev_t *dev);
```

Arguments

addr Pointer to the **scsi_ad** (device address) structure; the pass-through device number is returned in the **sa_major** and **sa_minor** members of the structure.

dev Device major/minor number pair.

DESCRIPTION

sdi_getdev translates a device major/minor number pair into the pass-through interface major/minor number pair for that device. The pass-through major/minor number is returned in the **addr** structure.

Return Values

None.

USAGE

A target driver uses the pass-through device number when logging non-buffer related errors.

Level

Base or Interrupt.

Examples

The following example shows how **sdi_getdev** can be used after an unsuccessful call to **sdi_icmd**:

```
struct sb       *sb_ptr;
struct scsi_ad   dk_addr;
dev_t            pt_dev;
...

/* Call sdi_icmd to send an immediate command */
   if (sdi_icmd(sb_ptr) != SDI_RET_OK)
{
   /* The call was unsuccessful.  Print an error message,
    * get the pass-through device number, and log an error
    * against the device.
    */
    cmn_err(CE_WARN, "DISK: Bad SB type to SDI. ");
    sdi_getdev(&disk_addr, &pt_dev);
}
...
```

REFERENCES

sb(D4I), **scsi_ad**(D4I), **sdi_getdev**(D3I), **sdi_icmd**(D3I)

sdi_gethbano (D3I)

NAME

sdi_gethbano – get/validate host bus adapter controller number

SYNOPSIS

```
int
sdi_gethbano(int cntlnum);
```

Arguments

cntlnum

Requested HBA controller number.

DESCRIPTION

If *cntlnum* is negative, **sdi_gethbano** returns the next available controller number. Positive values of *cntlnum* are checked for validity. In this case, **sdi_gethbano** returns *cntlnum* if valid or a negative value if not.

Return Values

A positive value represents a valid and available controller number. A negative value indicates the requested controller number is is either invalid or unavailable, or there are no available numbers to allocate.

USAGE

sdi_gethbano is typically called by the **init** routines of HBA drivers to obtain a controller number for later use by **sdi_register**.

Level

Base only.

REFERENCES

sdi_register(D3I)

NAME

sdi_icmd – perform requested operation immediately

SYNOPSIS

```
int
sdi_icmd(struct sb *pt);
```

Arguments

pt Pointer to the **sb** (command block) structure; the *sb_type* member of the **sb** structure must be set to either **SFB_TYPE** or **ISCB_TYPE**.

DESCRIPTION

sdi_icmd sends an immediate **sb** to a device. Immediate means that this function bypasses queued **scb**'s and immediately accesses the device to perform the requested operation.

Return Values

A return code of **SDI_RET_OK** indicates that the request is in progress and the target driver interrupt routine will be called. A return code of **SDI_RET_ERR** indicates that the type field is invalid. After a logical unit queue is resumed, all outstanding immediate control and function blocks are returned before the next normal command is returned.

USAGE

The **sdi_icmd** function typically is used during error handling.

In contrast to an operation using an **sfb**, operations using an **scb** send the job to the requested logical unit.

Coming in at immediate-priority, operations using an **sfb** are executed in the order submitted and take priority over **scb** operations. Only one instance of each immediate command type (**SFB_TYPE** or **ISCB_TYPE**) may be outstanding to a particular logical unit.

Level

Base or Interrupt.

Examples

The following example shows how an **sb** is re-sent using **sdi_icmd** when the completion code indicates that a retry (**SDI_RETRY**) is requested. **diskint** is an example of a disk target driver interrupt routine.

```
void
diskint(sb_ptr)
struct sb *sb_ptr;
{
    ...

    /* Check the completion code of the SCB to see if the
     * command needs to be retried.
     */
```

```
        if (sb_ptr->SCB.sc_comp_code & SDI_RETRY )
        {
            /* Retry the command request using sdi_icmd */
               if (sdi_icmd(sb_ptr) != SDI_RET_OK)
        {
            /* If the return value of sdi_icmd is not OK,
             * print an error message.
             */
             cmn_err(CE_WARN, "DISK: Bad SB type to SDI.");
        }
        return;
    }
    ...
```

REFERENCES

sb(D4I), scb(D4I), sdi_translate(D3I), sfb(D4I)

NAME

`sdi_init` – initialize the SDI driver

SYNOPSIS

```
extern int sdi_started;

void
sdi_init();
```

DESCRIPTION

sdi_init initializes the SDI driver to accept SDI functions. The *sdi_started* flag is provided so that a target driver can determine if another target driver may have already called **sdi_init**.

Return Values

None.

USAGE

Level

Base only.

Examples

This example shows the sequence of instructions used to test **sdi_started** and call **sdi_init**:

```
extern int sdi_started
...
/* Check to see if the Host Adapter driver has
 * already been started.
 */
if( !sdi_started )
{
        /* Call the Host Adapter driver init routine */
        sdi_init();
}
...
```

sdi_name (D3I)

NAME

`sdi_name` – get name of addressed PDI controller

SYNOPSIS

```
void
sdi_name(struct scsi_ad *addr, char *name);
```

Arguments

addr Pointer to the `scsi_ad` (device address) structure.

name String containing the device *name*.

DESCRIPTION

`sdi_name` decodes a device number into a character string so that the device number can be displayed (with `cmn_err`).

Return Values

None.

USAGE

The controller name is copied into *name*. The returned string may be as long as 48 bytes (you must allocate 49 bytes). Access to the controller name can only be used for display; the driver should not attempt to decode the string for other uses.

The string returned is *"SLOT # TC #"*, with the slot number of the host adapter card and the target controller ID filled in.

Level

Base or Interrupt.

Examples

This example is a sample `print` routine in a disk target driver. The arguments to the `cmn_err` function are the device number and a string to display (on the system console).

```
diskprint(dev, str)
dev_t dev;
char *str;
{
    char name[49];        /* Character array for device name */
    struct scsi_ad addr; /* SCSI address structure          */

    /* Fill in SCSI device address based on device number */
    addr.sa_major = emajor(dev);
    addr.sa_minor = eminor(dev);
    addr.sa_lun = LUN(eminor(dev));

    /* Call sdi_name with the address of the SCSI address
     * structure and a pointer to the character array.
     */
    sdi_name(&addr, name);

    /* Print the error message */
       cmn_err(CE_WARN, "%s, Unit %d, Partition %d:  %s", name,
               addr.sa_lun, eminor(dev) & PARTMASK, str);
}
```

REFERENCES

scsi_ad(D4I)

sdi_poolinit (D3I)

NAME

`sdi_poolinit` – initialize a dynamic structure pool

SYNOPSIS

```
void
sdi_poolinit(struct head *headp);
```

Arguments

headp Pointer to a partially intialized head structure; the *f_isize*, *f_maxpages*, and the *f_freelist* must be initialized.

DESCRIPTION

`sdi_poolinit` initializes the head structure for the new pool of memory.

Return Values

None.

USAGE

You must call this routine before the first **sdi_get** call. Before calling **sdi_poolinit**, the *f_isize*, *f_maxpages*, and *f_freelist* fields of **headp** must be initialized to the needed values.

The *f_isize* field will contain the size in bytes of the structures for this pool. The *f_maxpages* field is the number of pages to be requested for each allocation of kernel memory for structures. Unless the structures are very large, a good value for *f_maxpages* is `1`. The *f_freelist* field must point to a **struct jpool** structure which is initialized with both pointers pointing back at itself (to serve as a terminating element of the freelist).

Level

Base only.

Examples

This example shows the sequence of instructions used to initialize a **struct head** and the call to `sdi_poolinit`.

```
struct head     sm_poolhead;
struct jpool    smfreelist;

sm_poolhead.f_maxpages = 1;
smfreelist.j_ff = smfreelist.j_fb = &smfreelist;
sm_poolhead.f_freelist = &smfreelist;
sm_poolhead.f_isize = 28;
sdi_poolinit(&sm_poolhead);
...
```

NAME

`sdi_redt` – search the EDT for an existing entry

SYNOPSIS

```
struct sdi_edt *
sdi_redt(int hba, int scsi_id, int lun);
```

Arguments

hba HBA number for the device.

scsi_id Target number of this device on the HBA.

lun Logical unit number of this device on the given target and HBA.

DESCRIPTION

sdi_redt returns a pointer to an Equipped Device Table (EDT) entry for the device specified by the *hba, scsi_id* and *lun* given if such an entry exists. If the EDT is empty or no matching entry exists, a **NULL** pointer is returned. The value for *hba* used must be the same as the value returned by **sdi_gethbano** when the Host Bus Adapter (HBA) was initialized.

Return Values

Pointer to an **sdi_edt** structure.

USAGE

sdi_redt is typically used in a global open/close/command routine. Rather than maintaining a local table of valid **hba:scsi_id:lun** tuples, PDI drivers should use the existing EDT through this function to determine the validity of such a tuple.

sdi_redt is also the approved interface for obtaining a pointer to an existing **sdi_edt** structure. This pointer can then be used for calls to **sdi_wedt** to modify an EDT entry.

Level

Base only.

REFERENCES

sdi_gethbano(D3I), **sdi_wedt**(D3I)

sdi_register (D3I)

NAME

sdi_register – register a Host Bus Adaptor (HBA) device instance to controller number

SYNOPSIS

```
int
sdi_register(struct hba_info *infop, struct hba_idata *idatap);
```

Arguments

infop Pointer to the HBA driver's information structure.

idatap Pointer to the instance data for the specific device being registered.

DESCRIPTION

This routine registers the correspondence between a controller number and a specific HBA hardware instance.

Return Values

Upon successful completion, **sdi_register** returns the controller number to which the device is registered. If the value in **idatap->cntlr** is invalid, or the hardware is not installed in the machine, a negative value is returned indicating the error.

USAGE

This function is typically called by the **init** routines of HBA drivers to register configured device instances of the given HBA.

The **hba_info** structure contains information about the device driver for the HBA type, and is defined as follows:

```
/*
 * Per-module HBA information.
 */
struct  hba_info        {
        int     *hba_flag;
        ulong   max_xfer;
        /*
         * Entry points.
         */
        long                (*hba_freeblk)();
        struct  hbadata *(*hba_getblk)();
        long                (*hba_icmd)();
        void                (*hba_getinfo)();
        long                (*hba_send)();
        void                (*hba_xlat)();
        int                 (*hba_open)();
        int                 (*hba_close)();
        int                 (*hba_ioctl)();
};
```

The **hba_idata** structure contains data describing a specific hardware instance of the HBA type:

```
/*
 * Per-instance HBA information.
 */
struct  hba_idata        {
        int              version_num;
        char             *name;
        unsigned char    ha_id;
        ulong            ioaddr1;
        int              dmachan1;
        int              iov;
        int              cntlr;
        int              active;
};
```

The controller number to which the device is to be registered must be placed in the *cntlr* field of the **hba_idata** structure before the call. This value should have been obtained from, or validated by, the **sdi_gethbano** routine.

Level

Base only.

REFERENCES

sdi_gethbano(D3I)

sdi_send (D3I)

NAME

`sdi_send` – send a command to a PDI HBA driver

SYNOPSIS

```
long
sdi_send(struct sb *pt);
```

Arguments

pt Pointer to the **sb** structure.

DESCRIPTION

sdi_send accepts a pointer to an **sb** command block structure, and sends the command to the controller for routing to a specific device.

Return Values

The return value **SDI_RET_OK** indicates that the request is in progress and the target driver interrupt handler will be called. The value **SDI_RET_RETRY** indicates that PDI cannot accept the job at this time, and that it should be retried later. **SDI_RET_ERR** indicates the **sb_type** is invalid. When a device is opened for pass-through, **SDI_RET_RETRY** is returned.

USAGE

The command block must be allocated from the host adapter pool of command blocks, and the addresses translated using the **sdi_translate** function. The *type* field must be **SCB_TYPE**. Commands sent through this function are executed in the order they are received.

Level

Base or Interrupt.

Examples

This example shows how **sdi_send** is used. **disksend** is an example disk target driver routine, called internally within the target driver to send a command to a device. It is passed a pointer to a command block.

```
disksend(sb_ptr)
struct sb *sb_ptr;
{
        int sendret;          /* sdi_send return value */
        extern int sendid;    /* timeout ID for retry  */

        /* Call sdi_send with the SB pointer for the job */
        if ((sendret = sdi_send(sb_ptr)) != SDI_RET_OK)
        {
           /* If sdi_send returned retry, set up a timeout to
            * submit the job later
            */
           if (sendret == SDI_RET_RETRY)
           {
              /* Call timeout and save the ID */
                 sendid = timeout(disksendt, sb_ptr, LATER);
                 return;
           }
```

```
        else
        {
            /* The Host Adapter driver could not process the job.
             * Print an error message.
             */
            cmn_err(CE_WARN, "DISK: Bad SB type to SDI. ");
            continue;
        }
    }
    ...
```

REFERENCES

sb(D4I), sdi_icmd(D3I), sdi_translate(D3I)

sdi_swap16 (D3I)

NAME

sdi_swap16, **sdi_swap24**, **sdi_swap32** – swaps bytes in a 16-, 24-, or 32-bit data type

SYNOPSIS

```
short sdi_swap16(unsigned int arg);

int sdi_swap24(unsigned int arg);

long sdi_swap32(unsigned long arg);
```

Arguments

arg Value to be swapped.

DESCRIPTION

sdi_swap16 swaps the two bytes of the 16-bit argument, *arg*, and returns the swapped result.

sdi_swap24 swaps the three bytes of the 24-bit argument, *arg*, and returns the swapped result.

sdi_swap32 swaps the four bytes of the 32-bit argument, *arg*, and returns the swapped result.

Return Values

The return value is the value of the swapped argument.

USAGE

This function is typically used by HBA drivers to convert 16-, 24-, or 32-bit binary values for a control block, returned by or sent to the Host Adapter, when the byte orientation of the Intel *x*86 CPU and the Host Adapter card are opposite.

Level

Base only.

NAME

sdi_translate – translate **scb** virtual to physical address for a PDI Host Bus Adapter (HBA) driver

SYNOPSIS

void
sdi_translate(struct sb **pt*, **int** *bflags*, **proc_t** *procp*);

Arguments

pt Pointer to the **sb** structure.

bflags The *b_flags* member of the **buf_t** (buffer header) structure.

procp Pointer to the **procp_t** process pointer.

DESCRIPTION

sdi_translate allows PDI to perform machine-specific base level virtual to physical address translation for the host adapter.

Return Values

None.

USAGE

sdi_translate is called each time an **scb** is assembled for transmission before the **sdi_send** or **sdi_icmd** functions are called. The *sb_type, sc_cmdpt, sc_cmdsz, sc_datapt, sc_datasz,* and *sc_link* fields must be valid. The *bflags* argument is the same as the *b_flags* member of the **buf_t**(D4P) structure. The **B_READ** and **B_PHYS** flags are used by **sdi_translate**. The target driver must guarantee that the data area and command area are locked into memory and are accessible by the requester. **sdi_translate** should not be called if the data address is supplied by PDI.

In the case of a block read or write, the data area is locked automatically by the kernel.

This function may sleep and must be called while executing as the requesting process.

It is the CDB aspect of the **scb** that requires translation; therefore, the **sfb** must never be run through **sdi_translate**. Another important consideration is that if the data area is not a contiguous segment of memory, the **B_PHYS** flag must be set, especially when allocating more than 2K (2048 bytes) of memory. (This flag is defined in **ddi.h**.)

Level

Base only.

Examples

In this example, the values that must be initialized before the call to **sdi_translate** are set in the **sb** structure.

```
struct sb  *sb_ptr;       /* SCSI Block */
struct scb *scb;          /* SCSI control block */
struct scs *cmd;          /* SCSI command */
buf_t  *bp;               /* Buffer pointer */
char *buffer;             /* Buffer for data */
unsigned int size;        /* Size of the buffer */
```

```
unsigned short mode;     /* Direction of the transfer */

...

/* Set the command address and the command size */
scb->sc_cmdpt = SCS_AD(cmd);
scb->sc_cmdsz = SCS_SZ;

/* Set the data address and the data size */
scb->sc_datapt = buffer;
scb->sc_datasz = size;

sdi_translate(sb_ptr, bp->b_flags, procp());

...
```

REFERENCES

sb(D4I), scb(D4I), sdi_icmd(D3I), sdi_send(D3I)

NAME

sdi_wedt – modify an existing Equipped Device Table (EDT) entry

SYNOPSIS

```
int
sdi_wedt(struct sdi_edt *edtp, int devtype, char *inq);
```

Arguments

edtp Pointer to an EDT entry to modify.

devtype
New device type value to set for this EDT entry.

inq Pointer to the new inquiry string to set for this EDT entry.

DESCRIPTION

sdi_wedt modifies the device type and inquiry string of an existing EDT entry pointed to by *edtp*.

Return Values

On success, **sdi_wedt** returns **SDI_RET_OK**. On failure, it returns **SDI_RET_ERR**.

USAGE

If the EDT is empty or no matching entry exists, an error is returned. The value for *edtp* used must be the same as the value returned by **sdi_redt** for a given PDI device.

No validity checking is performed on the value specified for *devtype*. *inq* must be a valid pointer to a null-terminated string.

sdi_wedt is not regularly used, but allows modification of the inquiry string and device type for an existing EDT entry.

Level

Base only.

REFERENCES

sdi_redt(D3I)

NAME

`intro` – introduction to SDI data structures

DESCRIPTION

This section describes the structures that are accessed in SDI target drivers. Five data structures are used by SDI to handle data transmission between the target drivers and the host adapter. Additional structures, the **scm** and the **scs** structures, are used to send a command from a user program to a device using the pass-through interface.

The structures discussed in this section are:

`sb` block structure

`scb` control block structure

`scm` command structure

`scs` command structure

`scsi_ad` device address structure

`sfb` function block structure

`ver_no` version number structure

sb(D4I)

NAME

sb – command block structure

SYNOPSIS

`#include <sys/sdi.h>`

DESCRIPTION

The **sb** structure defines the command block, which can be either an **scb**(D4I) structure or an **sfb**(D4I) structure. The **sb_type** field indicates whether the **sb** structure contains an **scb** (control block) or an **sfb** (function block) structure.

USAGE

Use the **sb** structure when you call an SDI function that sends a request to a PDI device [either **sdi_send**(D3I) or **sdi_icmd**(D3I)].

The method for using the **sb** structure is:

1. Use the **sdi_getblk** function to allocate a command block
2. Set **sb_type** appropriately
3. Assign values to the members of the structure as appropriate
4. Call the appropriate function to send the data structure

See **scb**(D4I) and **sfb**(D4I) for more information on structure use.

The target driver must only allocate a command block using **sdi_getblk**(D3I).

If one **sb** structure is copied, the new structure must be processed with **sdi_translate**(D3I).

Structure Members

The **sb** structure is defined as follows:

```
unsigned long     sb_type;   /* Type of SDI block */
union{
  struct scb      b_scb;     /* SCSI control block */
  struct sfb      b_sfb;     /* SCSI function block */
}sb_b;
```

sb_type indicates whether the **sb_b** structure is an **scb** or an **sfb**. structure. Values may be:

ISCB_TYPE	**sb_b** is an immediate **scb** (used with **sdi_icmd**).
SCB_TYPE	**sb_b** is an **scb** (used with **sdi_send**).
SFB_TYPE	**sb_b** is an **sfb** (used with **sdi_icmd**).

b_scb The SCSI control block structure.

b_sfb The SCSI function block structure.

REFERENCES

scb(D4I), **sdi_getblk**(D3I), **sdi_icmd**(D3I), **sdi_send**(D3I), **sdi_translate**(D3I), **sfb**(D4I)

NAME

scb – command control block structure

SYNOPSIS

#include <sys/sdi.h>

DESCRIPTION

The command control block structure, **scb**, is used to send a command to a PDI device. The **scb** contains a pointer to a command descriptor block (CDB) that describes the command to the target controller. The CDB command information is created using either the **scm** structure or the **scs** structure, both described in **scm**(D4I). The CDB contains the operation code of the instruction you wish to send and other command-specific data.

Return Values

The following table is an alphabetic list of the values that may be returned in the **sc_comp_code** field of the **scb** structure. The third column indicates the hexadecimal value associated with the completion code value. The fourth column indicates on which computer type the use of the completion code is supported. The fifth column describes which flags in bit positions 28–31 of **sc_comp_code** are enabled by the completion code. E is **SDI_ERROR**, M is **SDI_MESS**, R is **SDI_RETRY**, S is **SDI_SUSPEND**, and "-" indicates that the respective flag is not enabled.)

sc_comp_code	Description	Hex Value	Computer Type	Flags
SDI_ABORT	Command was aborted	0x05	unsupported	EMRS
SDI_ASW	Job completed normally	0x01	3B2, 386, i860	----
SDI_CKSTAT	Check the status byte	0x0e	3B2, 386, i860	E-RS
SDI_CRESET	Reset caused by this unit	0x07	386	E-RS
SDI_HAERR	Host adapter error	0x0b	3B2, 386, i860	EM-S
SDI_LINKF0	Linked cmd done without flag	0x02	unsupported	----
SDI_LINKF1	Linked cmd done with flag	0x03	unsupported	----
SDI_MEMERR	Memory fault	0x0c	unsupported	E-R-
SDI_MISMAT	Parameter mismatch	0x12	unsupported	EMRS
SDI_NOALLOC	This block not allocated	0x00	3B2, 386	----
SDI_NOSELE	SCSI bus select failed	0x11	3B2, 386, i860	E--S
SDI_NOTEQ	Addressed device not present	0x08	386	EM--
SDI_ONEIC	More than one immediate request	0x17	3B2, 386	E---
SDI_OOS	Device out of service	0x10	3B2, 386, i860	EM--
SDI_PROGRES	Job in progress	0x13	3B2, 386, i860	----
SDI_QFLUSH	Job was flushed	0x04	3B2, 386	EMR-
SDI_RESET	Reset detected on the bus	0x06	3B2, 386, i860	EMRS
SDI_SBUSER	SCSI bus error	0x0d	None	E-RS
SDI_SCBERR	SCB error	0x0f	3B2, i860	E---

sc_comp_code	Description	Hex Value	Computer Type	Flags
SDI_SFBERR	SFB error	0x19	3B2, 386, i860	E---
SDI_SHORT	TC did not transfer all data	0x1b	unsupported	E-RS
SDI_TCERR	Target protocol error detected	0x1a	unsupported	E--S
SDI_TIME	Job timed out	0x09	3B2	E-RS
SDI_UNUSED	Job not in use	0x14	3B2, i860	----
SDI_V2PERR	**vtop** failed	0x08	unsupported	EM--

The supported **sc_comp_code** values are defined as follows:

SDI_ASW — All seems well. The job completed without an error.

SDI_CKSTAT — Check the status byte. This value is set when the target controller returns a status other than good.

SDI_HAERR — A problem occurred between PDI and the host adapter controller. Possible causes are I/O bus parity or a failed host adapter.

SDI_NOALLOC — The requested block was not allocated to a target driver by PDI. If a target driver detects this value, panic the system (using the **cmn_err**(D3P) function). **sc_comp_code** is set to this value when the command block is released from the target driver.

SDI_NOSELE — SDI timed out trying to select the controller.

SDI_ONEIC — More than one immediate request has been sent.

SDI_OOS — The firmware is not operational.

SDI_PROGRES — The job is not complete (set by PDI in the **sdi_icmd** and **sdi_send** functions).

SDI_QFLUSH — When the target driver requested a job queue flush for a device, all jobs in the queue are returned with this completion code set.

SDI_RESET — PDI detected a reset on the HBA bus. All outstanding or jobs queued at the target controller are returned to the target drivers with this condition code set. If the job is being controlled by PDI, but has not been sent out on the bus, the job is not returned. This code is also returned if a target driver requests that a target controller be reset.

SDI_SCBERR — The control block contains an error or an invalid type.

SDI_SFBERR — There is an error in one of the fields in the **sfb** structure.

SDI_TIME — SDI timed out a job.

SDI_UNUSED — The host adapter is not using the control structure. SDI sets the **sc_comp_code** to this value when it allocates a block for a target driver.

The following values are listed in **sdi.h** but are not supported at this time:

SDI_LINKF0 This linked command completed normally and the command value bit was zero.

SDI_LINKF1 This linked command completed normally and the command value bit was one.

SDI_MISMAT A controller attempted to perform an operation that did not agree with the data supplied in the SCB. For example, this error can occur when the controller attempts to transfer data in and the **SCB_READ** value is not set in the **sc_mode** member.

SDI_SBUSER The host adapter encountered a problem on the SCSI bus and all recovery action failed. A controller with a faulty bus driver can cause such an error. TP **SDI_TCERR** The host adapter detected a protocol error while performing this request.

USAGE

After the **scb** is sent, do not change the information in this structure or anything referenced by it (for example, in the structure that describes the CDB) until after the job completes.

The method of using the **scb** structure is:

1. Fill in the appropriate information in the CDB, and put the address of the CDB in the **sc_cmdpt** member of the **scb** structure, and set **sc_cmdsz**.
2. Set the **sb_type** member of the **sb** structure to indicate whether this structure is being used by **sdi_icmd**(D3I) or by **sdi_send**(D3I).
3. Set the **sc_link** member of the **scb** structure to **NULL**.
4. Set the **sc_datapt** member of the **scb** structure to the virtual address of the data area, and set **sc_datasz**. Always assign values to **sc_datapt** and **sc_datasz** if the command requires a data area. You must set these two fields to **NULL**.
5. Call **sdi_translate**(D3I) to resolve virtual to physical addressing. Before calling this function, these fields must be set: **sb_type**, **sc_cmdpt**, **sc_cmdsz**, **sc_datapt**, **sc_datasz**, and **sc_link**.
6. Call either **sdi_send** or **sdi_icmd** to send the CDB to the PDI device.

On successful job completion, **sc_comp_code** is set to **SDI_ASW** (all seems well).

For an error condition, check **sc_comp_code** for **SDI_CKSTAT**, then check **sc_status** to determine the type of error that was returned by the target controller. (When an error occurs on a PDI device, the error is passed to the controller and then through the firmware of the host adapter. PDI acknowledges this interaction and sets the error code from the target controller in **sc_status** and sets **sc_comp_code** to **SDI_CKSTAT**.)

If **sc_comp_code** is not **SDI_CKSTAT** or **SDI_ASW**, then the value in bits 0–27 of **sc_comp_code** indicates the nature of the error and the value in bits 28–31 indicates how to process the error. As an alternative, you may wish to check bits 28–31 for **SDI_ERROR**, and then test bits 0–27 for more specific information.

A scenario for this usage is shown in the structure members explanation for sc_comp_code, earlier in this manual page.

Structure Members

The **scb** structure is defined as follows:

```
unsigned long    sc_comp_code; /* Current job status */
void             (*sc_int)();  /* Target driver intr handler */
caddr_t          sc_cmdpt;     /* Target command */
caddr_t          sc_datapt;    /* Data area */
long             sc_wd;        /* Target driver word */
time_t           sc_time;      /* Time limit for job */
struct scsi_ad   sc_dev;       /* PDI device address */
unsigned short   sc_mode;      /* Mode flags for current job */
unsigned char    sc_status;    /* Target status byte */
char             sc_fill;      /* Fill byte */
struct sb        *sc_link;     /* Link to next scb command */
long             sc_cmdsz;     /* Size of command */
long             sc_datasz;    /* Size of data */
long             sc_resid;     /* Bytes to transfer after data */
```

The fields that the host adapter can change are: sc_comp_code, sc_status, and sc_time.

More information on each member of the **scb** structure follows:

sc_comp_code
: The job completion status. This member is tested in the interrupt routine after the job has completed. Use **sc_comp_code** by testing for **SDI_ASW** (normal return). If **SDI_ASW** is not present, test bits 28–31 to determine if **SDI_ERROR** was set to indicate an error occurred. The remaining values in bits 28–31 indicate how to process the error. The values for bits 28–31 are covered in the following text. Values for bits 0–27 are covered at the end of the **scb** structure section. Refer to the header file for more information on how to extract the values in each bit position. Values for bits 28–31 are:

  SDI_ERROR
  : An error occurred.

  SDI_RETRY
  : The error is unrelated to this job, and the job should be retried (device dependent).

  SDI_MESS
  : A message describing this event has been printed on the console and logged.

  SDI_SUSPEND
  : The host adapter has suspended sending normal commands to the logical unit and the target driver is responsible for resuming the queue. Immediate commands can still be sent with the **sdi_icmd** function, but the SCSI device cannot be opened for pass-through.

sc_int
: A pointer to a target driver interrupt routine. This routine is called when the job associated with the control block completes. The interrupt routine is called with a single argument which is a pointer to the address of the **sb** of the job. The functions in the

interrupt routine must not call **sleep**(D3K), have user context, or run in the context of any particular process. **sc_int** is called when the job sending the information to the PDI device completes. If **sc_int** is **NULL**, no interrupt routine is called when the job completes.

sc_cmdpt A virtual address pointing to the start of a target controller command, with the size indicated by the **sc_cmdsz** member. The command pointed to by **sc_cmdpt** is sent with no interpretation by the SDI software. The command area must be in kernel space and contiguous in physical memory. You must allocate your own data structure to ensure contiguous physical memory.

sc_datapt A virtual address pointer pointing to the start of the data area for the given command, with the size indicated by the **sc_datasz** member.

sc_wd Provided for use by the target drivers. This member is not examined or changed by PDI; you can use this member for any purpose.

sc_time The maximum number of milliseconds PDI should wait for the job to complete. The timing begins when the command is sent to the controller. The completion status must be returned before the timer runs out. If a time-out occurs, the processing of queued jobs for that controller is suspended until resumed by the target driver. If the **sc_time** member is zero, the job is not timed. This timing should only be used to ensure the completion of the job and not for performance measurements. The returned value of **sc_time** indicates the actual amount of time that the job took and the resolution is in minutes.

sc_dev Device address (an instance of the **scsi_ad**(D4I) structure).

sc_mode (Not supported.) This member specifies any special modes for this job. The **SCB_HAAD** bit in the **sc_mode** field refers to the data address, pointed to by the **sc_datapt** element. If the **SCB_HAAD** bit is set in the **sc_mode** field, the data address was supplied by PDI, otherwise it was supplied by the target driver.

When **SCB_PARTBLK** is set in the mode field, it should indicate that the data area does not define the complete transfer. In this case, the **sc_resid** field indicates how many more bytes to expect in the transfer. These extra bytes are not transferred between system memory and the HBA bus. If the transfer is a write, zeros are sent to the controller.

sc_status Contains the value returned by the target controller. If a CHECK CONDITION status is returned, the host adapter suspends processing of commands to that device.

sc_fill (Not supported.) A character with which an incomplete data block is padded. All incomplete data blocks are always padded with zeros.

sc_link	(Not supported.) You must set this member to **NULL** before calling sdi_translate.
sc_cmdsz	Command size in bytes.
sc_datasz	Data size in bytes of the requested input or output buffer.
sc_resid	(Not supported.) The number of bytes not transferred to or from the target controller. This is used for partial block transfers. Residue bytes which are received from the target controller are discarded by PDI.

REFERENCES

scb(D4I), scm(D4I), sdi_icmd(D3I), sdi_send(D3I)

NAME

scm, **scs** – Portable Device Interface (PDI) command structures

SYNOPSIS

```
#include <sys/scsi.h>
```

DESCRIPTION

Both the **scm** and **scs** structures are used by target drivers, and with the pass-through interface to send a command to a PDI device. The **scs** structure defines the layout for a group 6 (six-byte command length) command descriptor block (CDB); **scm** is a group 10 (ten-byte command length) CDB. Both types of CDBs are described in the *ANSI Small Computer System Interface (SCSI), X3T9.2/82-2, Revision 17B*, December 16, 1985. Refer to the ANSI manual for more information on individual structure members. The **sm_pad0** member ensures that the **sm_addr** member does not cross a 32-bit word boundary.

USAGE

Structure Members

The members of the **scm** structure are:

```
int       sm_pad0 : 16;    /* 16-bit pad */
int       sm_op   : 8;     /* Opcode */
int       sm_lun  : 3;     /* Logical unit number */
int       sm_res1 : 5;     /* reserved field */
unsigned  sm_addr;         /* Block address */
int       sm_res2 : 8;     /* reserved field */
int       sm_len  : 16;    /* Transfer length */
int       sm_cont : 8;     /* Control byte */
```

Because of the **sm_pad0** member, you must add 2 to the address of the **scm** structure when specifying it in the **scb** structure.

The members of the **scs** structure are:

```
int       ss_op   : 8;     /* Opcode */
int       ss_lun  : 3;     /* Logical unit number */
int       ss_addr : 21;    /* Block address */
int       ss_len  : 8;     /* Transfer length */
int       ss_cont : 8;     /* Control byte */
```

scsi_ad (D4I)

NAME

scsi_ad – PDI device address structure

SYNOPSIS

```
#include <sys/sdi.h>
```

DESCRIPTION

The PDI device address structure, **scsi_ad**, is used by every **scb**(D4I) or **sfb**(D4I) structure with the appropriate PDI device. PDI interprets the external major and minor numbers, the logical unit number, and the extended logical unit number to send the **scb** or **sfb** to the correct device.

USAGE

The major number is decoded by PDI to determine the host adapter and target controller. The minor number typically is used only by the target driver to determine the logical unit and any other device specific information (partition of a disk or density of a tape). PDI determines the logical unit from **sa_lun**. This member may have the values 0 to 7, except when extended unit numbering is used. In this case, the **EXLUN** value is set in the **sa_lun** member, and the **sa_exlun** member is set the appropriate value.

For example, if the target controller wanted to access extended logical unit 0x021a, then **sa_lun** would equal 0x82, and **sa_exlun** would equal 0x1a.

Structure Members

The **scdi_ad** structure is defined as follows:

```
long           sa_major;    /* Major number */
long           sa_minor;    /* Minor number */
unsigned char  sa_lun;      /* logical unit number */
unsigned char  sa_exlun;    /* extended logical unit number */
short          sa_fill;     /* Fill word */
```

This structure consists of the device number, which is passed to the target driver by the kernel, and the logical unit number. The **sa_major** and **sa_minor** members (external major and minor numbers) are long integers to allow for future expansion of the major and minor numbers.

REFERENCES

scb(D4I), **sfb**(D4I)

NAME

`sfb` – function block structure

SYNOPSIS

`#include <sys/sdi.h>`

DESCRIPTION

The function block, **sfb**, serves as a mechanism for sending control information from a target driver to the host adapter or to a PDI device. (The **scb**(D4I) is sent to the device; the **sfb** is generally sent to all other receiving entities.)

An **sfb** is sent to the device when an abort or reset message is required. (Abort and reset messages have a different protocol than do the commands sent to the PDI device with a CDB.)

USAGE

Structure Members

The **sfb** structure is defined as follows:

```
unsigned long    sf_comp_code;    /* Current job status */
void             (*sf_int)();     /* Target driver intr handler */
struct scsi_ad   sf_dev;          /* SCSI device address */
unsigned long    sf_func;         /* Function to be performed */
int              sf_wd            /* Target driver word */
```

The **sf_comp_code** is identical to the **sc_comp_code** in the **scb**, and it takes on the same values.

The **sf_int** and **sf_dev** entries are used the same way as in the **scb** structure. The only field which the host adapter changes in the **sfb** structure is **sf_comp_code**.

The **sf_func** member indicates the operation to be performed:

SFB_ABORTM Send an abort message to the addressed logical unit.

SFB_FLUSHR Flush a logical queue unit.

SFB_NOPF The target driver is not to perform an operation.

SFB_RESETM Send a bus device reset message to the addressed controller.

SFB_RESUME Permit normal job flow to a logical unit. This command is used after **SFB_SUSPEND**, but no error results if **SFB_RESUME** is called first.

SFB_SUSPEND Suspend a queue. This indicates that normal job flow to the logical unit is halted until the queue is resumed by the target driver.

REFERENCES

scb(D4I)

ver_no(D4I)

NAME

`ver_no` – PDI version number structure

SYNOPSIS

```
#include <sys/sdi.h>
```

DESCRIPTION

The version number structure, **ver_no**, is used to ensure that the version of PDI is appropriate for the target drivers.

USAGE

Structure Members

The **ver_no** structure is defined follows:

```
unsigned char   sv_release;    /* Release number */
unsigned char   sv_machine;    /* Computer type */
short           sv_modes;      /* PDI Release Number */
```

sv_release indicates the PDI release number (set to 1 for the first release).

sv_machine indicates the type of computer you are using.

sv_modes indicates the PDI functionality that is supported. Modes are added together with the bitwise OR operator.

Migration from Release 3.2 to Release 4.0

The *UNIX System V Block and Character Interface (BCI) Reference Manual* defined the functions, routines, and structures appropriate for use by drivers in the UNIX System V 3.2 environment. Many, but not all, of the routines in the BCI have been incorporated into the Device Driver Interface/Driver-Kernel Interface as is or, in the case of macros, reimplemented as procedures.

The functionality of some other BCI routines has been incorporated into the DDI/DKI either by renaming the BCI routine, but otherwise providing the identical interface, or by replacing the BCI routine with a different, but similar, interface. Still other BCI routines provide functionality that is obsolete; these routines have been dropped, and there are no DDI/DKI routines that provide similar functionality. In all cases the BCI routine is provided in Release 4.0 for backwards compatibility.

While backward compatibility for BCI routines is provided, it is still desirable to convert drivers to use the DDI/DKI if possible because the older routines will not be supported in future releases. Table A-1 is intended to assist developers in this task by summarizing the correspondence between routines in the BCI and routines in the DDI/DKI.

Each entry in the table lists the name of the BCI routine, some comments about changes made to the routine in the DDI/DKI, and the name of the corresponding DDI/DKI routine. Commonly occurring comments are:

- No change. The BCI routine has been retained in the DDI/DKI with the same name, interface, and functionality.
- Macro reimplemented as procedure. A BCI macro has been retained in the DDI/DKI, but has been implemented as a procedure with the identical calling and return syntax.
- Renamed. The BCI routine has been retained in the DDI/DKI with a different name, but otherwise provides the same interface and functionality.
- Replaced. The BCI routine has been removed from the DDI/DKI. The DDI/DKI provides a new interface that provides a similar function.
- Obsolete interface supported for backward compatibility only. The BCI routine has been removed from the DDI/DKI. The DDI/DKI does not provide a new interface; the interface itself is obsolete. For instance, the DDI/DKI does not support clist-based drivers; thus any routines dealing with clists have been removed from the DDI/DKI.

Again, please note that this table is a guide for programmers attempting to convert old driver source from BCI to DDI/DKI. All BCI routines, regardless of their status in the DDI/DKI, are provided in System V/386 Release 4.0 for backwards compatibility.

Table 3: 3.2 to Release 4.0 Migration

BCI	Comments	DDI/DKI
`adjmsg`	No change	`adjmsg`
`allocb`	No change; for memory-mapped I/O, use `esballoc`	`allocb`
`backq`	Obsolete interface supported for backward compatibility only	—
`bcopy`	No change	`bcopy`
`brelse`	No change	`brelse`
`btoc`	Replaced	`btop`, `btopr`
`bufcall`	No change; don't use with `esballoc`	`bufcall`
`bzero`	Word alignment no longer required	`bzero`
`canon`	Obsolete interface supported for backward compatibility only	—
`canput`	No change; use `bcanput` to test specific priority band	`canput`
`clrbuf`	No change	`clrbuf`
`cmn_err`	No change	`cmn_err`
`copyb`	No change	`copyb`
`copyin`	No change	`copyin` or `uiomove`
`copymsg`	No change	`copymsg`
`copyout`	No change	`copyout` or `uiomove`
`ctob`	Replaced	`ptob`
`datamsg`	No change	`datamsg`
`delay`	No change	`delay`
`dma_alloc`	Obsolete interface supported for backward compatibility only	—
`dma_breakup`	Replaced	`dma_pageio`
`dma_enable`	No change	`dma_enable`
`dma_param`	Replaced	`dma_prog`
`dma_relse`	Obsolete interface supported for backward compatibility only	—

Table 3: 3.2 to Release 4.0 Migration (continued)

BCI	Comments	DDI/DKI
`dma_resid`	Obsolete interface supported for backward compatibility only	—
`dma_start`	Replaced	`dma_swstart`
`dupb`	No change	`dupb`
`dupmsg`	No change	`dupmsg`
`enableok`	Macro reimplemented as function	`enableok`
`flushq`	No change; use `flushband` to flush specific priority band	`flushq`
`freeb`	No change	`freeb`
`freemsg`	No change	`freemsg`
`fubyte`	Replaced	`copyin`, `uiomove`, or `uwritec`
`fuword`	Replaced	`copyin`, `uiomove`, or `uwritec`
`getc`	Obsolete interface supported for backward compatibility only	—
`getcb`	Obsolete interface supported for backward compatibility only	—
`getcf`	Obsolete interface supported for backward compatibility only	—
`geteblk`	No change; use `ngeteblk` or `getrbuf` for alternate buffer sizes	`geteblk`
`geterror`	Macro reimplemented as function	`geterror`
`getq`	No change	`getq`
`inb`	No change	`inb`
`ind`	Renamed only	`inl`
`insq`	No change	`insq`
`inw`	No change	`inw`
`iodone`	Renamed only	`biodone`
`iomove`	Replaced	`uiomove`
`iowait`	Renamed only	`biowait`
`kseg`	Obsolete interface supported for backward compatibility only	`kmem_alloc`
`linkb`	No change	`linkb`

Table 3: **3.2 to Release 4.0 Migration** (continued)

BCI	Comments	DDI/DKI
longjmp	Obsolete interface supported for backward compatibility only	—
major	Renamed; macro reimplemented as function	**getmajor**
makedev	Renamed; macro reimplemented as function	**makedevice**
malloc	Renamed only	**rmalloc**
mapinit	Renamed only	**rminit**
mapwant	Renamed only	**rmsetwant**
max	No change	**max**
mfree	Renamed only	**rmfree**
min	No change	**min**
minor	Renamed; macro reimplemented as function	**getminor**
msgdsize	No change	**msgdsize**
noenable	Macro reimplemented as function	**noenable**
OTHERQ	Macro reimplemented as function	**OTHERQ**
outb	No change	**outb**
outd	Renamed only	**outl**
outw	No change	**outw**
physck	Replaced; functionality included in **physiock**	**physiock**
physio	Replaced; functionality included in **physiock**	**physiock**
psignal	No change	**psignal**
pullupmsg	No change	**pullupmsg**
putbq	No change	**putbq**
putc	Obsolete interface supported for backward compatibility only	—
putcb	Obsolete interface supported for backward compatibility only	—
putcf	Obsolete interface supported for backward compatibility only	—
putctl	No change	**putctl**
putctl1	No change	**putctl1**
putnext	Macro reimplemented as function	**putnext**
putq	No change	**putq**
qenable	No change	**qenable**
qreply	No change	**qreply**

Table 3: 3.2 to Release 4.0 Migration (continued)

BCI	Comments	DDI/DKI
`qsize`	No change	`qsize`
`RD`	Macro reimplemented as function	`RD`
`repinsb`	No change	`repinsb`
`repinsd`	No change	`repinsd`
`repinsw`	No change	`repinsw`
`repoutsb`	No change	`repoutsb`
`repoutsd`	No change	`repoutsd`
`repoutsw`	No change	`repoutsw`
`rmvb`	No change	`rmvb`
`rmvq`	No change	`rmvq`
`signal`	Obsolete interface supported for backward compatibility only	—
`sleep`	No change	`sleep`
`spl`	No change	`spl`
`splx`	No change	`splx`
`sptalloc`	Obsolete interface supported for backward compatibility only	`kmem_alloc` or `physmap`
`sptfree`	Obsolete interface supported for backward compatibility only	`kmem_free`
`strlog`	No change	`strlog`
`subyte`	Replaced	`copyout`, `uiomove`, or `ureadc`
`suser`	Replaced	`drv_priv`
`suword`	Replaced	`copyout`, `uiomove`, or `ureadc`
`testb`	Obsolete interface supported for backward compatibility only	—
`timeout`	No change	`timeout`
`ttclose`	Obsolete interface supported for backward compatibility only	—
`ttin`	Obsolete interface supported for backward compatibility only	—
`ttinit`	Obsolete interface supported for backward compatibility only	—

Table 3: 3.2 to Release 4.0 Migration (continued)

BCI	Comments	DDI/DKI
ttiocom	Obsolete interface supported for backward compatibility only	—
ttioctl	Obsolete interface supported for backward compatibility only	—
ttopen	Obsolete interface supported for backward compatibility only	—
ttout	Obsolete interface supported for backward compatibility only	—
ttread	Obsolete interface supported for backward compatibility only	—
ttrstrt	Obsolete interface supported for backward compatibility only	—
tttimeo	Obsolete interface supported for backward compatibility only	—
ttwrite	Obsolete interface supported for backward compatibility only	—
ttxput	Obsolete interface supported for backward compatibility only	—
ttyflush	Obsolete interface supported for backward compatibility only	—
ttywait	Obsolete interface supported for backward compatibility only	—
unkseg	Obsolete interface supported for backward compatibility only	kmem_free
unlinkb	No change	unlinkb
untimeout	No change	untimeout
useracc	Replaced; functionality included in physiock	physiock
vtop	No change	vtop
wakeup	No change	wakeup
WR	Macro reimplemented as function	WR

The **size**(D2) entry point was not defined in Release 3.2. Drivers without a **size** routine have the following peculiarities:

- They may not be able to use the last few sectors on the device partition. (The number of unusable sectors is *disk_sectors_in_partition* % *disk_sectors_per_logical_block*. Typically this is zero; it must be smaller than the logical block size.)
- They pay a performance penalty because the kernel avoids some pre-fetches on devices without a **size** routine.

Migration from Release 4.0 to Release 4 Multi-Processor

To make the UNIX System V Release 4 DDI/DKI more amenable to a multiprocessing environment, some Release 4.0 DDI/DKI kernel utility routines have been changed or removed. In addition, many new routines have been added. This appendix contains two tables: one shows how existing routines have been changed or removed, and the other lists new routines.

Changes to Release 4.0 DDI/DKI Routines

The functionality of some Release 4.0 DDI/DKI routines has been incorporated into the Release 4 Multi-Processor DDI/DKI by providing a new routine with a different, but similar, interface. Still other routines provided functionality that was obsolete; these routines have been dropped, and there are no DDI/DKI routines that provide similar functionality. In all cases the Release 4.0 routine is provided in Release 4 Multi-Processor for compatibility.

While compatibility with Release 4.0 routines is provided, it is still desirable to convert drivers to use the Release 4 Multi-Processor DDI/DKI if possible because the older routines will not be supported in future releases. Table B-1 is intended to assist developers in this task by summarizing the correspondence between routines in Release 4.0 and routines in Release 4 Multi-Processor.

Each entry in the table lists the name of the routine, some comments about changes made to the routine in the DDI/DKI, and the name of the corresponding Release 4 Multi-Processor DDI/DKI routine. Routines are categorized as follows:

- Replaced. The routine has been removed from the Release 4.0 DDI/DKI. The Release 4 Multi-Processor DDI/DKI provides a new interface that provides a similar function.
- New restrictions. The routine remains in the DDI/DKI with the same interface and functionality, but new restrictions are placed on its use.
- Extended. The interface to the routine remains the same, but the semantics have been changed in a compatible manner.
- Interface changed. The interface to the routine has changed, but the semantics remain the same.

Again, please note that this table is a guide for programmers attempting to convert old driver source from Release 4.0 to Release 4 Multi-Processor. All routines in the Release 4.0 DDI/DKI, regardless of their status in the Release 4 Multi-Processor DDI/DKI, are provided in System V Release 4 Multi-Processor for Intel Processors for compatibility.

Table 4: Release 4.0 to Release 4 Multi-Processor Migration

Release 4.0 DDI/DKI	Comments	Release 4 Multi-Processor DDI/DKI
`bcanput`	New restrictions; use `bcanputnext(q, pri)` instead of `bcanput(q->q_next, pri)`; stream cannot be frozen	`bcanput`
`biowait`	New restrictions; cannot hold basic locks or read/write locks	`biowait`
`bp_mapin`	New restrictions; cannot hold basic locks or read/write locks	`bp_mapin`
`canput`	New restrictions; use `canputnext(q)` instead of `canput(q->q_next)`; stream cannot be frozen	`canput`
`chpoll`	New restrictions; size of `pollhead` structure is not guaranteed; may not call any function that sleeps	`chpoll`
`cmn_err`	New restrictions; cannot hold locks if *level* is `CE_PANIC`	`cmn_err`
`copyin`	New restrictions; cannot hold basic locks or read/write locks	`copyin`
`copyout`	New restrictions; cannot hold basic locks or read/write locks	`copyout`
`delay`	New restrictions; cannot hold basic locks or read/write locks	`delay`
`dma_pageio`	New restrictions; cannot hold basic locks or read/write locks	`dma_pageio`
`enableok`	New restrictions; stream cannot be frozen	`enableok`
`flushband`	New restrictions; stream cannot be frozen	`flushband`
`flushq`	New restrictions; stream cannot be frozen	`flushq`
`geteblk`	New restrictions; cannot hold basic locks or read/write locks	`geteblk`
`getq`	New restrictions; stream cannot be frozen	`getq`
`getrbuf`	New restrictions; cannot hold basic locks or	`getrbuf`

Table 4: Release 4.0 to Release 4 Multi-Processor Migration (continued)

Release 4.0 DDI/DKI	Comments	Release 4 Multi-Processor DDI/DKI
	read/write locks if *flag* is **KM_SLEEP**	
hat_getkpfnum	Replaced	**kvtoppid**
hat_getppfnum	Replaced	**phystoppid**
insq	New restrictions; stream must be frozen	**insq**
kmem_alloc	New restrictions; cannot hold basic locks or read/write locks if *flag* is **KM_SLEEP**	**kmem_alloc**
kmem_zalloc	New restrictions; cannot hold basic locks or read/write locks if *flag* is **KM_SLEEP**	**kmem_zalloc**
ngeteblk	New restrictions; cannot hold basic locks or read/write locks	**ngeteblk**
noenable	New restrictions; stream cannot be frozen	**noenable**
physiock	New restrictions; cannot hold basic locks or read/write locks	**physiock**
physmap	New restrictions; cannot hold basic locks or read/write locks if *flags* is **KM_SLEEP**	**physmap**
psignal	Replaced	**proc_signal**
pullupmsg	Replaced	**msgpullup**
putbq	New restrictions; stream cannot be frozen	**putbq**
putctl	New restrictions; use **putnextctl(q, type)** instead of **putctl(q->q_next, type)**; cannot hold locks; stream cannot be frozen	**putctl**
putctl1	New restrictions; use **putnextctl1(q, type, param)** instead of **putctl1(q->q_next, type, param)**; cannot hold locks; stream cannot be frozen	**putctl1**
putnext	New restrictions; cannot hold locks; stream cannot be frozen	**putnext**
putq	New restrictions; stream cannot be frozen	**putq**
qenable	New restrictions; stream cannot be frozen	**qenable**
qreply	New restrictions; cannot hold locks; stream cannot be frozen	**qreply**
qsize	New restrictions; stream cannot be frozen	**qsize**
RD	Extended. Accepts both read and write	**RD**

Table 4: Release 4.0 to Release 4 Multi-Processor Migration (continued)

Release 4.0 DDI/DKI	Comments	Release 4 Multi-Processor DDI/DKI
	queue pointers	
rminit	Replaced	rmallocmap
rmsetwant	Replaced	rmalloc_wait
rmvq	New restrictions; stream must be frozen	rmvq
SAMESTR	New restrictions; argument cannot reference **q_next**; stream cannot be frozen	SAMESTR
sleep	Replaced	SV_WAIT_SIG
spl	Replaced; **spl0, spl1, spl4, spl5, spl6, spl7** functions eliminated; **splbase, spltimeout, spldisk** added	spl
strqget	New restrictions; stream must be frozen	strqget
strqset	New restrictions; stream must be frozen	strqset
timeout	Replaced	itimeout
uiomove	New restrictions; cannot hold basic locks or read/write locks if *uio_segflg* is **UIO_USERSPACE**	uiomove
unbufcall	Interface changed and new restrictions; argument type changed from **int** to **toid_t**; cannot hold locks	unbufcall
untimeout	Interface changed and new restrictions; argument type changed from **int** to **toid_t**; cannot hold locks	untimeout
ureadc	New restrictions; cannot hold basic locks or read/write locks if *uio_segflg* is **UIO_USERSPACE**	ureadc
uwritec	New restrictions; cannot hold basic locks or read/write locks if *uio_segflg* is **UIO_USERSPACE**	uwritec
wakeup	Replaced	SV_BROADCAST
WR	Extended. Accepts both read and write queue pointers	WR

Additions to the DDI/DKI in Release 4 Multi-Processor

Many new routines and one data structure have been added to the DDI/DKI for Release 4 Multi-Processor. Many of the additions are locks to enable drivers to be multithreaded. Use of some of these routines is described in the *Integrated Software Development Guide,* in the chapter on device drivers.

The table below lists all the new routines and data structures in the Release 4 Multi-Processor DDI/DKI, along with their section numbers and a brief description.

Table 5: Additions to the DDI/DKI in Release 4 Multi-Processor

Routine	Section	Description
LOCK	D3	acquire a basic lock
LOCK_ALLOC	D3	allocate and initialize a basic lock
LOCK_DEALLOC	D3	deallocate an instance of a basic lock
RW_ALLOC	D3	allocate and initialize a read/write lock
RW_DEALLOC	D3	deallocate an instance of a read/write lock
RW_RDLOCK	D3	acquire a read/write lock in read mode
RW_TRYRDLOCK	D3	try to acquire a read/write lock in read mode
RW_TRYWRLOCK	D3	try to acquire a read/write lock in write mode
RW_UNLOCK	D3	release a read/write lock
RW_WRLOCK	D3	acquire a read/write lock in write mode
SLEEP_ALLOC	D3	allocate and initialize a sleep lock
SLEEP_DEALLOC	D3	deallocate an instance of a sleep lock
SLEEP_LOCK	D3	acquire a sleep lock
SLEEP_LOCKAVAIL	D3	query whether a sleep lock is available
SLEEP_LOCKOWNED	D3	query whether a sleep lock is held by the caller
SLEEP_LOCK_SIG	D3	acquire a sleep lock
SLEEP_TRYLOCK	D3	try to acquire a sleep lock
SLEEP_UNLOCK	D3	release a sleep lock
SV_ALLOC	D3	allocate and initialize a synchronization variable
SV_BROADCAST	D3	wake up all processes sleeping on a synchronization variable
SV_DEALLOC	D3	deallocate an instance of a synchronization variable
SV_SIGNAL	D3	wake up one process sleeping on a synchronization variable

Table 5: Additions to the DDI/DKI in Release 4 Multi-Processor (continued)

Routine	Section	Description
SV_WAIT	D3	sleep on a synchronization variable
SV_WAIT_SIG	D3	sleep on a synchronization variable
TRYLOCK	D3	try to acquire a basic lock
UNLOCK	D3	release a basic lock
bcanputnext	D3	test for flow control in a specified priority band
bioerror	D3	manipulate error field within a buffer header
canputnext	D3	test for flow control in a stream
dtimeout	D3	execute a function on a specified processor, after a specified length of time
freezestr	D3	freeze the state of a stream
getnextpg	D3	get next page pointer
itimeout	D3	execute a function after a specified length of time
kvtoppid	D3	get physical page ID for kernel virtual address
msgpullup	D3	concatenate bytes in a message
pcmsg	D3	test whether a message is a priority control message
phalloc	D3	allocate and initialize a pollhead structure
phfree	D3	free a pollhead structure
phystoppid	D3	get physical page ID for physical address
pptophys	D3	convert page pointer to physical address
proc_ref	D3	obtain a reference to a process for signaling
proc_signal	D3	send a signal to a process
proc_unref	D3	release a reference to a process
put	D3	call a put procedure
putnextctl	D3	send a control message to a queue
putnextctl1	D3	send a control message with a one byte parameter to a queue
qprocsoff	D3	disable put and service routines
qprocson	D3	enable put and service routines
rmalloc_wait	D3	allocate space from a private space management map
rmallocmap	D3	allocate and initialize a private space management map

Table 5: Additions to the DDI/DKI in Release 4 Multi-Processor (continued)

Routine	Section	Description
`rmfreemap`	D3	free a private space management map
`unfreezestr`	D3	unfreeze the state of a stream
`lkinfo`	D4	lock information structure

Additions to the DDI/DKI in Release 4.2

14 new routines have been added to the DDI/DKI for Release 4.2. Some of the additions are entry points and utilities to enable drivers to be dynamically loaded into (or unloaded from) a running system. Use of these routines is described in the *Device Driver Programming* guide, in the chapter on dynamically loadable modules.

Table C-1 lists all the new routines in the Release 4.2 DDI/DKI, along with their section numbers and a brief description.

Table 6: Additions to the DDI/DKI in Release 4.2

Routine	Section	Description
`_load`	D2	initialize a loadable kernel module
`_unload`	D2	clean up a loadable kernel module
`bcmp`	D3	compare data between two kernel address locations
`bioreset`	D3	reset a private buffer for reuse after completed I/O
`drv_gethardware`	D3	retrieve hardware information
`mod_drvattach`	D3	install interrupts for a loadable device driver
`mod_drvdetach`	D3	remove interrupts for a loadable device driver
`rdma_filter`	D3	filter transfers to use only DMA-able memory
`strcat`	D3	concatenate strings
`strcpy`	D3	copy a string
`strlen`	D3	determine the length of a string
`strncat`	D3	concatenate strings appending a specified number of characters
`strncmp`	D3	compare strings using a specified number of characters
`strncpy`	D3	copy a string using a specified number of characters

C. ADDITIONS TO THE DDI/DKI IN RELEASE 4.2

Introduction to the Permuted Index

The Permuted Index that follows is a list of keywords, alphabetized in the second of three columns, together with the context in which each keyword is found. The manual page that produced an entry is listed in the right column.

Entries are identified with their section numbers shown in parentheses. This is important because there is considerable duplication of names among the sections, arising principally from commands and functions that exist only to exercise a particular system call.

The index is produced by rotating the NAME section of each manual page to alphabetize each keyword in it. Words that cannot fit in the middle column are rotated into the left column. If the entry is still too long, some words are omitted, and their omission is indicated with a slash ("/").

How the Permuted Index Is Created

Many users find that understanding a few things about how the permuted index is created helps them to read it more effectively and clarifies what kind of information can and cannot be obtained from it.

The basic building block for the index is the one-line description given in the NAME line on the top of each manual page. For example, this is what the top of the `mountall`(1M) manual page looks like:

---

mountall(1M) **mountall(1M)**

NAME

`mountall, umountall` – mount, unmount multiple file systems

Each NAME line includes:

- the command, file format, system call or other utility for which the manual page is named (this is the primary utility; `mountall` is the primary utility in the example)

PERMUTED INDEX

- secondary utilities, which are also described on that manual page and do not have a separate manual page of their own (**umountall** is a secondary utility in the example)
- a brief description of the utility function(s)

For each manual page NAME line, the indexing software generates several index entries, generally one entry for each keyword in the phrase. The middle column of the index is alphabetized on these keywords.

For:

NAME

mountall, umountall – mount, unmount multiple file systems

This is generated:

mount, unmount multiple	file systems. /umountall:	mountall(1M)
systems. mountall, umountall:	mount, unmount multiple file	mountall(1M)
unmount multiple file systems.	mountall, umountall: mount,	mountall(1M)
/umountall: mount, unmount	multiple file systems.	mountall(1M)
mount, unmount multiple file	systems. mountall, umountall:	mountall(1M)
multiple file/ mountall,	umountall: mount, unmount	mountall(1M)
mountall, umountall: mount,	unmount multiple file systems.	mountall(1M)

How to Use the Index

Look in the middle column of the index for the word of interest. Then read the complete phrase by starting with the utility name, which may appear in the left or middle column. Utility names are followed by a colon.

The NAME line phrase is contained in the two columns, with long phrases wrapping around to the beginning of the left column. The right column of the index provides the manual page name and section number.

A slash (/) sometimes appears in the index entry to indicate that space limitations were exceeded and one or more words from the phrase were deleted.

Permuted Index

UNIX SYSTEM LABORATORIES

What do YOU think?

USL values your opinion. Please indicate your opinions in each of the following areas. We'd like to know how well this document meets your needs.

Book Title:____

	Excellent	Good	Fair	Poor
Accuracy - Is the information correct?	❑	❑	❑	❑
Completeness - Is information missing?	❑	❑	❑	❑
Organization - Is information easy to find?	❑	❑	❑	❑
Clarity - Do you understand the information?	❑	❑	❑	❑
Examples - Are there enough?	❑	❑	❑	❑
Illustrations - Are there enough?	❑	❑	❑	❑
Appearance - Do you like the page format?	❑	❑	❑	❑
Physical binding - Do you like the cover and binding?	❑	❑	❑	❑

Does the document meet your needs? Why or why not?

____

____

____

What is the single most important improvement that we could make to this document?

____

____

____

Please complete the following information.

Name (Optional): ______________________________

Job Title or Function: ______________________________

Organization: ______________________________

Address: ______________________________

____

Phone: (   ) ______________________________

If we need more information may we contact you? Yes ❑ No ❑

Thank you.

NO POSTAGE
NECESSARY
IF MAILED
IN THE
UNITED STATES

BUSINESS REPLY MAIL

FIRST CLASS MAIL PERMIT NO. 199 SUMMIT, NJ

POSTAGE WILL BE PAID BY ADDRESSEE

UNIX System Laboratories, Inc.
Director
USL Documentation Department
Room F–313
190 River Road
Summit, NJ 07901-9907